CHOREOGRAPHING **DIFFERENCE**

CHOREOGRAPHING DIFFERENCE

Ann Cooper Albright

CHOREOGRAPHING DIFFERENCE

CHOREOGRAPHING DIFFERENCE

CHOREOGRAPHING DIFFERENCE

CHOREOGRAPHING DIFFERENCE

CHOREOGRAPHING **DIFFERENCE**

CHOREOGRAPHING DIFFERENCE

CHOREOGRAPHING DIFFERENCE

The Body and Identity in Contemporary Dance

CHOREOGRAPHING DIFFERENCE

CHOREOGRAPHING DIFFERENCE

Wesleyan University Press

CHOREOGRAPHING DIFFERENCE

PUBLISHED BY UNIVERSITY PRESS OF NEW ENGLAND • HANOVER AND LONDON

CHOREOGRAPHING DIFFERENCE

Wesleyan University Press

Published by University Press of New England

Hanover, NH 03755

Printed in the United States of America

5 4 3 2 1

CIP data appear at the end of the book

To my parents,

Marilyn Cooper Albright

and

R. Christian Albright

—for believing in me—

Contents

List of Illustrations

Acknowledgments

Many different communities have supported the writing of this book. One of the most important has been my interdisciplinary feminist study group, The Flaming Bitches, especially Yopie Prins, Wendy Hesford, Wendy Kozol, and Sibelan Forrester, who all read early, early versions of these chapters and encouraged me to articulate the importance of dance as a cultural discourse. To them and all the bitches who have come together during my time at Oberlin College, thank you for your support. I would also like to thank various dance scholars for their support of this project in encouraging me or inviting me to speak on their campuses: Sally Banes, Cynthia Jean Cohen Bull (Cynthia Novack), David Gere, Heather Elton, Sharon Friedler, Jane Desmond, and Linda Caruso Haviland. Susan Manning was especially helpful as the reader; I found her comments insightful and encouraging. In addition, Veta Goler and Ananya generously shared their dissertations with me.

Most of my research was carried out not in libraries but in active dance organizations and in the theater. I want to acknowledge two hubs of contemporary dance activity: Movement Research, Inc., in New York City (especially Audrey Kindred and Julie Muz), and the International Festival of New Dance in Montreal. Dena Davida, Aline Gélinas, and Anne Viau were particularly helpful in Montreal. I also want to acknowledge my editor at *Dialogue* magazine, Lorrie Dirkse, for giving me the opportunity to write about the issues I felt were vital in contemporary dance.

ACKNOWLEDGMENTS

If my research initially happens while away from Ohio, much of my thinking takes place in and around my classes. To all my students at Oberlin College and Ohio State University: I appreciate your willingness to engage with these issues and to push my own thinking into new areas. Thanks also to Caroline Jackson-Smith and Adenike Sharpley for conversations about African-American performative traditions.

Several people helped me get this book to its destination and they include my wonderfully encouraging and cool editor, Suzanna Tamminen, and my two student assistants, Sadie Zea Ishee and Chlöe Hopson, as well as my husband, Tom Newlin, and my children, Isabel and Cyrus.

Oberlin College and the Ohio Arts Council have supported this project in various ways, but mostly through much-needed funds to go see dances!

I acknowledge permission to use sections of "Incalculable Choreographies," which was published as an essay in *Bodies of the Text*, edited by Ellen Goellner and Jacqueline Shea Murphy (Rutgers University Press, 1995).

Introduction: Witnessing Dance

Choreographing Difference: The Body and Identity in Contemporary Dance is the result of over a decade of my involvement with dance as a performer, choreographer, improvisor, educator, and feminist scholar. This book grew out of a conviction that contemporary dance could shed light on the current debates about how cultural identities are negotiated and embodied.[1] The project has acquired an urgency over the past few years as I see more and more dancing bodies becoming invisible and arts funding increasingly becoming a political minefield. My hope is that not only will this work contribute to current dialogues about corporeality, but that it will also expose both scholars and dancers to some of the ways in which dance can be a central, indeed, a crucial discourse for our time. It is my contention that contemporary dance foregrounds a responsive dancing body, one that engages with and challenges static representations of gender, race, sexuality, and physical ability, all the while acknowledging how deeply these ideologies influence our daily experience. It is through the act of choreographing these differences that the dances I discuss in this book mobilize cultural identities, unleashing them from their overly deterministic moorings while at the same time revealing their somatic ground.[2]

I am interested in the tensions between dance and the plethora of cultural discourses about the body. Throughout this book, I will be engaging on the one hand with academic theories, which often perceive the body as a passive surface onto which society inscribes its political and social ideologies, and, on the other hand, with conceptions of the body as an essentially natural phenomenon that precedes cultural conditioning. Close analyses of contemporary choreography, however, reveal the ways in which the dancing body confounds these easy distinctions. Because dance comprises the daily technical training of the dancer's body as well as the final choreographic production, dance can help us trace the complex negotiations between somatic experience and cultural representation—between the body and identity. For instance, while the audience may at first recognize a dancer onstage in terms of male or female, black or white, disabled or nondisabled, these visual categories can be disrupted by the kinesthetic meanings embedded in the dancing itself. Is the style of movement consistent with or resistant to this configuration of social identity? Does the performance situation (staging, lighting, costuming, etc.) reinforce or refuse these categorizations? How is this particular body interacting with other bodies? Much contemporary dance takes up and plays with these questions of movement and meaning, giving us some brilliant examples of how physical bodies are both shaped by and resistant to cultural representations of identity.

I first began dancing seriously in college. Although I was ostensibly studying philosophy and French literature, much of my time was being spent in the dance studio, exploring movement and dance. I came to see this physical inquiry as a way of knowing and experiencing the world; one that was no less sophisticated than other forms of knowledge. Because I had come to dance within an academic setting, it seemed entirely natural to me to integrate my academic interests with my physical ones, at once reading and writing about dance as well as dancing and making dances about what I was studying in school. I quickly realized, however, that my college (and indeed, American culture in general) rarely accepted dance as a fully legitimate artistic pursuit or academic discipline. This realization was a product of my budding feminist consciousness as I became increasingly aware that the legacy of women-centeredness that I valued so highly in modern dance was inextricably linked to the marginalization of this body-centered artform. Thus, as I solidified my commitment to dance over the next several years, I did so as an act of resistance, fully determined (as only a nineteen-year-old can be) to make dance a much more central cultural institution.

At the same time, I was gradually becoming aware of various feminist critiques in philosophy and literature, I was also becoming (less gradually) dissatisfied with what I was reading in dance theory. Besides the work of dance theorists and critics such as Edwin Denby and John Martin (both of whom wrote from the universalized perspective of white, middle-class men), and Don McDonagh's infamous *The Rise and Fall and Rise of Modern Dance*, as well as the mostly anecdotal biographies of famous dancers, there was little substantial dance scholarship on the library shelves. (One exception was Marcia Siegel's seminal study of early American modern dance, *Shapes of Change*.) As a philosophy major, I had read Suzanne Langer's work (*Feeling and Form*) and that of Maxine Sheets-Johnson (*The Phenomenology of Dance*).[3] Yet, both of these philosophical treatises universalized and abstracted dance to such a degree that it didn't seem to matter who produced the movement image that was being analyzed for its essential kinesthetic and physical properties. Meanwhile, my studies in feminist thought were convincing me that actually it did matter whether the dancer was a woman or a man, black or white, fat or thin. My academic interests coupled with my own reluctance to dance a Graham number in a long skirt during the annual spring concert convinced me that I wasn't very good at seeing movement abstractly—as movement for movement's sake. I found that I couldn't escape (or repress) the social meanings that those dancing bodies held for me. Although I wasn't completely articulate about why this was important at the time, I knew that dance theory needed to break through the veneer of abstraction in describing "human movement" so as to engage with the dancing body in its very specific social situatedness.

Fortunately, I am not alone. The emergence of interdisciplinary scholarship and the rise of cultural studies have given dance scholars valuable critical tools with which to analyze the network of social and physical discourses in dance. As a result, a new generation of dance scholars trained in a wide range of methodologies is incorporating critical paradigms from a host of intellectual sources, including feminist theory, cultural studies, poststructuralist literary theory, anthropology, and sociology.[4] This fresh historical and theoretical work in dance has raised the stakes of the field, resulting in several recent conferences focused on cultural issues and interdisciplinary dialogue, such as the 1990 Dance Critics Association "Looking Out: Critical Imperatives in World Dance" conference held in Los Angeles; the 1992 "Choreographing History" conference held at the University of California, Riverside; the 1995 "Border Tensions" conference at the University of Surrey; and the 1996 conference in "African-American Dance: Researching a Complex History" held at University of Illinois, Urbana-Champaign, to mention only a few.

The enthusiasm I have for this wonderful critical energy is dampened only by my concern for the physical bodies and economic conditions of professional dancers. The last decade has witnessed an unprecedented reduction of government funding for dance (and the arts in general). In addition, the devastation of the dance community as a result of AIDS-related deaths has taken a large physical and spiritual toll. Even though I am writing this book as a dancer in academia, I try to keep the material realities of professional dancing bodies present throughout my work. One way to keep the bodies of contemporary choreography at the center of my discussions is to evoke the experience of watching a dance by luxuriating for a moment in a more lyrical and descriptive style of writing. My attempts thus to engage the reader's kinesthetic imagination come from a dual desire to recreate textually the dancing through descriptive movement analysis and to keep those real live bodies in the reader's mind as well.

It is useful, I think, to introduce my project by looking briefly at the two dances that frame the decade or so of contemporary dance that this book documents. A comparison of *Active Graphics II*, choreographed in 1987 by Pooh Kaye for her company Eccentric Motions, with the 1996 American premiere of *La Tristeza Complice* (*The Shared Sorrow*) by Les Ballets C. de la B. can help both to flesh out the different kinds of choreographic works I analyze in this book, and to position my own body and identity within this critical project.[5] Both dances are based on extremely physical, frequently virtuosic dancing. Both use intense movement styles that push the dancers' bodies to the limits of physical possibility and endurance. But the choreographic priorities of these works are radically divergent and they involve very different kinds of spectatorial engagement. While *Active Graphics II* is visually inviting, physically exciting, and kinesthetically pleasurable to watch, *La Tristeza Complice* has a more overtly political agenda.

Of course, it is tempting to discuss the differences between the two dances in terms of a historical evolution from abstract dance to content-oriented dance, from playful postmodernism to social commentary, and to see this progression as an inevitable response to the bleak cultural climate for the arts at the end of the century. While I do not believe that this shift between *Active Graphics II* and *La Tristeza Complice* is merely a coincidence, or that it can be explained simply in terms of their geographic difference (New York City vs. Belgium), neither am I comfortable with a teleological argument that suggests that the second piece is necessarily more sophisticated than the first. It is true that dancers have become much more politically active and aware of the cultural issues surrounding differences of race, class, sexuality, and ability over the past decade. And certainly this growing consciousness has shaped much of the contemporary choreography I discuss in this book. Yet *Active Graphics II* is visionary in its own way, reimagining movement possibilities while refiguring the traditional frames of dance performance.

Active Graphics II begins and ends in complete darkness, which merges the stage space with that of the rest of the theater, subverting the literal frame of the proscenium arch and confusing the standard divisions between the audience and stage space. The suspenseful, pulsing music by Pat Irwin pours into this blackness that surrounds the audience with a strange, yet compelling intimacy. As the driving rhythms momentarily recede and a single note chimes repeatedly, a white rectangle of light appears suspended in a sea of blackness that includes the whole theater. The rectangle appears to be floating in midair. A dancer wavers on one edge of this block of light. Like a surfer, she tests her balance. First a leg, then an arm and head enters this rectangle of white. Luxuriating in being off balance, the dancer suspends her body in an arc and then dives toward the lighted space, landing chest first. Her body rebounds into a series of jumps that intensify as she adds a flick of her arm, a twist of her torso. Finally a thrown head propels her into a back arch. Sometimes the dancer moves along the center of the mat and is fully lit. Other times a leg or an arm gesture will float into the blackness and out of the audience's sight. In the middle of this initial solo, the dancer turns for the first time toward the audience. As she expands her arms in an open gesture, she simultaneously moves into the shadows.

The first section of *Active Graphics II* is a curious subversion of the conventional frames of theatrical lighting. Usually, the light moves in order to keep the dancer within view, thus stabilizing her in a choreographic frame. Here, the dancers' freedom to move in and out of the light shifts the active and passive functions of the frame. It is as if they choose when to dive into the light, when to allow the audience to see their dancing. The costumes, black bicycle outfits with a thick white stripe running down the front and across the back, reinforce this play of shadow and light. The movement vocabulary also contributes to the audience's growing sense of the dancers' physical willfulness by flaunting a looping, explosive energy that rarely, however, addresses the audience in a frontal, presentational manner. Whirling, tumbling, and swooping in and out of the lights, the dancers project a physical aliveness that conveys a sense of their own movement experience.

When I first saw this dance in 1987, I was enthralled by the combination of feisty, gymnastic movements with the very sensuous physicality of the dancing. Trained as I was in Contact Improvisation, I felt a real kinesthetic empathy for the tumbling, upside-down motions that flowed through the dancers' bodies. There was something very powerful and very present in this dancing that satisfied many of my own movement desires. At the same time, I was taking a graduate course in feminist theories of representation that depressed me on a weekly basis. Most of the readings pointed out in gruesome detail just how completely women's bodies had been written over (and their own desires

INTRODUCTION

Robin Simmonds in *Active Graphics*. Choreography by Pooh Kaye/Eccentric Motions.
Photo © Beatriz Schiller 1997.

written out) by the inevitable repressiveness built into cultural representations
of the female body. This was back during the heyday of the "male gaze," when
most of the theories we were reading came from art history or film studies.
While the writer in me was becoming a more critical reader of these images,
the dancer in me was sure that dance, as a representation grounded in live
moving bodies, held the potential to resist and disrupt this repressive paradigm. Seeing *Active Graphics II* absolutely convinced me that something else
was going on in contemporary dance, and I was inspired then to begin a critical and physical journey through the multiple layers of cultural meanings in
the dancing body. Combining my dancerly and critical perception about this
dance, I wrote a short essay in which I argued that works like *Active Graphics
II* both literally and figuratively subverted the traditional spectatorial frames
of dance.[6] In place of this male gaze was a way of looking at dance that, I suggested, opened up the possibility of seeing not only the dancer's body in motion but her subjective experience of that motion as well.

In retrospect, I realize that my discussion of this piece was connected to my desire to articulate how dance performances engage the audience differently than other artforms. Perceiving dance means more than a flat visual gaze, it also means attending to kinesthetic, aural, somatic, and spatial sensations. In his discussions of how modern dance communicates to its audience, dance critic John Martin uses the term "metakinesis." "Because of the inherent contagion of bodily movement, which makes the onlooker feel sympathetically in his own musculature, the dancer is able to convey through movement the most intangible emotional experience."[7] By writing about *Active Graphics II*, I was attempting to theorize my own metakinetic experience. Yet my pleasure at watching this dance was clearly augmented by my own identification with the dancers as a young, white, female, able-bodied, "downtown" dancer. Caught up in the fallacy of believing my experience was a universal one, I wrote about a different kind of spectatorship without taking into account the cultural differences between spectators.

Although it is true that movement necessarily engages the viewer's bodily presence, the viewer is not necessarily engaged in the same manner. While almost everybody would feel a clenching of the gut to see someone free fall through space and then get caught at the last moment, we all have very different expectations about what kind of dancing is pleasurable to see or do. These expectations are culturally constructed and yet experienced somatically on a very deep muscular level. Dances like *Active Graphics II* excite my physical desire for movement. Other dances, however, confuse this sort of direct kinesthetic empathy. *La Tristeza Complice* is such a dance.

I first heard about *La Tristeza Complice* before I saw it, when a heated discussion about the politics of the dance broke out in the midst of my graduate seminar at Ohio State University. While some of the students were enthralled by the highly risky and intense dancing, others were deeply repelled by its brutally realistic style and violent overtones. Even though I was familiar with the company's work and had witnessed its provocative effect on my students, I was still surprised when people walked out of the performance during the New York City premiere of the work in October 1996. While some people objected to the overly realistic presentation of street characters ("Why should I go to the theater to see what I see all the time outside my door?") and others to what they perceived as the physical risk to the dancers, I believe that the most difficult moments of the dance came when the audience members were forced to become accountable for their own spectatorial position.

Set in a theatrical *huis clos* of a public waiting area, *La Tristeza Complice* features the particular neurosis or despair of each vagrant character as they enter

Les Ballets C. de la B. in *La Tristeza Complice*. Photo by Laurent Philippe.

the space one by one. We see the crazed man in his underwear careening through the space on one roller blade, at times gliding gracefully and at other times limping around the stage. Then there enters the tall, lanky drag queen, precariously balanced on his heels as he fights off the taunts and abuses of two adolescent boys. More characters enter the fray, including a bag lady whose compulsive arranging and rearranging of her possessions bespeaks a spiritual searching for her self. Punctuating the existential landscape of the set is a rope and noose hanging from one corner. In the midst of all this loneliness, however, there are several extraordinary moments of physical communion. Often these moments arise from the kinesthetic dynamics of the movement itself rather than from a specific dramatic intention. In this public no-man's-land, there is little direct interpersonal connection, but physical energy is contagious, and when one person begins a rhythmic, repetitious stamping combination, others are drawn in to his dance. Sometimes this exchange of energy becomes destructive, but at other times it suggests a kind of curious, almost unconscious *communitas*.

This edge between aggression and empathy is played with again and again in *La Tristeza Complice*. In one section, for instance, a drag queen (played by Koen Augustijnen) repeatedly grabs a woman's body (Angélique Wilkie).

Koen Augustijnen and Angélique Wilkie in *La Tristeza Complice*. Photo by Chris Van der Burght.

Pulling and picking at her skin, her hair and her clothes, he seems at once abusive and yet also desirous of becoming her. Watching a white man touch a black woman in such an abusive manner emphasized her passivity and at first I felt very uncomfortable with the sexual and racial politics of this scene. Nonetheless, these politics were complicated by the fact that this man was wearing a bra and lipstick, as well as the fact that he had earlier been the object of sexual harassment. In addition, the woman endured the whole event while doggedly singing a slow ballad. While I found the work to be disturbingly ambiguous at times like this, I also found it powerful and compelling, particularly during the moments when the dancers followed the intensity of a movement exchange so long that its disturbing qualities seemed to transform into a communal ritual.

While commenting on the intensity of Angélique Wilkie's theatrical presence, Jawole Willa Jo Zollar (artistic director of Urban Bush Women) described her performance as "staying in the fire." Zollar used this expression to point out the performer's commitment to experiencing a physical and psychic disorientation in performance, her willingness to stay in the experience even when it was not completely controlled or comfortable.[8] Pushing the edges of theatrical realism like this is clearly a hallmark of Les Ballets C. de la B., and the company spends a good deal of time working through these highly volatile scenes. But Zollar's expression is also, I believe, an apt description of the audience's experience here as well. For dances like *La Tristeza Complice* ask the audience to be willing to stay with the performance, even when the situation becomes disturbing or uncomfortable. For me, this is when the act of watching transforms into the act of witnessing.

To witness something implies a responsiveness, the response/ability of the viewer toward the performer. It is radically different from what we might call the "consuming" gaze that says "here, you entertain me, I bought a ticket, and I'm going to sit back and watch." This traditional gaze doesn't want to get involved, doesn't want to give anything back. In contrast, what I call witnessing is much more interactive, a kind of perceiving (with one's whole body) that is commited to a process of mutual dialogue. There are precedents for this responsive watching in Quaker meetings, African-American notions of bearing witness, the responsive dynamic of many evangelistic religions, as well as the aesthetic theory of *rasa* in Classical Indian Dance, to mention only a few such examples.[9] This act of witnessing, however, raises the stakes of audience engagement, sometimes making the audience member uncomfortable, sometimes provoking highly charged responses to the work. This is particularly true of dances that foreground issues of social, political, and sexual difference in ways that make the spectator aware of the performer's cultural identity as well as his or her own cultural positioning. Much of the contemporary dance I discuss in this book sets up a performance situation that seeks to engage the audience's responsiveness on this level. Certainly not all performances do this, or even try to do this, but I believe that shifting the dynamics of the traditional gaze is one of the hallmarks of contemporary dance.

Watching *La Tristeza Complice*, like watching *Active Graphics II*, engages the audience on many different levels. This complexity has everything to do with the bodily nature of dance. When I watch dance, I consciously approach the experience with my physical as well as my visual, aesthetic, and intellectual faculties. The meanings that dances hold for me shift as I digest them through journal writings, physical associations, and conversations with choreographers, dancers, and audience members. Dances have a way of taking up residence in my body. They often start out whispering to me, but eventually their voices become clearer and clearer and then I begin to know which words might follow that motion. I never pretend to understand the dance once and for all (I don't try to stabilize the meaning of each gesture), and yet neither do I assume that I've lost the importance of that physical experience as I begin to articulate the cultural implications of those dances.

This process of unraveling the various meanings of movement images, physical bodies, and cultural identities can take time, and I frequently find myself thinking about dances long after the choreographer and dancers have moved on to new projects. In this way, the public performance of a dance is taken inside my body, refigured in writing, and then resurfaces in the public realm as an article or a book. That this is an intensely subjective process is self-evident. But I do not believe that by acknowledging the bodily source of my own scholarship I am invalidating my critical perceptions.[10] For, although *Choreographing Difference: The Body and Identity in Contemporary Dance* is grounded in my embodied experience, it is also necessarily influenced by the cultural context and intellectual environment of this particular historical moment. At times, of course, there is an uncanny synchronicity between my intellectual interests and my physical situation. For instance, two years after I became interested in issues of disability and dancing I experienced a temporary but profoundly disabling back injury. Thus the story of this book is, in some ways, the story of my physical and critical responses to the work I see, and I have attempted to write these responses in a way that is self-conscious of my own positionality—historically, culturally, bodily. Sometimes I approach the dances that propel this book as a dance historian or a cultural critic. Other times, however, I situate myself as a dancer, a white woman, a writer. Each chapter of this book marks differently the shifting relationship betweeen the issues of representation that I articulate through examples of contemporary dancing and my own experience of those issues. This interconnectedness between self and other—my body and the bodies of contemporary dance—becomes, then, the choreography of authorial voice and critical positioning staged by this book on contemporary dance.

My first chapter, "Mining the Dancefield," inverts the title of Annette Kolodny's seminal essay "Dancing Through the Minefield" in order both to claim my allegiance to the critical agenda of feminist theory and to foreground my particular interests in the dancing body. The title puns on the two meanings of "mining," for I want both to explode the intellectual complacency of much dance writing as well as to dig out the theoretical potential embedded in this artform. In this first chapter, I lay the groundwork for much of my later discussion of dance by challenging the ways in which the body (and, by extension, dance) has been situated within Western epistemology. I describe how dance comprises what I see as a double moment of representation in which bodies are both producing and being produced by cultural discourses of gender, race, ability, sexuality, and age. I argue that this double moment allows for a slippage between what I call a somatic identity (the experience of one's physicality) and a cultural one (how one's body renders meaning in society). In the second half of the chapter, I use this theoretical frame to look briefly at three historical examples: the nineteenth-century romantic ballerina Fanny Cerrito, as well as two icons of twentieth-century American modern and postmodern dance, Isadora Duncan and Yvonne Rainer. I then turn to a discussion of the contemporary Congolese-Canadian choreographer Zab Maboungou in order to demonstrate how her dancing elicits the audience's witnessing by doubling her somatic and cultural identities in order to resist both the colonial and the male gaze.

My next chapter, "Techno Bodies: Muscling with Gender in Contemporary Dance," begins with a discussion of how we tend to define dancers' gender identities in terms of the actual musculature and physical presentation of the dancing body. I look at the ways that the muscularly built-up female body is presented in the work of Elizabeth Streb and La La La Human Steps. Referencing feminist discussions of female body sculpting and body conditioning, I analyze how these "physical machines" both challenge and reinscribe traditional definitions of feminine beauty and comportment. In my discussion of the choreography of Édouard Lock (specifically his work for Louise Lecavalier) and Streb/Ringside, I examine how these built-up bodies are resituated by a traditional gaze in spite of their incredibly intense and powerful dancing. I argue that, in contemporary dance, gender needs to be deconstructed not only in terms of the musculature of the body, but also in terms of the ways in which that body is represented in motion. Finally, I elaborate my own belief that the intense, built-up physicality of dancers like Lecavalier is an anxious embracing of the "constructed" or technologically built-up body in the face of the mysterious dis/eases of contemporary society. Looking at Jennifer Monson's choreography, I explore the implications of working within the legacy of fit and frail bodies and show how some dance affirms a passion for physical movement in spite of the incredible losses of fit bodies within the dance community.

Chapter 3, "Dancing Across Difference: Dance and Disability," builds on the previous discussions of how identity is inscribed on the musculature and physicality of a body, and examines the social construction of a quintessentially "able" body in Western dance. How is this gendered ideal of a graceful, youthful, beautiful dancing body thrown off balance by dance performances that include disabled dancers? I describe recent work with "disabled" dancers in companies such as Cleveland Ballet Dancing Wheels, Candoco, Light Motion, and Joint Forces to show how this work can (but doesn't always) challenge implicit assumptions about just what constitutes "ableness" when it comes to dance. Comparing various performances that include both able-bodied and wheelchair dancers, I ask, for instance, if ability is necessarily always a visible category. Next, I demonstrate how these dancers are often merely tok-enized within a representational frame that emphasizes and reinscribes the *dis* of disability. Finally, I discuss a number of other dancing projects grounded in Contact Improvisation that challenge and deconstruct the category of ableness in dance, creating a continuum of abilities rather than an either/or situation.

The next chapter, "Incalculable Choreographies," plays with the intertex-tuality of dancing and writing. Drawing on the literary and theoretical work of Jacques Derrida and Hélène Cixous, I extend their metaphorization of sex-ual difference as a fluid, mobile category—a *dance*—by including another kind of text, that written by and on the live dancing body of contemporary Cana-dian performer Marie Chouinard. I explore how her solo work reframes the traditional dynamic of desire in dance performances, confusing categories of gender and sexuality. When Chouinard literally and figuratively appropriates Nijinsky's body (including his phallus) in her interpretation of *L'après-midi d'un faune*, for instance, she opens the question of what it means to be a man by refusing to stay in the role of a woman. Playing with various enactments of choreography as writing the dancing body, I also insert my own dancing body into the writing of this chapter.

Chapter 5, "Dancing Bodies and the Stories They Tell," expands the cen-tral issues of identity and the body into a specific analysis of autobiography in dance. I ask how one "writes the self" through movement, focusing on the ways the dancing body shifts back and forth between a literary narrative (telling a story) and a physical one (embodying it). Through a discussion of Blondell Cummings's and David Dorfman's solo works, I show how the danc-ing body both enacts its identity and confuses these cultural markings through the combination of movement, autobiographical text, and visual image. Spe-cifically, I contrast the images of race and gender in Cummings's *Chicken Soup* (1982) and the complex network of physical, social, economic, and political references that radically destabilizes her identity in "Blues II," a solo in *Basic Strategies* (1988), with the autobiographical work of David Dorfman, a white male whose solo dancing frequently foregrounds the political implications of that identity. I argue that works like Cummings's and Dorfman's provide a model for a theory of identity that is both radically destabilized and yet also lo-cated in the specific social markers of race, gender, ability, and class embedded within the material body.

The final chapter of the book, "Embodying History: Epic Narrative and Cultural Identity in African-American Dance," explores the question of cul-tural identity within the evening-length epic performance work of contempo-rary African-American choreographers Bill T. Jones and Jawole Willa Jo Zollar. The main focus of this chapter is a comparative analysis of Bill T. Jones/ Arnie Zane Dance Company's *The Last Supper at Uncle Tom's Cabin/The Promised Land* and Urban Bush Women's recent work *Bones and Ash: A Gilda Story*. I am interested in how these epic performance works both enact and rework mythic and historical images of slavery, colonial power, and religious faith within contemporary parables that allow each dancer to infuse the story with his or her own history and physicality.

Before I turn to my core arguments of the opening chapter, however, I want to make one more point. Despite my interest in feminist theory and my personal involvement in contemporary dance, *Choreographing Difference: The Body and Identity in Contemporary Dance* would never have been written without the courageous and outrageous artistic forays into issues of identity and representation by dancers and choreographers over the last decade. During that time, I witnessed performances that forced audience members to confront the cultural meanings of both the bodies they were watching and their own position as spectators. Twenty years ago, the dancing body was seen as a wonderful source of movement possibilities. Today, however, more and more dancers and choreographers are asking that the audience see their bodies as a source of cultural identity—a physical presence that moves with and through its gendered, racial, and social meanings. With a renewed emphasis on text, narrative, and autobiography, much contemporary dance focuses on the dancer's specific physical, emotional, and cultural experiences within the moment of dancing. It is their commitment to movement as an expressive artform and their resourcefulness in finding ways to continue their work within an era of shrinking financial and spiritual support that first set this book in motion. Based on their work, I invite the reader to join in the dance.[11]

CHOREOGRAPHING **DIFFERENCE**

Mining
the Dancefield

Feminist Theory

and Contemporary Dance

INTRODUCTION

In 1979, Annette Kolodny wrote an essay entitled "Dancing Through the Minefield: Some Observations on the Theory, Practice and Politics of a Feminist Literary Criticism." Tracing the expansion of a feminist inquiry within the academy, particularly in literary studies, Kolodny outlined various ways in which an emerging generation of feminist scholars was re-envisioning its relationship to the literary canon. Kolodny's essay described three propositions that reflected important shifts in scholarly paradigms, laying out the critical foundations for future feminist work within her discipline: "1. Literary history (and with that, the historicity of literature) is a fiction. . . . 2. Insofar as we are taught to read, what we engage are not texts, but paradigms. . . . 3. Since the grounds upon which we assign aesthetic value to texts are never infallible, unchangeable, or universal, we must reexamine not only our aesthetics but, as well, the inherent biases and assumptions informing the critical methods which (in part) shape our aesthetic responses."[1] Kolodny's essay summarized several ways in which feminist theory was attempting to dismantle the ideologies embedded within the production and consumption of cultural knowledges. Although her discipline is literary studies, Kolodny's three statements reflect a broader shift in feminist inquiry from discussing visual and textual images of women as empirical, historical data, to unraveling the complex network of representation and identity in the making and receiving (reading) of these images. Perhaps one of Kolodny's most important points, however, concerns her declaration that literature is, in fact, a social institution, one that both reflects and constitutes power relations within our culture as a whole. This commitment to politically engaged scholarship gives her conclusion a tone of urgency as she appeals to academic feminists to remember that "ideas are important *because* they determine the ways we live. . . . In my view, it is a fine thing for many of us, individually, to have traversed the minefield; but that happy circumstance will only prove of lasting importance if, together, we expose it . . . so that others, after us, may literally dance through the minefield."[2]

The title of this chapter, "Mining the Dancefield," consciously inverts Kolodny's own title in order to reveal both my indebtedness to the last quarter-century of feminist scholarship and the very particular slant with which I approach these studies. I am a dancer and performer, as well as a feminist scholar. I like to think and move at the same time. While the body has become the latest trendy discursive site in contemporary cultural theory, dance—which is arguably one of the most extensive physical and intellectual cultural discourses of (about, on, with, for) the body—has received scant serious attention outside of its own scholarly community. Jane Desmond makes this point abundantly clear in a recent essay when she declares, "Dance remains a greatly undervalued and undertheorized arena of bodily discourse. Its practice and its scholarship are, with rare exception, marginalized within the academy."[3] The irony is that dance research can help ground the troped or metaphorized body of much contemporary theory by analyzing actual cultural practices. As Desmond notes, dance can bring lived experience into our discussions of representation and cultural constructions of the body. "By enlarging our studies of bodily 'texts' to include dance in all of its forms—among them social dance, theatrical performance, and ritualized movement—we can further our understandings of how social identities are signaled, formed, and negotiated through bodily movement."[4]

One sense of "Mining the Dancefield" comes from my desire to shake up dance studies, to figuratively explode the traditions of aesthetic evaluation and abstract philosophical inquiry that have so long guided the scholarship within the field. Like Kolodny, I want to examine and critique the ideologies of dance criticism and research, and to ask which bodies and whose experiences are being overlooked in these texts. The other sense of "mining" that my title implies parallels Desmond's critique of the continued marginalization of dance studies. While feminist theory has helped me to mine (in the sense of explode or shake up) the critical complacency of earlier dance scholarship, it is important to acknowledge that dance can, in turn, provide feminist theory with rich intellectual resources as well. If I spent the latter part of the eighties trying to understand and incorporate feminist critiques into my discussions of contemporary dance, I spent the first half of the nineties trying to "talk back" to feminist theory—trying to demonstrate how dance can stretch and reinvigorate feminist discussions of the body, representation, social differences, and cultural identity. While this book as a whole is written at the intersection of feminist theory and dance, my introductory discussion will directly address what I see as the imaginative and intellectual limits of much contemporary theorizing about bodies. By analyzing how the embodied experience of dancing can provide a counter (and resistant) discourse to representations of the body *even while* creating those representations, I take up and respond to central questions in feminist theory such as: (a) how is the body defined in Western culture? (b) how is lived experience theorized? (c) what is important about feminist conceptualizations of the "male" gaze and how does this spectatorial dynamic work in dance? and finally (d) how does dance perform, revise, or reinscribe notions of cultural identity, including representations of gender, race, sexuality, and ability?

THE BODY OF DANCE

Unlike most other cultural productions, dance relies on the physical body to enact its own representation. But at the very moment the dancing body is creating a representation, it is also in the process of actually forming that body. Put more simply, dancing bodies simultaneously produce and are produced by their own dancing. This double moment of dancing in front of an audience is one in which the dancer negotiates between objectivity and subjectivity—between seeing and being seen, experiencing and being experienced, moving and being moved—thus creating an interesting shift of representational codes that pushes us to rethink the experience of the body within performance. In a historical moment when the "body" is considered to be a direct purveyor of identity and is thus the object of so much intellectual and physical scrutiny, a moment when academics and scientists, as well as artists and politicians, are struggling to understand the cultural differences between bodies, dance can provide a critical example of the dialectical relationship between cultures and the bodies that inhabit them.

Because it carries the intriguing possibility of being both very abstract and very literal, dance can foreground a body's identity differently. Some contemporary choreography focuses the audience's attention on the highly kinetic physicality of dancing bodies, minimizing the cultural differences between dancers by highlighting their common physical technique and ability to complete the often strenuous movement tasks. Other dances foreground the social markings of identity on the body, using movement and text to comment on (often subvert) the cultural meanings of those bodily markers. Tracing the layers of kinesthetic, aural, spatial, as well as visual and symbolic meanings in dance can help us to understand the complex interconnectedness of personal experience and cultural representation so critical to contemporary cultural theory. Indeed, much contemporary dance makes visible the movement between these personal and social realities.

This slippage between the lived body and its cultural representation, between a somatic identity (the experience of one's physicality) and a cultural one (how one's body—skin, gender, ability, age, etc.—renders meaning in society) is the basis for what I consider some of the most interesting explorations of identity in contemporary dance. Much of the choreography that I will be discussing over the course of this book plays with, challenges, and questions idealized images (of love, femininity, family, health, etc.) and traditional narratives, consciously bringing to the audience's attention the gaps between the stereotypes and the reality of the dancers' physical lives. These dances often focus on the negotiation between how one defines one's body in face of how that body is defined by society. Although it is *of* the body, dance is not just *about* the body, it is also about subjectivity—about how that body is positioned in the world as well as the ways in which that particular body responds to the world. By foregrounding the way identity is figured corporeally, by challenging which bodies are allowed which identities, and by fracturing the voyeuristic relationship between audience and performer, these contemporary dances refute traditional constructions of the body. As we shall see, their work addresses the (dis)connections between physical bodies and their cultural identities, refiguring the relationship between the "eyes" of the audience and the "I's" of the dancers in order to open up new ways of moving and being in the world.

Even though my subject is contemporary dance, my intellectual focus centers on the epistemological status of the body. I use the term epistemological (to know, to understand, literally to stand upon a place) because what is at stake in discussions about the body is often not simply an issue of knowledge (how do we best come to know the body—through language, images, sensations, or experiences?) but also one of place (where do we place the body—in nature or in culture?). Because dance is primarily a nonverbal artform that places the physical body at the center of its representational structure, dance in the West has been perceived as existing in a semiotic vacuum, outside of language and meaning. Elusive and ephemeral, the dancing body has evoked a whole series of fantastic images and metaphors that, unfortunately, tend to gloss over the more profound implications of an art that is so fully grounded in the physical body. For dance is not only about long legs, grace, or specific movement styles. It can also tell us a lot about the social value of the body within a particular culture. Learning to perceive the multiple layers of cultural meanings of the body in dance requires, however, a willingness to converse in different languages—both physical and verbal—at once. Thus, to understand the ways the dancing body can signify within a culture, one must engage with a variety of discourses: kinesthetic, visual, somatic, and aesthetic, as well as intellectual.

The body is currently a site of much critical debate, as contemporary theorists wrangle over the questions of how people's bodies are affected by cultural representation. Growing up female and a feminist has convinced me of what so many other feminists have taken pains to analyze, namely that a network of social ideologies imbues the body in Western culture with ablist, racist, classist, sexist, and often just downright repressive ideals. On the other hand, being involved with contemporary dance as both a dancer and a critic for the last fifteen years has convinced me that bodies, while inscribed by social practices, are rarely passive receptacles of these structures. Lived bodies strain at the seams of a culture's ideological fabric. Inherently unstable, the body is always in a paradoxical process of becoming—and becoming undone. As any dancer or athelete will readily admit, the body never reaches a stable location, no matter how disciplined the training. The daily practice required to keep that body "in shape" exposes the body's instability, its annoying tendency to spill over its appropriate boundaries. Yet at the same time, that daily practice also structures a physical identity of its own making. Simultaneously registering, creating, and subverting cultural conventions, embodied experience is necessarily complex and messy. That is precisely what I find so exciting about contemporary dance.

It is my project here to articulate how culture is embedded in experiences of the body and how the body is implicated in our notions of identity. As a representational system concentrated in the live body, contemporary dance can help us trace this interconnectedness of bodies and identities by foregrounding the cultural significance of somatic experience. Before I begin to address these issues in terms of specific dances, however, it is important to recognize just what is at stake in bringing the physical body into the center of a discussion about representation and identity.

In the introduction to her book *Volatile Bodies*, Elizabeth Grosz describes the origins of what she calls a "profound somatophobia" in Western philosophy.[5] Here she discusses the enduring legacy of Platonic idealism, which relegated bodies, particularly female bodies, to the realm of unformed matter. This material substance—messy and excessive, refusing to be bound—needs to be controlled by the mind and ruled over by reason. If Plato is one of the earliest proponents of this dualistic philosophy, Descartes is one of its most famous theoreticians, for he not only distinguished mind from body and consciousness from the natural world, but he also considered the self as an exclusive function of the mind, pulling subjectivity completely away from any aspect of bodily existence. "I think therefore I am" not only places the self squarely in the realm of a dematerialized consciousness, but it also implies a rather static notion of selfhood. His "I am" is a state simply attained for some and not (as one's experience might suggest) a situation of constant negotiation and struggle.

In the last two decades feminists have provided us with a litany of examples documenting just how pervasive the separation of body and mind is in our culture. As they have aptly demonstrated, the foundational philosophies and religious ideologies of Western civilization first constructed and then sought to naturalize a dualistic paradigm that divided the world into oppositional categories such as body/mind, nature/culture, private/public, spirituality/corporeality, and experience/knowledge. These schematic polarizations created, in turn, unavoidable hierarchies that positioned the body as the material "other" to the transcendence of the mind. Sidonie Smith, in her book *Subjectivity, Identity and the Body*, describes the misogynistic legacy of this disembodiment of the universal subject and shows how it developed into a gendered separation of self and other, where the "other" was essentialized as being nothing but her body, left with a material void as her identity.[6] Judith Butler makes a similar point when she claims that:

By defining women as "Other," men are able through the shortcut of definition to dispose of their bodies, to make themselves other than their bodies. . . . From this belief that the body is Other, it is not a far leap to the conclusion that others are their bodies, while the masculine "I" is the noncorporeal soul. The body rendered as Other—the body repressed or denied and, then, projected—reemerges for this "I" as the view of others as essentially body. Hence, women become the Other; they come to embody corporeality itself.[7]

Not only women, of course, but also people of color, gay men, the disenfranchised, as well as people with disabilities, have historically been tied to the material conditions of their bodies, structuring an identity that has repeatedly been constructed as oppressively and basely physical, as a lack of selfhood—a lack of moral, spiritual, and social agency. Indeed, the repressive implications of this tradition are felt most strongly by those individuals whom the society associates with bodily being. One of the central questions that *Choreographing Difference* deals with is: what happens, then, when people who are already marginalized as being *only* their bodies enter an artform that is similarly positioned as physical, intuitive, emotional, and nonintellectual? Of course, dancers are constantly being confronted with this particular cultural legacy, which has historically denigrated art composed of, for, and by physical bodies. Marginalized as being *only* their bodies because they work intensively *with* their bodies, dancers are often seen as pretty but dumb, inarticulate, childlike, irresponsible, and physically disciplined but morally loose—all because their bodies are available for visual consumption.[8] These cultural stereotypes reflect the hierarchical dichotomies in Western culture, revealing rather simplistic notions about the separateness of mind and body. The genres of modern, postmodern, and contemporary dance have confronted these stereotypes in an effort to articulate the complex reality of bodily being.

Not surprisingly, dance has run into many of the same hurdles as the women's movement of the 1970s. In its desire to reclaim the female body as a valuable place of knowledge and identity, seventies feminism sought to refute the body/mind dualism so prevalent in our culture. Indeed, much of the political energy of that time came from women's efforts to accept their bodies as a crucial part of their selfhood, to understand the cultural implications of menstruation and maternity, and to forge political alliances with other women based on the commonality of the female body. Yet because they claimed the body as a place of knowledge and physicalized their movement with public displays of rebellion (making real "spectacles" out of themselves in the process), these feminists were quickly marginalized as hysterical women— seen as being overly influenced by their bodies, rather than as having their bodies tempered by a large dose of rational thought. One of the lessons to be learned from that historical moment (besides the fact that we can't ignore the very real differences of class, race, and ideology, etc. between women) is that it is impossible simply to shift the power dynamic within the somatophobic structures of Western culture in order to reify bodies, particularly women's bodies, as a locus of personal agency. It isn't enough to claim that women's bodies are oppressed by the patriarchal order and then wax nostalgic about the possibility of an unfettered, liberated physicality that would render one "free to be me." Rather, we need to interrogate and deconstruct ideas that situate the body as precultural, as the "natural" ground onto which society builds its own image.

Over the last decade, the relationship between women's bodies and their sense of selfhood has become increasingly perplexing. Indeed, some feminist critics are now beginning to question not only the connection between a given biology (female) and a given gender (feminine), but the entire cultural construction of biology as well. Why privilege the body's genitalia as a category of difference at all? The problems with this intellectual position for a feminist movement in America quickly become self-evident. If in the course of a rigorous feminist questioning of cultural constructions of sex and gender we lose the category of women altogether, then how can we form any kind of political coalition focused on the rights of women to control our own bodies? On the other hand, by uniting in the name of women (even if we acknowledge all the important differences of class, race, sexuality, and age that separate our experiences as women), we risk reifying the very distinction that so often denies us political power to begin with. This tension between establishing a sense of collectivity based on a bodily distinction, be it race, gender, ability, or sexuality, and recognizing the important differences within each group, is inherent in almost every political movement, and it is particularly striking in the identity politics of the last decade. How can we affirm a sense of unity without essentializing the body and falling into eugenic stereotypes? One way out of this dilemma is to begin to think of identity as a cultural performance in which one can strategically highlight different aspects of the body. Judith Butler begins her book *Gender Trouble* with Simone de Beauvoir's famous line: "One is not born a woman, but rather becomes one." Over the course of a stunning analysis of the interdependent constructions of sex, gender, and identity, Butler increasingly problematizes this historic sentence. Not only is the present indicative of the verb "to be" destabilized into a continuous process of becoming, but the very notion of a "one" who can become anything at all is rendered a logical impossibility. "If there is something right in Beauvoir's claim that one is not born, but rather *becomes* a woman, it follows that woman itself is a term in process, a becoming, a constructing that cannot rightfully be said to originate or to end."[9] The "becoming" of women, then, is an enactment—a performance of sorts—and as such resists both a biological teleology and a cultural ontology. Although Butler first defines gender as "the repeated stylization of the body, a set of repeated acts within a highly rigid regulating frame that congeal over time to produce the appearance of substance, of a natural sort of being,"[10] she recognizes the existential limits of performance and the ways in which "repeated acts" undermine the stability of the very gender they are said to express. Performances (whether theatrical events or framed moments in everyday life) are physicalized within a specific time and space, often (although not always) with a live audience, and therefore can never be *exactly* repeated. This ephemeral nature of performance makes for a very intriguing slippage.

In a later essay on the politics of announcing one's identity as a lesbian (the performance of coming out), Butler describes the way in which repetition at once enacts and displaces that identity. "Rather, it is through the repeated play of this sexuality that the 'I' is insistently reconstituted as a lesbian 'I'; paradoxically, it is precisely the *repetition* of that play that establishes as well the *instability* of the very category that it constitutes."[11] Like Butler, I am quite interested in the ways in which this sense of identity, figured as performance, can serve to destabilize cultural notions about the essential nature of bodily categories. But I am struck by a critical distinction in Butler's two notions of repetition. When she describes gender as a "repeated stylization of the body," or "repeated acts . . . that congeal over time," Butler is talking about bodily habits that become so automatic they begin to seem completely "natural." In "Performative Acts and Gender Constitution: An Essay in Phenomenology and Feminist Theory," Butler reiterates her definition of gender as a "stylization of the body [that] must be understood as the *mundane* way in which bodily gestures, movements, and enactments of various kinds constitute the illusion of an abiding gendered self" [emphasis added].[12] The "repeated play" of sexuality in the above citation concerning a lesbian identity, however, is a much more conscious kind of repetition, one that knows the stakes of its own self-representation and can imagine an empowering "strategic intervention" within the very cultural codes that determine its currency. The question I have for Butler is: how does one interrupt the "naturalized" gendered physicality (the repetitions of which create a sense of stability) in order to stage the more "performative" one (whose repetitions establish instead an unstable category)?

My point here is that so often in feminist theorists' discussions of gender and identity, the body is associated with a series of internalized cultural regulations that tend to come under the guise of socially defined "natural" attributes. Once the ideological "naturalness" of those conventions is deconstructed, however, their physical remnants are not so automatically displaced. Pulled away from its overdetermined psychic (and psychoanalytic) relationship to the body, sexuality, on the other hand, is often figured as a place of resistance without accounting for the bodily echoes of those physically ingrained cultural patterns. The delightful instability of Butler's "I" no longer seems to be tied to a material body as the one she earlier evokes is. Are we to assume, then, that the body is now also a site of instability? If the categories of gender and sex can be destabilized, then what about the categories of race or physical ability? Can they too be destabilized? In theory? In practice? Perhaps more to the point, what does this destabilized body actually look like? A lot of feminist theory becomes pretty confusing when one insists on keeping the physical reality of material bodies within the conceptual framework. Butler's theory of gender as performance marks sexual identity as a shifting category (one that is consciously "played" out), but it never accounts for how the body receives, produces, and interacts with that very potent psychic instability.

My frustration with much recent cultural theory comes to a head at the moments when the body is either described as an object of social control, as when cultural conventions are inscribed upon the seemingly passive body, or, conversely, when it is discussed as a signifier whose sign has conveniently evaporated. The message is there, but the medium is gone. Either way, the impact of embodied experience on our concepts of identity is glossed over. I am intrigued by Butler's notion of a "performative" identity, but my focus on contemporary dance compels me to wonder what it would mean (practically as well as conceptually) to destabilize a cultural identity without denying the very real materiality of that body. Addressing this question requires a full recognition of how a shifting "performative" identity is nonetheless experienced as variously, yet continuously, embodied.

THEORIZING EXPERIENCE

It is hard to talk about bodily experience. It has always been hard, and the recent deluge of critical thinking about how experiences of the body and identity are culturally constructed hasn't—ironically enough—made it much easier. Like the dancing body in performance, experience is elusive, and discussing it requires the strategic negotiation between a subject (whose experience are we talking about?) and an object (exactly what experience are we trying to articulate?). But the hardest part is linking the two, for although one is obviously affected by one's experience (of privilege, racism, age, etc.), one is never completely determined by that experience. Hence the verb *to be* is too restrictive, while the verb *to have* seems overly possessive. The dialectic between who one is, what one lives through, and how one makes sense of all that, creates a particularly complex interweaving of identity, experience, and representation. The desire to explain, catalogue, and control phenomena that is embedded in Western rationalism has driven many a theorist to try to determine a causal relationship within this triad. It is not my interest here to enter into that kind of inquiry. Rather, I would like to discuss experience, specifically experience of the body, in order to trace the context and contours of its role in mediating between representation and identity. Of course, as I have noted earlier, this means that we must be willing to talk about the body's sensations, kinesthetic impressions, emotional reactions, and physical comportment as well as its historically and culturally inflected signification. In order to theorize about bodies, we must be willing to engage with their physical as well as their metaphysical meanings.

At the end of her book *Alice Doesn't: Feminism, Semiotics, Cinema,* Teresa deLauretis tries to build a bridge from her discussions of narrative and desire in representation over to experience and subjectivity. Leading off with the famous passage from Virginia Woolf's *A Room of One's Own,* where Woolf's female character is chided by a male academic for walking aross the lawn where women are not allowed, deLauretis redefines Woolf's use of instinct ("Instinct rather than reason came to my help: he was a Beadle; I was a woman") as cultural knowledge or habit. Instinct, for deLauretis, has "too strong a connotation of automatic, brute, mindless response."[13] She prefers experience: "The notion of experience seems to me to be crucially important to feminist theory in that it bears directly on the major issues that have emerged from the women's movement—subjectivity, sexuality, the body, and feminist political practice."[14] However, once deLauretis evokes the political relevancy of experience, she steers clear of the theoretical murkiness of material lived bodies. "I use the term not in the individualistic, idiosyncratic sense of something belonging to one and exclusively her own . . . but rather in the general sense of a *process* by which, for all social beings, subjectivity is constructed. Through that process one places oneself or is placed in social reality, and so perceives and comprehends as subjective (referring to, even originating in, oneself) those relations—material, economic, and interpersonal—which are in fact social and, in a larger perspective, historical."[15]

While I appreciate deLauretis's articulation of experience as interactive process, I find her too quick to pass over aspects of experience, particularly physical experience, that are not so easily categorized. To be sure, this experience of Woolf's character—the "I" of the story—is a prime example of the social positioning of women, but suppose for a moment that deLauretis had started to quote Woolf earlier in her essay.

Thought . . . had let its line down into the stream. It swayed, minute after minute, hither and thither among the reflections and the weeds, letting the water lift it and sink it, until—you know the little tug—the sudden conglomeration of an idea at the end of one's line. . . . But however small it was, it had, nevertheless, the mysterious property of its kind—put back into the mind, it became at once very exciting, and important; and as it darted and sank, and flashed hither and thither, set up such a wash and tumult of ideas that *it was impossible to sit still*. It was thus that I found myself walking with extreme rapidity across a grass plot. (Emphasis added)[16]

This wonderful stream of consciousness description evokes a certain affective quality of physical experience that gets dropped out of deLauretis's discussion. It is the energizing engagement with her thoughts that brings Woolf's character to her feet, propelling her across the grass and smack into that black-robed keeper of those awesome patriarchal lawns. Mediated through a series of lived events in which the narrator excitedly and literally follows the thread of an idea right up to the threshhold of a (male) academic institution, this section of *A Room of One's Own* represents the interaction between somatic experience and social definitions that constitutes the ongoing process of subjectivity. I would argue that the "I" of this first passage doesn't evaporate as she confronts the Beadle who puts her back in her place. Indeed, it was not the thoughts per se but the somatic attitude of her body that was transgressive, not simply the geographic fact of her (mis)placement, but its energized concentration. At the time that Woolf's character gets put in her place as a woman, she still has the experience of refusing that place—the experience of not being able to "sit still."

I am elaborating on this example because it is indicative of a certain myopia about what constitutes meaningful experiences. Too often feminists speak of the body only in terms of the cultural constructions of the female body. This constructed body is seen as a sort of material blank page onto which society etches its own image. But I have spent too much time working with bodies to want to gloss over the implications of a physical engagement with the world. Cultural identity is not necessarily synonymous with somatic identity. Yet neither is a somatic identity any more "real" or essential than a social one simply because it is anchored in the body. Rather, the two are interconnected in the process of living that we call experience. Understanding the multiple features of that experience will help us to articulate how the dancing body can at once enact and resist its own representation.

LOOKING AT DANCE

Once we accept that bodily experience lies in the intersection of the personal and the social, the question that immediately arises is: "can we see that experience?" I have argued that dance is a radically different form of representation because of the presence of live bodies, those of the performers as well as those of the viewers. How do these live bodies affect our seeing? Can we actually learn to see the dancer's bodily experience? How can we include the bodily experience of the performer (and not just the desire of the spectator) in theories of representation? As I suggested earlier, dance performances encompass what I consider to be a fascinating double moment in which performing bodies are both objects of the representation and subjects of their own experience. I envision this dual moment in dance as a sideways figure eight, with the dancing body situated at the intersection of two loops circumscribing the realms of representation and physical experience. Although these two loops are separated here for the purposes of my analysis, it is important to understand that there is a continual flow of the body along the pathway of the figure eight such that the dancing body is constantly crossing and crisscrossing both realms. The ambiguity of this situation creates the possiblity of an interesting slippage of viewing priorities. In what follows, I engage with several theories of representation in order to understand how dances and dancers can elicit different ways of seeing.

Let us begin with her physique. . . . Cerrito is blonde, with very gentle and tender blue eyes and a pleasant smile that is possibly a little too much in evidence. Her shoulders and bust have nothing of that skinniness that is usually the mark of a ballerina, whose entire substance seems to have sunk into the legs. Her rounded, well-covered arms do not offend the eye with sorry anatomical details, but unfold gracefully and with suppleness. Her charming figure gives no hint of the fatigue of the studio or the sweat of training. . . . Her feet are small and well arched, her ankles slender, and her legs shapely. . . . In short, she is young and attractive, and makes a good impression.[17]

This description of a dance performance by the celebrated Romantic ballerina Fanny Cerrito was written by an equally celebrated nineteenth-century writer and dance critic, Théophile Gautier. Although Cerrito, by the time of this review in 1846, had fashioned a half dozen ballets in her own right, Gautier elides any reference to her unusual status as both a soloist and a choreographer. Indeed, Gautier's description of Cerrito gives the reader very little sense of what her dancing actually looked like. The fact that she moves instead of standing still seems, finally, of scant importance—as if dance were simply an interesting and novel frame in which to display more effectively the female body.

Twenty-some years ago, feminist film studies helped to revolutionize cultural studies of representation by moving away from the meticulous documentation of archetypal female characters found in mainstream movies to an exploration of how the very mechanical apparatus of cinema itself (the form rather than the content, that is) conveyed a gendered structure to the visual positions of viewer and viewed. Deeply informed by psychoanalytic theory, film studies sought to uncover the voyeuristic underpinnings that ground the traditional workings of cinema. Beginning with Laura Mulvey's influential essay "Visual Pleasure and Narrative Cinema," attempts to articulate what has come to be known as "the male gaze" outline a central dilemma in film: "Going far beyond highlighting a woman's to-be-looked-at-ness, cinema builds the way she is to be looked at into the spectacle itself."[18] Mulvey positions this process within a series of predominantly male looks—those of the camera, the director, and, by extension, the spectator.

Not surprisingly, given the history of dance as a showcase for bodies to be displayed, certain genres of dance also have a series of looks that parallel those which Mulvey and other feminists outline in film and the visual arts. While it is dated by a century and a half, Gautier's description of Cerrito's dancing body reveals the gendered dynamics of representation still present in various forms of theatrical dancing, where the female (or feminized) body is set up on a stage as a spectacle to be viewed by an implicitly male audience member.[19] For instance, classical ballet choreography often constructs a triad of gazes remarkably similar to that of the camera, film director, and spectator. Women ballerinas are traditionally placed and displayed by a male partner, whose gaze reflects that of the (usually male) choreographer and guides that of the audience (who, whether they are male or female, are positioned in the role of the male spectator and/or critic). Indeed, much of the choreography and dynamic phrasing of ballet works to highlight the various signature poses of the ballerina, which become a series of mini-pictures punctuating the dancing with recognizable moments. Even in less obviously patriarchal genres of dance, it is often difficult to escape or deconstruct the implicit power dynamic of this powerful gaze.

More recently, cultural critics have articulated a notion of multiple gazes, that is, visual gazes based not only on sexual difference (as in the male gaze) but also on racial, class, ethnic, and physical differences as well.[20] Obviously who you are and what you are looking at will determine a great deal about how you look. Even though theories of multiple gazes point out how these various gazes conflict with or contradict one another (for instance, the powerful social institution of the male gaze may be disrupted by a counterdynamic of a racial gaze), they tend to assume that whatever is being gazed at is a static image. Ironically enough, while these theories acknowledge that we may be looking *for* different things and *with* different cultural priorities, the very act of looking itself is hardly questioned. The physical presence of the dancer—the alive-ness of her body—radically challenges the implicit power dynamic of any gaze, for there is always the very real possibility that she will look back! Even if the dancer doesn't literally return the gaze of the spectator, her ability to pre-sent her own experience can radically change the spectatorial dynamic of the performance.

Years of watching experimental dance and performance work has con-vinced me that different kinds of performances can elicit different kinds of gazes. This observation seems so simple as barely to warrant saying, but it rubs up against an almost monolithic notion in theories about representation, of the viewer as subject and the viewed as object. (As I have already pointed out, even the more recent conceptualizations of multiple gazes still tend to regard what is being looked at in terms of static or passive images.) I want to compli-cate this paradigm by evoking, with a slightly different goal this time, the process of "becoming" that Butler articulates in her discussions of identity. For it is important to recognize that the gerund that refuses the coming-to-be-any-one-thing nonetheless posits a physical reality—a presence—that incorporates a meaning of its own.

In her insightful essay "On the Pedestal: Notes on Being an Artist's Model," Elizabeth Hollander confronts the issue of being looked at in her description of a classic moment in the history of representation.

I got onto the stand and, before I had time to start feeling funny about being naked, I was told to take four five-minute poses, a prospect which did far more to confuse and unnerve me than mere physical exposure could have done. I had had, however, some experience on the amateur stage, and so, summoning all my powers of composure, I turned and stood.[21]

The question of an artist's model's subjectivity presents a curious paradox, which is signaled grammatically by the double possessive. Can we ever see the traces of her subjectivity and experience within a painted representation? How can we figure the model's experience within a picture authorized by someone else's signature and point of view? In the course of this article Hol-lander elucidates the contradictions of being both an "object of attention" and a "subject for art." Ostensibly, there is little to do and yet the doing itself can be rewarding, even personally satisfying. As Hollander navigates through the foreboding swells of feminist guilt at positioning herself (consciously, no less) in terms of the gaze, and through a lesser hesitation at making a profession out of such an inherently narcissistic concern, she begins to chart the possibility of a subjectivity not in face of, but rather in the middle of, a traditional artistic frame. Importantly, she locates this experience in terms of a performative presence.

The most important virtue a model can have, however, is the least easily definable: presence. Modeling is a kind of performance, and so it requires the performer to command her stage. . . . The difficulty here is that we usually associate drama with action, be it internal or external, while the model's presence must be still, both physically and emotionally. . . . To achieve a powerful or suggestive effect without benefit of action, motion, clothes or speech requires a consciousness of one's physical presence as expressive in and of itself.[22]

As she "turned and stood" in that very first drawing class, Hollander started to affect the visual reception of her body. In that initial act of taking a stand she was able to physically express—in the literal sense of extending outside of one's self—her own image.

Now Hollander never pretends to upstage the real business of making art. She knows that whatever quiet authority she wields in the drawing studio will most likely be overlooked within the context of the stock and trade of painting. Nonetheless, Hollander's essay demonstrates just how significant her experience can be. Coming of age in the midst of the women's movement, Hollander takes her stand consciously and historically, positioning herself on that pedestal among the many images of women in art history.

The first time I had to pose for a drawing, I immediately began to think of great paintings and drawings I had seen, and while not every model has had my experience of art history, there is some way in which every model must refer to her own experience or images of women, whatever their range, whenever she takes a pose. The model must become, at some level, part of the history of art for three hours. . . .[23]

What interests me is that Hollander places herself on both sides of the picture. Regardless of whether her painted image actually disrupts the male gaze, Hollander's work is important because she forces us to open the myopic tunnel of vision and recognize the possibility of another perspective, another kind of experience. But perhaps what is most valuable is that Hollander takes her stand in print, contributing from behind the frame to an ongoing discourse about women and vision. I appreciate Hollander's willingness to travel through various landscapes, from the personal place of her body on the pedestal, through cultural histories of painted images, and onto the written page, and I admire the fact that she is prepared to brush up alongside a well-heeled feminist polemic and risk the uncertainty of theorizing about her lived experiences.

While it would admittedly be simplistic to assume that the authority of experience is any more real or authentic than the complex cultural mechanisms embedded in representation, reproduction and reception, neither do I believe that sophisticated theoretical paradigms should completely erase other, perhaps more awkward, sources of information. Written at the intersection of art history and feminist thought, "On the Pedestal: Notes on Being an Artist's Model" carves out the possibility of seeing a model's experience, which is particularly relevant to my discussion of representation in dance.

The aura of "presence" that Hollander invokes suggests a certain authority (which Hollander calls "command"), a sense of both physical positioning and metaphysical subjectivity. This notion of a performing presence—the power of physical beingness—is an integral part of dance. Unfortunately, it has often been romanticized as a magical, ineffable quality that can transcend the specificities of movement style, cultural context, and historical moment to posit a universal aesthetic *communitas* between audience and performer. I am interested in cracking the glass bubble of mystery surrounding this particular experience in order to recognize its historical and cultural basis, for it seems to me that presence is a word that covers (and sometimes covers over) the interrelationship of bodies and gazes in dance. In the section that follows, I will look at two examples of exceptional presences in the history of American dance: Isadora Duncan, the pioneer of modern dance who crystalized an image of the new woman early in the twentieth century, and Yvonne Rainer, whose dance work during the sixties and seventies consolidated a postmodern approach to movement. These women, I will argue, became noteworthy because they refocused the conventions of viewing dance that were popular during their time, thus allowing their audiences to see their dancing with a different kind of spectatorial focus.

Quite still. . . . Then one step back or sideways, and the music began again as she went on moving on before or after it. Only just moving—not pirouetting or doing any of those things which we expect to see, and which a Taglioni or a Fanny Elssler would have certainly done. She was speaking in her own language—do you understand? her own language: have you got it?—not echoing any ballet master, and so she came to move as no one had ever seen anyone move before.[24]

This description of the first time he had ever seen Isadora Duncan dance by Gordon Craig, son of the famed British actress Ellen Terry and later one of Duncan's lovers, underscores one of the most radical qualites of Duncan's performing presence. When he writes of how Duncan established "her own lan-

guage" of the body, Craig is describing not only Duncan's innovative movements, but also her reordering of the visual priorities of dance. Although she is
most (in)famous for her bare feet and uncorseted body, her evangelistic insistence on dance as a "high" and spiritual art, and her use of "great" classical
composers, Duncan was taken seriously in her day because she radically
shifted the structural dynamic of dance performances. Her wave-like motions
—the rush, suspension, and retreat of her body back and forth across the space
—refused the visual poses of previous dance forms, establishing in their stead
an exchange based on a strong kinesthetic experience.

Duncan's spatial and spiritual generosity, the virtual flooding of imaginary
water and light that energized her dancing, must have affected her viewers'
bodies, encouraging them by way of her movement to join in this kinesthetic
dialogue. Rushing forward as she scooped through space to arrive at the edge
of the stage, her body fully extended and her arms and head facing upward,
Duncan's extraordinary presence—that activating luminosity which infuses
the performance with a sense of aliveness in the spectators and testifies to an
expressive power within the performer—engaged the audience to such a degree that they must have felt literally swept up in her dancing. Despite her
Hellenistic rhetoric, Duncan's body was never as cool as a marble sculpture,
making it difficult to watch her in only a distanced, aestheticized fashion. Pro-
jecting a physical energy out through the monumental spaces that inspired her
dancing, she brought to the stage an insistent awareness of her own lived
physicality, generating a responsiveness in the viewers which, I want to suggest, includes their own bodily experience.

In her article "Dance History and Feminist Theory: Reconsidering Isadora
Duncan and the Male Gaze," Ann Daly discusses Duncan's seminal influence
on the development of American modern dance in terms that refute simplistic
notions of the male gaze. "[T]he metaphor of representation as a 'gaze' is not
as suited to dance as it is to static visual media such as cinema and art. Dance,
although it has a visual component, is fundamentally a kinesthetic art whose
apperception is grounded not just in the eye, but in the entire body."[25] Drawing on Julia Kristeva's notion of the "chora" (Kristeva places nonverbal gesture and corporeal knowledge in this realm of cultural meaning), Daly argues that the dancing body expresses meaning *differently* than most forms of
discourse.[26]

Daly's analysis of Duncan's visionary physicality and musical expressivity
allows her to describe how Duncan engaged her audience without positioning
her body as object of the gaze. "Instead of dancing squarely on the beat, she
played with the elasticity of her accompaniment's rhythm, embedding hesi-

tancy, fear, longing, or a whole host of inner states by variously quickening or suspending her movement through time."[27] What made Duncan's dancing so extraordinary, then, was her ability to share with the audience her experience while moving. This, I would argue, is what helped to create her powerful presence onstage. In language that parallels much of what I have been arguing, Daly describes Duncan's dancing body as "no longer a product—of training, of narrative, of consumption—but rather a process. The dance was about becoming a self (the subject-in-process/on trial) rather than about displaying a body."[28]

Duncan used her dancing to create a kinesthetic relationship with her audience, drawing on their rapt attention to bring out her own performing energy. Although the physicality and musicality of her movement brought her audience into contact with the contagious quality of kinesthetic sensation and thus challenged the usual gazes in dance at that time, Duncan still retained some of the traditional framing of women dancers as spectacle. Certainly it would be no overstatement to say she had star quality. Although various dance subcultures such as the 1930s Worker's Dance League tried to crack this packaging of the dancer as spectacle, it wasn't until the beginnings of postmodern dance that this cultural frame was consciously dismantled.

In 1965, Yvonne Rainer signaled a major shift in the focus of American experimental dance with her infamous "NO" manifesto.

NO to spectacle no to virtuosity no to transformations and magic and make-believe no to the glamour and transcendency of the star image no to the heroic no to the anti-heroic no to trash imagery no to involvement of performer or spectator no to style no to camp no to seduction of spectator by the wiles of the performer no to eccentricity no to moving or being moved.[29]

Written after a period of intensive physical research in which Rainer was trying to expunge narrative or rhythmic development and physical emotiveness, this sentence reflects one of the first attempts not only to create new, innovative movement, but also to alter the representational context of dance by resisting the implicit spectacularization of the dancing body. In her working journal of the time, Rainer encapsulated her motivation: "Basically, I wanted it to remain undynamic movement, no rhythm, no emphasis, no tension, no relaxation. You just *do* it, with the coordination of a pro and the non-definition of an amateur."[30]

A year later, in 1966, Rainer crafted a piece that sought to live up to her own manifesto by eliminating or at least minimizing certain aspects of theatricality in dance. Originally performed as three simultaneous solos, *Trio A* was an on-going series of pedestrian movements that were often juxtaposed in odd or difficult ways (such as picking up something from the floor while standing on one leg). The choreography was to be executed in a neutral, task-like manner, thereby thwarting the audience's expectation and desire to see a virtuosic dancer and forcing them to see, instead, the body as a simple object in motion. One of the dance's most striking aspects was the fact that the performer's face was almost always averted, involved in the movement rather than with the audience. Another point of resistance was the way the dance finished with the dancer's back to the audience, refusing the traditional frontal final pose.

In her essay on this period of Rainer's work entitled "Yvonne Rainer: The Aesthetics of Denial," Sally Banes calls *Trio A* a "paradigmatic statement of the aesthetic goals of post-modern dance."[31] For Banes, *Trio A* marked a radical shift from the binary opposition of ballet and modern dance. "The possibility is proposed that dance is neither perfection of technique nor of expression, but quite something else—the presentation of objects in themselves."[32] Banes's use of the word "objects" is telling here, for the work of Judson Dance Theater in the sixties and that of the Grand Union in the early seventies (both of which Rainer actively participated in) was concerned with using the body simply as a thing that senses, moves, and responds rather than as a physicalization of a dramatic persona. Rainer's desire to conceptualize the dancing body as an object came out of her attempt to resist its scopic objectification within the gendered economy of the male gaze. In other words, by emphasizing the earthy materiality of the physical body—its quality of thingness—Rainer was trying to demystify the female dancing body and refuse the traditional position of the dancer as an object of desire by making visible what was previously elided by showing the process of dancing, the effort, decision making, even its awkwardness. The irony here is the fact, attested to by so many of her contemporaries, that watching Rainer do *Trio A* was an incredibly riveting experience. Rather than making her body object-like, or distancing herself from her viewers, Rainer's resistance to the conventions of spectacle in *Trio A* compelled her audience to witness her own movement experience much more fully.

Although their individual movement styles and aesthetic desires were separated by a half century and a world of difference, both Rainer and Duncan radically shifted the terms of their (self-) representations. Duncan's musicality and Rainer's casually internal movement style brought the audience's attention to the process of making and remaking the self through movement. Because they were conscious of the stakes involved in performing their female selves, their dancing traveled back and forth across the dual loops of representation and experience to create two powerful physical presences.

DANCING ACROSS IDENTITY

Her knee lifts in a step that gets caught in mid-air, suspended while the underbeat of the drums gradually coaxes its way through her torso and out her shoulders, arms, and wrists until it reaches a final parting caress in her hands. Then another, and another, each step rising like the tide through her body while she tilts her head to listen and wait for another impulse to move. Her eyes are lulled by the soothing rhythms of the drums and her face seems almost sleepy as it shifts from one side to another. A deep breath pulls her out of her reverie and her chest rises up, swelling with a call that fills the space with the sound of her voice.

I wrote this description of Zab Maboungou's dancing after seeing the beginning section of *Reverdanse*, an evening-length solo work. As she steps from the darkness into the light onstage, Maboungou immediately introduces the viewer to the aesthetic prioirities in her dancing by focusing our attention on the intricate dialogue in her body between the rhythms of the drums and the motion of her dancing. Sometimes she surfs over the beat by drawing out a sustained arching of her upper torso. Sometimes she rides the sound of the drums, slowly sinking and rising as her shoulders punctuate the drummers' shifting cadences. There is a certain thoughtfulness to her moving, a self-reflexivity suggested in her program notes. "'Reverdance' is a celebration of movement which emphasizes the intimate over the flamboyant; nuances of internal adventure unravel through a progession of pieces, a saraband of small metamorphoses emerging from alternating melodies. . . ." "Rever" is French for to dream, and yet Maboungou doesn't translate it in the English version of the title (which sounds like both reverdance and riverdance), a choice that serves to underscore both the dream-like quality of her dancing and the continuous flow of the motion (like a river) throughout her body.

I saw an excerpt from *Reverdanse* in the fall of 1995, while I was in Montreal for the biannual Festival International de Nouvelle Danse (FIND). Maboungou's showing was part of an alternative festival of local Quebec dance (fondly called the OFF-FIND) and it included a discussion with the artist afterward. Zab Maboungou is a Congolese-Canadian dancer who describes her work as "contemporary African dance," a denotation that, as we shall see, rests uneasily with stereotypes about the place and function of traditional ethnic dance both in the Eurocentric as well as the Afrocentric dance communities. In the discussion of *Reverdanse* that follows, I use Clifford Geertz's notion of a "thick" description—that is, an analysis that elucidates the multiple layers of meaning in cultural performances—to demonstrate how *Reverdanse* resists

Zab Maboungou in
Reverdanse.
Photographer: Xavier Lluis.
Courtesy of "Cercle
d'Expression Artistique
Nyata Nyata."

the stereotypical production values of what often gets presented as "African" dance in the new world. Drawing on Butler's notion of the inherent instability of a "performative" identity, I argue that her work *re*fuses and *con*fuses the polarization of contemporary and traditional labels in African dance, provoking a debate about the politics of naming in dance.

Visually, *Reverdanse* presents us with many of the iconic signs of African dance. There are musicians onstage who set the atmosphere for the dancing with their drumming. The dancer is barefoot, wearing a raffia skirt and an elaborate raffia necklace with shells and beads. She is clearly of African descent, with medium brown skin and a short Afro. Her movements are multifocused and multirhythmic, composed of the isolations of the shoulders, central torso, and the hips. And yet, the deep internal focus of her solo and the subtle shifts of emotion differ radically from the African dance that usually gets presented in Canada and the United States. Typically, in a company that performs traditional African dance such as the Chuck Davis African American Dance Ensemble, a celebratory village setting is simulated with all the dancers and musicians forming a circle in which the performers take turns. The dancing is usually quite spectacular, aerobic, and frequently acrobatic, with the movement paralleling the musical accents of the drumming. The drums dictate the tempo and the steps, with each change signaled by the drummers. The atmosphere is most often exuberant, with a sense of dancerly one-upmanship encouraged by those on the sidelines.

Maboungou's dancing, however, seems to have a much more dialogic relationship with the music, and she often sustains a gesture across many beats. Her movement is rarely punctuated in an emphatic or forceful manner. Rather, the rhythms seem to mull around in the center of her body, her hips in conversation with her shoulders, or her belly responding to the movements of her arms. Sometimes, such as in the section of *Reverdanse* entitled "Savanes" (Savannah), she dances in silence, continuing the music through her vibrating body. It is this striking difference in performative intent from what often gets marketed as "African" dance that, I would argue, opens up a space for Maboungou's own experience of that identity to become visible. Because Maboungou refuses to enter the popular construction of an African woman dancer, her audience can't easily plug her into a stereotype. The looping of similar movement with subtle variations in attack or rhythm in Maboungou's dancing illustrates the double (and doubling) effect of repetition that Butler discusses in her theory of a "performative" identity. The fact that Maboungou is always in motion, always at once creating and dissolving images, allows her both to enact an identity and refuse its stability. Her dancing is about the process of becoming, not the "what" one has become. The gap created by this difference forces the viewer to look again, asking us to follow the nuances in her very personal experience of that identity.

Maboungou's choreography, her dancing signature, resists any simple categorization. While the cultural basis for her dancing is primarily African, her performances also evoke for me the shifting musicality of Duncan as well as the internalized focus and nonpretentious attitude of Rainer's postmodern dance. Because her presence vibrates between various cultural and aesthetic identities, Maboungou has, until recently, eluded popular and critical attention.[33] Her dilemma is one that many contemporary minority artists face. Splayed between different communities, these artists must negotiate a minefield of strategic alliances and shifting identities. Because her work is so individual and departs from typical mainstream notions of what constitutes "African" dance, the African communities in Montreal have had trouble seeing her work as a cultural resource of traditional dance. At the same time, because she works with the vocabulary of African dance, the Eurocentric avant-garde dance scene in Quebec doesn't include her as one of its contemporary choreographers. Ironically, rather than her innovations serving to broaden our notions of what constitutes African dancing, the opposite effect takes place, with people questioning whether her work is really authentic or not.

Africanists have long debated whether it is more important to focus on the similarities and continuities across various African cultures as well as those in the African diaspora, or whether we should be recognizing the real differences not only among African experiences in the new world, but also among the diverse African cultures on the continent. A book such as Molefi Kete Asante's *African Culture: The Roots of Unity* argues stridently for a sense of connection among all African peoples. Later works, particularly those by African-American feminists in the late eighties and nineties, are more willing to recognize the dialectic of continuity and discontinuity, particularly concerning issues of gender and sexuality. This is, of course, an enormous debate that I cannot begin to do justice to in this context. Dance scholars such as Brenda Dixon Gottschild and Kariamu Welsh Asante are uncovering the pan-Africanist foundations of much Western dance.[34] This is important work in the dance field, but we must be careful not to assume uniformity in the name of unity. Indeed, we must also call attention to the ways in which only *certain* aspects of African dance (celebratory, acrobatic, presentational, energetic, etc.) get marketed as "African." This deconstructive analysis will allow us in turn to realize the ways that dance by African peoples can consciously resist the construction of these stereotypes, opening up the possiblity for a cross-cultural dialogue of multiple influences in contemporary African dance.

What is at stake here is not just what gets defined and presented as traditional African dance, but also how the spectator/performer relationship is constructed through the representational structures of the performance. How do we engage with Maboungou's dancing? Often, for instance, companies such as Chuck Davis African American Dance Ensemble will try to create the theatrical illusion of a community setting, but this serves more as a frame for their highly spectacular dancing than as an indication of the aesthetic priorities of their work. As with any commercial staging of an indigenous form of dance that has roots in a rural, communal, or ritualized setting (be it Native American, Classical Indian, or African dance), the director/choreographer must make decisions about ethnic visibility and cultural identity. The Chuck Davis African American Dance Ensemble is dedicated to showcasing the extraordinary heritage of dances from West Africa for a variety of Euro-American and African-American audiences, and it has a laudable and extensive outreach organization that seeks to give African-American children an appreciation of their cultural backgrounds. As a resident company at the American Dance Festival, a six-week long summer workshop that draws hundreds of dancers each year, the Chuck Davis African American Dance Ensemble has also exposed many people (including me) to their technique and repertory of African dance. In their performance, the director, Chuck Davis, serves as a sort of master of ceremonies, welcoming his audience in the name of peace, love, and respect for everyone. He then introduces each dance and often gives a short contextual background for the work. His company and companies like them have created an important visibility for African and African-American dance and I want to make clear how much I admire their work.

Nonetheless, all this usually takes place within a presentational format that I find problematic. Although the movement forms and the casual theatrical business surrounding the dancing are quite different from the status quo of American concert dance (in which there is rarely any verbal interaction between the audience and performers, or even among the performers themselves), I find that the representational structures of traditional gazes are not really challenged in these situations. That is why performances like these can easily slip back into a racist ideology that frames the dancers as spectacles of the "other," as black bodies that are inherently exuberant and naturally rhythmic. I am not suggesting that this racist gaze is monolithic or necessarily invoked in all of these performances. Much depends on the venue, the marketing, and the audience. For instance, I have witnessed building of *communitas* in the theater during a Chuck Davis performance that radically displaced this gaze. But I have received enough press releases advertising Latino, African-American, or Native American companies with adjectives such as "colorful," "sensuous," "exciting," and yes, even "exotic" to recognize how easily it can be reinscribed.

What struck me in the first minute of watching Maboungou's dancing was how she constructed a performance that resisted this colonial gaze. The excerpts of *Reverdanse* that I saw took place in an intimate studio setting where there was no proscenium arch to separate the audience's space from that of the performer. The makeshift lighting that illuminated her dancing body spread out to include the audience. In addition, her physical presence seemed to ride a fine line between an open generosity and a self-centered focus. We were, after all, able to see the minute details of her movements rippling through her torso, and yet it was clear from her internal focus, subdued face,

Zab Maboungou in *Reverdanse*. Photographer: Xavier Lluis. Courtesy of "Cercle d'Expression Artistique Nyata Nyata."

and three-dimensional (rather than exclusively frontal) use of space, that we were witnessing her dancing in a way that insisted on the integrity of that experience.

I want to return to Butler's notion of a performative identity to investigate more fully what I mean by this last sentence. Butler theorizes identity as a "becoming," a process that is continually in motion, one that can never begin or end. What interests her about this process is the way its ongoingness—the need to constantly reenact an identity—foregrounds that identity's instability. I see a similar process take effect in Maboungou's dancing. When she refuses to address the audience in the usual presentational format, when she doesn't step into any recognizable shapes or iconographic movements, when she insistently returns to repeat a choreographic phrase with only slight variations, Maboungou emphasizes a similar process of "becoming" that fractures any static notion of her identity as an African woman dancer and choreographer. The experience of watching her enter a movement phrase again and again, each time with a different emphasis, forces the audience to witness the reality of her experience within that motion, fracturing the power dynamic in traditional gazes where the object of sight is there for the viewer's pleasure, not the dancer's. Maboungou's "becoming" thus resists commodification as any one image, and the lights fade out with Maboungou still in motion.

As Maboungou's dancing body moves through the double moment of representation and experience that is the basis of live performance (which I earlier described as a sideways figure eight), the reality of her bodily experience (her motion) becomes intertwined with the fact of her physical traits (hair color, body size, race, etc.). Although her audience reads the visible signs of race and ethnicity, they have to reinterpret those signs in light of her somatic experience. Following her bodily rhythms, their gazes are pulled away from any static image of who she is or what she represents. As she moves with and through her race and ethnicity, she is revising how we come to know those terms. In dance, cultural representation flickers in and out of somatic identity like a high-frequency vibration, dissolving the boundaries of categories such as self/other, nature/culture, body/mind, and private/public. This interconnectedness of bodies and identities creates what I consider the transformative power of live performance, and contemporary dance makes the most of it.

Techno Bodies

Muscling

with Gender

in Contemporary Dance

The one overwhelming image I have of La La La Human Steps' multimedia extravaganza *Infante, C'est Destroy* is of Louise Lecavalier flying through the air like a human torpedo. She gets caught by another dancer, thrashes around with him for a while, then vaults right out of his arms and halfway across the stage, only to rebound back into his face. A few minutes and who knows how many heartbeats later, she rears up from the floor one last time, shakes her mane of bleached-blond hair and struts off the stage with an attitude that would make the most vicious heavy metal rocker look like Pete Seeger by comparison.

Louise Lecavalier is the star of Édouard Lock's dance 'n' rock creation, which I witnessed during the 1993 Festival International de Nouvelle Danse in Montreal. Throughout this nonstop 75-minute spectacle, Lecavalier's body—both its hardened aerobic energy and its filmed image—is continuously on display. Pitted against the pounding sounds of Skinny Puppy, Janitors Animated, David Van Tiegham, and Einsturzende Neubauten, her dancing uses the driving beat of the music to stretch dance movements to the outer limits of physical possibility and endurance. At one point, Lecavalier grabs one of the various mikes littered around the stage and, panting, begins to discuss the metaphysical dimensions of music, heartbeats, and physical energy. She then produces a mini-mike, which she solemnly attaches to percussionist Jackie Gallant's chest. With the kind of cosmic, synergistic intensity that makes heavy metal so seductive to teenagers, Gallant begins to pound away at her drum. The harder Gallant drums, the faster her heartbeat. The faster her heartbeat, the faster she drums to keep up. As Gallant builds quickly to the orgasmic peak of her auto-aerobic union with the drum, Lecavalier comes crashing back to center stage, riding the musical tidal wave just as Gallant finishes.

The first ten minutes of Lecavalier's dancing are absolutely awe-inspiring. Within a few minutes, her well-defined muscles are pumped-up and her body is practically pulsating with untapped energy. The way she launches her body across the floor and at various partners is phenomenal. Physically, she is immensely powerful, a fact noted by audience members and dance reviewers alike. Lecavalier is repeatedly described in the lobby as well as in the press as a "human torpedo," a "canonball," a "rocket," or a "bullet." Similarly, her physique is ubiquitously evoked through the popular language of body building as either "chiseled," "ripped," or "granite." One reviewer even took these pervasive images of violence to their logical extreme, comparing the dancing of La La La Human Steps to a war. "Arms swing menancingly like knives, legs flash like bayonets, hips are thrust forward with the aggressiveness and rapidity of machine-gun fire, and whole bodies fly like rockets through the air."[1]

I find the obsessiveness with which reviewers discuss Lecavalier's body and movement and their inevitable violent or machine-like metaphors indicative of a certain unease with Lecavalier's corporeality. Her all-encompassing focus on vaulting back and forth across the stage creates an intense physicality that both literally and figuratively *crosses over* gender norms, even in the midst of a cultural moment in which both men and women are encouraged to cultivate a muscularly defined look in their bodies. By taking on the musculature and powerful, explosive movement that mark the achievement of high masculinity in sports, martial arts, and Arnold Schwarzenegger movies, Lecavalier's dancing persona is not easily contained in the role of "prima ballerina," even though Lock's choreography is so obviously an elaborate vehicle for the display of her extraordinary physicality. After the first ten minutes of the spectacle, however, Lecavalier's dancing begins to feel increasingly coerced. Whether she is framed by the camera, as in the huge, blown-up films showing her falling slowly through space, or by the men onstage, Lecavalier never seems to be able to break out of Lock's own vision of her body.

Édouard Lock is a filmmaker, a photographer, and a director of mega pop spectacles. Critics frequently call Lecavalier his muse, likening her role in *Infante, C'est Destroy* to a blend of Madonna and Joan of Arc. Visually they have a point. In the filmed section of the dance, she is dressed in metal armor, and while she is performing live onstage, Lecavalier flaunts the same kind of sexualized power that Madonna has successfully commodified—what I call the

Louise Lecavalier in *Infante, C'est Destroy*. Photo by Édouard Lock.

black leather tits and ass and biceps, abs, and quads look. But unlike Madonna, Lecavalier doesn't immediately relieve the cultural anxiety produced by her cross-dressing with a reassuringly feminine voice. Neither, however, does she embody spiritual power or usurp the male prerogative in quite the way that I've always imagined Joan of Arc did. The powerful implications of her physicality are eventually diluted by the relentless repetition of the same old stunts. Most of the time, Lecavalier and her two female backups, Pim Boonprakob and Sarah Williams, dance around in various stages of undress, frequently throwing themselves at the male dancers, who are usually dressed in suits. In contrast to her male partners, Lecavalier is either totally naked, topless, or dressed in a black bustier and tight, see-through shorts. Occasionally she will sport a black leather jacket, but usually that is when she is wearing nothing else on top. My point, of course, is not that the women get naked onstage, it is that they are the *only* ones who do so.

I have introduced this chapter with the example of Lecavalier's dancing in order to foreground the complexities of talking about the physical body and gender in contemporary dance. How, for instance, can we account for the fact that Lecavalier's dancing at once provides the means for, and yet simultaneously resists the paternalistic gaze of Lock's choreography? In what ways can a woman physically break out of the traditional representation of the "feminine" body, and in what ways does the "feminine" become literally reincorporated to accommodate the changing fashions of physical being? For, as Judith Butler quite rightly warns us in her book *Gender Trouble*, "The female body that is freed from the shackles of the paternal law may well prove to be yet another incarnation of that law, posing as subversive but operating in the service of that law's self-amplification and proliferation."[2]

Thinking about Lecavalier's body, its delineated muscles and fierce physicality, as well as its position within Lock's spectacle, brings us right up against one of the most ferociously contested issues in feminist and cultural studies today. What is the status of the female body? Is it entirely a product of social discourse, or is there a precultural body that is connected to a natural realm of human existence? During the 1980s, feminist theory focused these questions in terms of a central debate between essentialism and constructivism. Diana Fuss's succinct book *Essentially Speaking* is a useful primer on this issue. She defines the theoretical differences in the following manner:

For the essentialist, the body occupies a pure, pre-social, pre-discursive space. The body is "real," accessible, and transparent; it is always there and directly interpretable through the senses. For the constructionist, the body is never simply there, rather it is composed of a network of effects continually subject to sociopolitical determination. The body is "always already" culturally mapped; it never exists in a pure or uncoded state.[3]

Over the course of her book, Fuss deconstructs the oppositional position of each ideology, suggesting that essentialist thinking underlies the constructivist viewpoint and vice versa. She wonders, finally, whether "it may be time to ask whether essences can change and whether constructions can be normative."[4] Her point is well taken. Modern dance, for instance, was founded on a rhetoric of the "natural" (barefoot, uncorseted) female body. Yet modern dance actually (although often unselfconsciously) deconstructs its own essentialist ideology by codifying and teaching movement forms and techniques that are said to be more *natural* than other kinds of dance training. What becomes clear to the student involved in modern or contemporary dance forms that emphasize the "natural" body is that this is a very conscious construction—one that, in fact, takes years to embody fully—and it feels quite different from one's everyday experience of corporeality. On the other hand, feminist theories of representation that emphasize the constructed nature of the female body often have a strongly deterministic tone, one that suggests that since this body is "always already" mapped out, there is little room for resistance or change. These writers tend to assume that the socialized body is an *essential* characteristic of our experience.

Of course, the body is precisely the place where these two realms interact. It is the place where sensation, representation, and physical experiences are interpreted both symbolically and somatically. In this chapter, I want to shift the terms of this debate from arguments over the body as either a natural or social product, to an investigation of the how—the process through which bodies make and are made by cultures. This focus on the *process* of embodiment rather than the *product* of a particular kind of body allows me to understand the ways bodies and cultures are mutually formative, but at the same time it helps me to avoid the depressingly deterministic effects of many contemporary discussions of the regulated or submissive body.

As an artform that relies on the body to enact its own representation, dance is one of the most intriguing and yet underexplored technologies of the female body. Dance techniques not only condition the dancers' bodies, they literally inscribe a physical ideology into dancers' physiques. The intensive daily training and performing can often radically reshape these bodies. And yet dance is certainly not *only* a discipline of the body. Anyone who has ever spent any time training to be a dancer knows in her bones and muscles that the body is constructed through physical practice, and that that physical practice has psychic consequences. Behind every different aesthetic orientation and style of movement within the field of dance dwells a view about the world that is transmitted (albeit often subconsciously) along with the dance technique. The physical training of dance takes place in a social situation, and the dance teacher and choreographer need to rely on verbal instructions and metaphoric images as well as the examples of their own dancing to convey the precise style and quality of movement they are interested in seeing.

These physical and verbal discourses concerning form, style, beauty, movement phrasing, and the like, combine to create a powerful ideology that can dramatically affect a dancer's own subjectivity. This is most obvious in the more traditional genres of dance such as classical ballet, where the construction of an idealized image of the female body has a long (and tortured) history that has been amply documented by historians, writers, artists, and choreographers, as well as dancers. Indeed, over the last fifteen years, the dance field has become increasingly conscious of the often debilitating effects (including body image problems, eating disorders, drug abuse, etc.) of the quest to embody such an image. Although most modern and contemporary dance forms have consciously expanded the narrow image of the dancer cum ballerina (thin, graceful, feminine, white), they also create specific world views grounded in the physical contours of the body. In this chapter, I am interested in probing what ideologies are represented in works that display energized female bodies such as that of Louise Lecavalier. I want to focus here on the question of how bodies and their social identities are dialectically constructed through physical practices that directly challenge traditional models of female dancing. In other words, is being physically powerful necessarily empowering for women in contemporary dance?

In dance, the choreographer uses human bodies to create physical experiences and theatrical images that exist in a world of her own making. The presentation of those bodies carries meaning regardless of the narrative or conceptual theme of the dance. Are these bodies grounded or do they sustain an image of lightness throughout the dance? Do they use a lot of space, or is their movement contained, bound to their body by some unknown force? Anyone even slightly familiar with the origins of modern dance in America cannot fail to remark on the sheer excessiveness of its liberatory rhetoric and the passion with which seminal figures such as Isadora Duncan condemned the artifice and repressiveness of ballet. Sometimes the physical being-in-the-world of the dancer's body and the artistic representation of that body reinforce one another to render a relatively seamless image in performance. At other times, however, there can be a disjunction between the dancer's physicality and what that movement represents. In Lecavalier's dancing, for instance, there is an intriguing slippage between her muscular strength and the representation of that physicality, and this jagged edge has everything to do with gender.

As its title suggests, *Infante, C'est Destroy* relies on the iconography of heavy metal rock concerts and videos, mimicking this genre's use of fantasy, androgyny, metal armoring, phallic imagery (such as guitars, mike stands, and swords), and a certain amount of implied violence. At once dancing rock star and imagistic muse, Lecavalier occupies two contradictory positions in relation to the spectacle as a whole. When she is dancing live onstage, she seems to control the sequence of events, jerking her partners into action or calling off the dancing by walking off the stage. Here, Lecavalier looks and acts like a male metal star, strutting, talking back to the audience, thrashing around the

Louise Lecavalier and Michael Dolan in *2*. Photo by Édouard Lock.

stage. Similarly, her shaggy hairstyle and tight leather clothing are clearly de-voted to a metal aesthetic. By vamping a hypermasculinity, all the while dis-playing her dancing body to the audience, Lecavalier embodies the same para-dox that Robert Walser identifies as a crucial component of the appeal of heavy metal to a diverse, largely male audience. In his book *Running With The Devil: Power, Gender, and Madness in Heavy Metal Music*, Walser explains this contradictory position by invoking Orpheus: "But his story contains a built-in contradiction: Orpheus must sing in such a way as to demonstrate his rhetori-cal mastery of the world, yet such elaborate vocal display threatens to under-mine Orpheus's masculine identity. Flamboyant display of his emotions is re-quired as evidence of his manipulative powers, but excess makes him into an object of display himself."[5]

For Lecavalier, the contradiction embedded in being at once subject of the show and object of the gaze (the choreographer's, her partner's, the audience's) is amplified in the film sequences of the spectacle. Projected on an enormous scrim at the front of the stage, the film shows Lecavalier at first clothed in a medieval suit of armor, complete with sword, and then later falling naked through a vast bleak space. There is no coherent narrative in this short film. Jumpcuts inexplicably move Lecavalier from knight in armor, to slain figure bleeding, to a Christ-like transcendence. She is alternately aggressor, victim, and saint, all the while imaged in larger-than-life celluloid. Iconographically, the dual position is not that unusual in the late twentieth century. But what makes this example particularly striking is the fact that Lecavalier has literally (as well as metaphorically) inscribed both genders onto her dancing body. She not only occupies both subject and object positions within the spectacle, she embodies them, physicalizing a liminal territory that challenges what we know about the traditionally gendered body in dance.

When I showed a video of *Infante, C'est Destroy* during a conference presentation, a number of audience members who were not familiar with Lecavalier thought that she was a he. Indeed, even after I had presented my paper, some people were still incredulous that this was a female body, believing that her body was too muscular to be that of a woman.[6] Although a close movement analysis reveals just how typically gendered Lecavalier's dancing really is, it is important not to overlook how radical her physique is for many people. Delineated muscles on women's bodies obviously challenge some very visceral beliefs about bodies and their appropriate(d) genders. I am interested in how we read muscles as marks of strength and how this affects our reading of the female body. As my discussion of Lecavalier's dancing shows, it would be wrong immediately to assume that this muscling of women dancers' bodies is inherently liberating. Nor should we assume that a woman choreographer would necessarily represent the built-up female body in a more progressive manner than Lock. Although it strains at gender conventions, the muscular female body has been incorporated in a wide variety of contemporary dances.

During the past decade, there has been a virtual explosion of dances that use upper body strength (particularly in women) and require the stamina to endure unprecedented athletic challenges. The romanticized image of the ballerina as an embodiment of feminine grace and beauty, or even the image of the early modern dancer poised proud and tall in her weighted stance has been displaced by a fearless, aerobicized physicality not unlike that of Lecavalier. Now it is not uncommon to see both women and men vaulting horizontally across the stage, catching themselves with their arms and rolling down through their chests to arch back into a diagonal one-handed handspring that takes them only momentarily to their feet before they dive across the space again. Lecavalier's dancing is one such example. The elaborate technological spectacle and punk-chic style of La La La Human Steps has obvious roots in mega rock shows. This kind of intense, driven movement can also be seen in the work of other companies, particularly contemporary European-based, or European-influenced dance/theater groups such as the British collective DV8, the work of AnneTeresa de Keersmaeker in *Rosas*, as well as Les Ballets C. de la B., to mention only a few of the companies working in this genre of Euro crash and burn dancing.

Perhaps the most extreme example of this kind of high-risk, aerobicized dancing in the United States is the work of Elizabeth Streb and her company, Ringside. Over the past fifteen years, Streb has been involved in making pieces that focus the audience's attention on how a human body (or bodies) interacts with various kinds of equipment such as poles, balls, hoops, plexiglass walls, a board on wheels, a coffin-like box suspended sideways in the air, two four-by-eight-foot birch plywood panels, trapeze harnesses, various kinds of adult-sized jungle gyms, and finally, in her 1995–1996 tour, a trampoline that can catapult people up to thirty feet in the air. Streb's dancers hurl themselves through space, slamming their bodies into the various pieces of equipment. Although the fierce physicality and built-up muscularity, as well as the way her dancers vault through the air, are analogous to the dancing in La La La Human Steps, Streb's work is much plainer, with a lot less theatricality, a lot less "attitude," and a lot less pretension than Lock's mega spectacles. Typically in a Streb concert, one walks into the theater while the technicians are testing and adjusting the equipment. The dances start with the dancers casually walking on stage, shaking a limb here and there to loosen up, and preparing themselves as if for a race or some kind of sports event. They are invariably dressed in bright colored bodysuits that reveal every muscle's contour. These bodysuits are standard Ringside gear, and while they make the dancers' bodies very visible to the audience, their full coverage and uniformity actually make them seem quite modest. In a way, this uniform deflects our gaze, rendering these bodies democratically equal (there are no stars here, no distinctions in costume between the men and the women) and slightly anonymous.

Once they have arranged themselves and glanced around to see if everyone is ready, the dancers launch into whatever physical challenge is being attempted in this particular dance. In a piece such as *Wall* (1991), five dancers throw their bodies against an upright bright red wall. Over the course of the short piece (and Streb's work often has a slightly clipped feel to it, as if to say, "Let's do it and move on"), these dancers support one another in their attempts (sometimes individual, sometimes communal) to climb the wall, slide down it, bash against it, and hang from various body parts on it. They coordinate their efforts by calling out instructions to one another, simple words such as "drop," "feet," or "arms." Just as suddenly as the piece began it is over, and the dancers walk unceremoniously offstage to prepare for the next physical contest.

Elizabeth Streb started making dances in 1979, and formed her company, Streb/Ringside in 1985. Although she began with simple props such as poles, hoops, and balls, Streb now designs and commissions very elaborate equipment that allows her dancers to scale walls, fling themselves through the air, and use trapeze-like harnesses to swing around a twenty-two-foot vertical pole. Despite her never-ending variety of props, Streb's choreographic goals remain basically the same from piece to piece. Her program notes for "POPACTION," her 1996 tour, spell out her vision: "Ringside is a platform for the investigation of movement, an attempt to expose movement, an attempt to expose movement's true nature by harnessing it, without debilitating it, within a confined space. Ringside's approach is to isolate the basic principles of time, space, and human movement potential."[7] In her pared-down, no-frills style of dancing as well as her narrow focus on the physics rather than the interpersonal dynamics of movement interactions, Streb's work is deeply connected to both the seminal work of Merce Cunningham and the early groundbreaking work of postmodern dancers such as Trisha Brown (who created a whole series of environmental equipment pieces in the seventies), Steve Paxton, and Yvonne Rainer. In an essay on Streb's choreography, Judy Burns discusses her connections to these artists: "Like Cunningham's chance dances and Trisha Brown's equipment pieces and number grids, to name just a few examples, Streb's choreographic structures remove dance from the realms of narrative, individual habit, or direct personal expression, demystify the choreographic process, and focus on movement for its own sake."[8]

Streb's intention to highlight the formal beauty of bodies in motion is absolutely clear in her recent work *UP!* (1995). In this piece, six dancers alternately dive off two facing platforms onto a trampoline and then rebound into the air, sometimes hanging onto pipes overhead and at other times bouncing back onto the platform. The effect of seeing bodies twirl in the air and fly past one another is quite awesome, and speaks to an archetypal desire of earthbound bodies to take flight. Also, the ways in which the dancers land back on the platform, as if they were butterflies alighting on a tree branch (without any visible rebound or dropping of their weight), is astonishing. Nonetheless, the wonder of these physical acts never entirely satisfies me. I find that the repetition quickly becomes relentless and the feats themselves eventually become pointless.

Watching Streb's dances is a bit like watching a sports event or a circus

Streb/Ringside Company in *UP!* Photo by Kevin Powell.

spectacle, an analogy invariably mentioned by critics in discussions of her work. (Streb herself acknowledges this aspect of her work with her tongue-in-cheek punning on both circus and boxing rings in her company's name Ringside.) Streb believes that her work, precisely because it gives the audience a kines-thetic thrill similar to sports and circus events, is essentially populist. She thinks that there is often an element of elitism in modern dance, and she sees her work as being different precisely because it is accessible. "Making action is what I do. I want my movement to read physically for everyone in the audience."[9]

This desire for her movement to read for everyone in the audience and her focus on (one could say fetishization of) human movement potential is con-nected not only to a belief that movement is a universal language, but also to an ideology embedded in the formalist aesthetics of postmodern dance that separates movement from the body that is moving. What interests Streb is the fact of a body in flight, not whose body is doing the flying. Her choreography frames dancers not in terms of their cultural identity, but rather in terms of their ability to master the different physical challenges she presents them with. Because she treats the human body as a sort of physical machine, Streb's dancers begin to strike us as automotons by the end of her concert. Ironically, the phys-

Elizabeth Streb in *Little Ease*. Photo by Kevin Powell.

ical strength of her dancers actually serves to mask their individuality, to hide the distinctiveness of their movement personalities.

Although she claims to be interested in movement for its own sake, Streb makes dances that give the performers very little time to register their own experience of movement. The relentless pace of most of her choreography combined with the spare directness of the dancers' instructions (climb here, jump here, hold on here, etc.) gives the dancers little opportunity to pay attention to more than their own safety. Because they need to be so focused on their own activities, they rarely acknowledge the spatial and rhythmic interactions between one another, giving each dancer an odd sense of isolation within the whole group. As a result, the audience receives a very flat and one-dimensional sense of the dancers; their movement begins to feel coerced and they become objects—missiles self-propelled in the air. There are exceptions, of course. I remember a moment where a dancer balanced on the edge of two boards before they suddenly opened, forcing him into a split and setting up a comic situation that the audience enjoyed immensely. Another exception is Streb's signature solo in a box, *Little Ease* (1985). In this dance, Streb is suspended in the air in a three-by-six-foot wooden box that looks like a coffin lying on its side. Moving urgently but not frenetically, Streb places her body in all imaginable positions: crouching, leaning, standing sideways, etc. Short but nonetheless poignant, this dance evoked a whole series of metaphors about both spatial and psychological confinement. Most of the moments in which a dancer emerges as an individual within the group dances, however, are moments performed by men dancers. Despite their strong bodies and intense, high-risk dancing, the women dancers in Streb/Ringside tend to be the most anonymous figures in the group.[10]

What does this mean? How can these women dancers who have such extraordinary bodies have so little physical presence? The answer, I believe, lies not only in their movements per se, but also in the bodily ideology of their physical training. During a postperformance discussion of Streb's "POPACTION" concert in Cleveland, an audience member asked Streb's dancers what they did to build their muscles. Many had gymnastics training as young adults, but almost all (including Streb) said that they lifted weights as part of their fitness regime. As I was leaving the theater, I heard two women joking about wanting to start lifting weights so that they could look like Streb's dancers. Their remarks made me realize that Streb's work is accessible not so much because it creates a kinesthetic experience in which the audience can participate, but rather because her dancers' bodies are recognizable icons within the syntax of the American fitness craze.

One of the most pervasive beliefs in popular culture is that building a fit and firm body, that is, building muscles, is tantamount to building one's self-confidence. Although for some people this may be right on the mark, it is important, nonetheless, to probe the popular myths that represent muscles as empowering (especially for women), in order to examine the somatic results of weight lifting. We need to ask: What are the physical effects of this kind of training? What kinds of movement priorities does it set up? For as Elizabeth Dempster points out in her essay on women and dance, "Social and political values are not simply placed or grafted onto a neutral body-object like so many old or new clothes. On the contrary, ideologies are systematically deposited and constructed on an anatomical plane, i.e. in the neuromusculature of the dancer's body, and a precise reading of this body can only proceed if the reader/spectator's gaze is not deflected by, but penetrates beneath, the brilliance of the body's surface."[11] In the section that follows, I will shift my focus from dance performances to women's bodybuilding in popular culture for a moment in order to "penetrate the brilliance" of the highly muscular female body. I will look at both the neuromuscular effects of weight training technologies, and various ways in which bodybuilding is portrayed as empowering for women.

Over the last twenty years, the fit and muscular body has become a privileged icon in contemporary American culture. Thirty years ago, it would have been unheard of for most middle class women to have desired clearly defined arm muscles. Today, not only are delineated biceps de rigeur, but the fashion industry has even provided women with the perfect apparel with which to display their upper body muscles in a variety of racing back dresses, jogging bras, and newly feminized versions of the muscle shirt. For the first time in Western history women are entering athletic clubs (traditionally bastions of homosocial bonding) in droves to "work out" with the Nautilus machines, Universal gyms, and free weights (to mention only the most common of the ever growing realm of exercise commodities). Given the ways that women's bodies have been physically constrained and historically represented as "naturally" passive and "weak," there can be no denying that sensing the rush of adrenaline and the aliveness of one's body after exercising can be an incredibly powerful experience. Certainly the physical realization of one's own strength can build one's self-confidence, and aid in the presentation of a physical demeanor that demands respect. This physical liberation comes with its own form of enslavement, however, for the development of a muscular body requires considerable resources and time if one is to avail oneself of the various contemporary fitness technologies. Although some feminists have argued that the new muscled body image represents an unfortunate diversion of women's energies away from the world and onto themselves, both the media and the fitness industry portray bodybuilding as a progressive opportunity for women.

Gloria Steinem's most recent collection of writings is entitled *Moving Beyond Words*.[12] The two epigraphs she uses to preface the book both contain the expression "moving beyond words" in some form, and suggest that the title of the book is a call to actualize the possibilities indicated by the rhetoric of seventies feminism. The essays in the book reveal how Steinem (who is now, as she puts it, "doing sixty") blends the political stances of feminist thought with her personal experience in order to come up with a kind of evangelical prose that is clearly meant to inspire other women to "realize" themselves more fully. This sort of inspirational writing is particularly striking in the section on women's bodybuilding. Although the introduction to this section is called "The Politics of Muscle," the essay is less a sociological analysis than a description of Steinem's conversion from a couch potato to a feminist fitness fan.

Like many women who came of age in America in the fifties, Steinem grew up more concerned with her visual image than with what her body could physically accomplish, believing that "the most important thing about a female body is not what it does but how it looks."[13] Steinem's epiphany comes much later in her life, by way of Bev Francis, an Australian athelete and women's powerlifting champion turned bodybuilder who is the underdog heroine of

George Butler's 1984 film *Pumping Iron II: The Women*. "But seeing Bev taught me there were frontiers of strength few women had even been allowed to glimpse. Just to give you an idea what an impact meeting one strong woman can have: I went out and bought weights. We're talking personal revolution here."[14] What Bev Francis represents for Steinem is a model of female strength who is so excessive in the bulk of her musculature that she cannot be readily incorporated into a commodified version of a "strong, yet sexy" identity. Although Steinem claims that "the strongest woman in the world can inspire you to go beyond . . . your limits of strength and daring," she repeatedly refers to Francis in terms that underline her otherworldliness—"Such a peak of muscularity that she seemed to represent another species."[15]

What is fascinating to me in Steinem's discussion of her own physicality and the whole budding phenomenon of women's bodybuilding is the way in which the external display of extremely developed muscles signifies, for her, an internal experience of personal strength, an experience of individual agency. Now this slippage of outside and inside, of reading the surface of the body as if it were a window to the soul (or at least the "inner self"), is a very common one. Indeed, capitalism and its resultant commodity fetishes have encouraged us to "read" one another's class, gender, and ethnic and sexual identities by way of our skin, clothing, jewelry, and other forms of bodily or-namentation. Even a cursory glance in women's magazines will give one a sense of the manner in which advertising conspires to convince women that, if they wear such and such a dress, or carry a particular bag, people will be more likely to pay attention to them.[16] Of course, what these ads leave out—what is not readily for sale—is the appropriate physical countenance to successfully wear the identity the styles evoke. Some of the most interesting examples of cultural subversion occur precisely when those dresses and those bags get worn by the "wrong" body, appropriated across race, class, or gender in order to sig-nify something entirely different. Rather than reading Francis's body within its performative situation, however, Steinem tends to read her muscles as di-rectly equivalent to an inner strength and subjectivity without accounting for the representational context of the bodybuilding contest for which Francis ac-tually produced her muscles. Although Steinem records in detail Francis's training regime and therefore has to recognize how constructed her body is, she nonetheless essentializes her surface musculature as indicative of an inner power and control.

By being at once internal and external, underneath the skin and yet read on the surface of the body, muscles force us to interrogate the meanings of the "natural" body. Often there is a tendency to think of the physical constructed-

ness of the female body in terms of aesthetic or scientific representations—
how bodies are most obviously culturally framed. Sure, we might think about
fashion, or makeup (remember how high heels, bras, and lipstick were the fa-
vorite iconic targets of seventies feminism?), but rarely of our own physical
contours and posture as part of that process. Although the fitness boom of the
eighties encouraged people to "wear" their muscles visibly as a kind of bodily
fashion, muscles are not, in fact, easily put on or taken off. In order to create a
clearly defined and visible musculature, most women need to do intensive
training with weight machines or free weights—straining the muscles until
they literally break down and then heal with more bulk. In addition to building muscles, most women also need to drop a significant percentage of fat
from their bodies, so that the muscles will show through their skin. As Susan
Bordo argues in her extensive work on body image in contemporary culture,
the last two decades have seen a radical shift in the social meaning inherent in
a visible musculature.

Given the racial and class biases of our culture, [muscles] were associated with the body as
material, unconscious, or animalistic. Today, however, the well-muscled body has become a
cultural icon; "working out" is a glamorized and sexualized yuppie activity. No longer signi-
fying lower-class status (except when developed to extremes, at which point the old association of muscles with brute, unconscious materiality surfaces once more), the firm, developed
body has become a symbol of correct *attitude*; it means that one "cares" about oneself and
how one appears to others, suggesting willpower, energy, control over infantile impulse, the
ability to "make something" of oneself.[17]

It seems to me that Bordo has identified exactly what Steinem is glorifying
under the trope of "strength"—a "correct" attitude toward one's body, which
includes a willingness to "master" its "natural" tendencies. Although in many
ways weight lifting can be seen as a powerful blow to the limitations imposed
on women's bodies by the patriarchal concept of their inherent weakness, it
still operates within contemporary culture as part and parcel of the various
body technologies (such as diet, fashion, breast enlargement, etc.) that women
are encouraged to participate in. It is with good reason that Steinem champi-
ons a woman who has shattered any previous notions about women's physical
limitations. At the same time, however, she fails to recognize the incredibly
disempowering social context in which Bev Francis, "the strongest woman in
the world," is forced to operate. In the section that follows, I propose to reread
Steinem's discussion of Francis's bodybuilding career in order to articulate the
various contradictory impulses embedded in contemporary feminist (re)con-
structions of the female body. Seeing the complex network of competing dis-

courses within the realm of bodybuilding cultures will, in turn, help us to identify the key contradictions at work in the dancing of Lecavalier and Streb/Ringside.

Although she acknowledges the "beauty contest" atmosphere of the women's 1983 Caesars World Cup Bodybuilding Competition—the importance of makeup, hair, bikinis, and, of course, the ubiquitous smiles—and although at one point Steinem provides a very cogent analysis of the racial dynamics of bodybuilding, she is curiously uncritical of the various bodily transformations that Francis goes through in her ten-year quest to win a woman's bodybuilding competition. In the 1983 contest (which is fictionally "documented" in Butler's film *Pumping Iron II: The Women*), Francis, who is by far the most muscular woman in the semifinal lineup, is relegated to last place in a move that is clearly meant to send a message to women contestants about the acceptable limits of an appropriately "feminine" muscularity.[18] Instead of delineating the ways in which Francis had been culturally "framed," Steinem touts Francis's continually unsuccessful attempts literally to remake her body for each different competition as the efforts of a champion athlete who sees defeat as a challenge to work harder next time. In trying to get "built-up" and still look appropriately feminine, Francis is negotiating a contradiction in terms, one that affects many women in contemporary culture, and one that will cause her alternately to get a nose job, dye her hair, lose more weight (including muscle mass), and then rebuild her musculature all over again in a futile attempt to outguess what the judges are looking for this year.

One of the most striking things about the 1983 competition as documented in *Pumping Iron II* is the frankly illogical shifting between the scenes of sweat and grimaces as the women exercise and lift weights in preparation for the contest—scenes that are clearly coded to foreground these women's extraordinary determination—and the vapid Miss Americaesque sound and light show of the actual contest, in which the women display their bodies but don't actually "do" anything except to pose. The strength that Steinem reads into Francis's body is never an issue in the contest. Muscles function as empty signifiers, visible, but apparently meaning nothing. Indeed, throughout all the behind-the-scenes shots of the film, the active consequences of these women's physical strength (as in "don't touch me or I'll beat the living daylights out of you") are continually downplayed. What is most troubling to me in this particular film is not the fact that some of these women's musculatures exceed gender norms, but rather that their behavior never follows suit: they remain perfect ladies from start to finish.

What for me is ultimately a pathetic story about one woman's desire to fit into a system that will always identify her as "other" than acceptably feminine is, for Steinem, an empowering narrative about the persistence of one woman's personal revolution. Steinem argues that Francis's example of the possibilities of bodybuilding for women, while it may not have won her any championship, created a ripple effect that has changed our preconceptions about women's strength. This may be so. However, what Steinem does again and again in her discussion of Francis's career is to confuse the individual experience of physical self-construction with that of social power and cultural change. Rather than being a testimony to how far we have come, I see women's bodybuilding contests as well as the majority of women's fitness programs as another normalizing practice, one that, to quote Bordo (referencing Foucault) again, trains the female body "in docility and obedience to cultural demands while at the same time being *experienced* in terms of power and control."[19]

This paradox throws an interesting wrench into a feminist discussion of the body's physical and social constructedness. Bodybuilding is, on the surface, an example of women refusing the social ideology that equates women with physical passivity. Muscular women actively participate in reconstructing their bodies for maximum bulk. Yet, as the example of Bev Francis illuminates, the fact that these muscular women contest conventional images of femininity does not mean that they don't also participate in a very traditional experience of being objectified—of making their bodies over to be judged and approved by men. (Indeed, women bodybuilders most often choose men to be their managers and trainers.) In his book *Little Big Men: Bodybuilding Subculture and Gender Construction*, Alan M. Klein devotes a chapter to women bodybuilders. In "Sally's Corner: The Women of Olympic," Klein reads his firsthand ethnographic experience of working out with and interviewing women bodybuilders in various "elite" gyms on the west coast against the swell of media attention and popular representations of women's bodybuilding. To his credit, Klein is one of the few theorists who try to take physical experience into account when they analyze cultural images of women. Klein cautions against easy interpretations of women's bodybuilding as an act of resistance without understanding the bodily experience of weight lifting. He argues that there is a great deal of internalized objectification of one's body in the very process of working out with weights and machines. "The bodybuilder's perception of the body as being made up of parts (chest, abs, back, arms, legs) and subdivided ('traps' [trapezius], front and rear 'delts' [deltoids]) . . . extends into the psychoperceptual realm, in that bodybuilders view each body part as objectified."[20] Here Klein touches upon the muscular effects of weight training, and begins to explain why built-up muscles don't necessarily constitute a powerful presence or somatic agency. I believe this is a direct result of the very static use of the body and the way weight training focuses only on building specific body parts, not on coordinating the entire body for maximum momentum and force. Bodybuilding practices don't address the ways in which women use their weight or physical space. Most of the time these women are, in fact, strapped into machines—a physical experience that reflects the ambiguity of identifying exactly who is controlling what.

There are, of course, experiences of weightlifting that can be very empowering and resistant to the status quo. In a footnote to a chapter on "The Body as Inscriptive Surface" in her recent book *Volatile Bodies*, Elizabeth Grosz identifies two possible approaches to bodybuilding: "On the one hand, it may, depending on the woman's goals, be part of an attempt to conform to stereotyped images of femininity, a form of narcissistic investment in maintaining her attractiveness to others and herself. On the other hand, it can be seen as an attempt on the part of the woman to take on for herself many of the attributes usually granted only to men—strength, stamina, muscularity—in a mode of defiance of patriarchal attempts to render women physically weak and incapable."[21]

Taking up the "other" hand, Diane Griffin Crowder describes the strategies of lesbian weight lifters in her essay entitled "Lesbians and the (Re/De) Construction of the Female Body." For Crowder, lesbian communities have long valorized defined muscles and the display of physical strength. At once a practical measure of self-defense and a way to define a new aesthetic, muscles help create what Crowder sees as a distinctly "lesbian" body. "If the conventionally feminine or even female body is unlivable and the masculine body unthinkable, then lesbians must re-create the body. The problem is how to do so."[22] Interestingly enough, in her explaination of "four major interrelated concepts underlying the various movements to "re-create" and make new "sense" of the lesbian body, Crowder discusses not only muscles but physical movement as well. "Lesbians often cultivate movements (gestures, stride, motion of arms and legs) that, unlike the circumscribed movements of most women, occupy the full volume of space around the body."[23] Although Crowder acknowledges that this lesbian body is purposefully constructed, she also describes a physical comportment that, over time, serves to "naturalize" this body—a performance that sinks so deeply into a body that it no longer seems presentational or overtly performative the way much women's bodybuilding does (in order to prove that deep down inside these are really "nice" women.)

In their recreation of the female body, lesbian weight lifters extend the physical experience of strength and muscle into the psychophysical movement of their lives. What Crowder is evoking in her discussion of lesbian embodiment is similar to what Merleau-Ponty calls "being-in-the-world." For Merleau-Ponty, the self cannot be separated either from the body or the world. Indeed, the self is constituted precisely as a lived body. This lived body is the source of our interaction in the world and, as such, is the place of both cultural inscription and resistance. Merleau-Ponty's work differs from Foucault's in that it focuses on the constant dialogue of sensory perception and individual reception, and he is committed to exploring aspects of our embodied existence that usually remain outside of theoretical language.[24] For Merleau-Ponty, I am not a self housed in a predominantly passive body. Rather, my body and my self are continually creating and being created by the world around me. This dialectical relationship of self and world can provide an important model for any discussion about the body's role in organizing reality. His being-in-the-world suggests the complex situatedness of both affecting and being affected by the material world. Even though I gave up philosophy in favor of dance as an organizing principle in my life, I am still fond of the down-to-earth quality of phenomenology and I find particularly useful the work of feminists who reinterpret Merleau-Ponty's insights about the body-in-the-world in terms of gender.

In her work on the physical attributes of gender conditioning, Iris Young tries to articulate the phenomenological basis of feminine bodily comportment by distinguishing three modalities of feminine movement: ambiguous transcendence, inhibited intentionality, and discontinuous unity. Basically this is fancy philosophical language for throwing like a girl—which is to say, using a body part in a manner that is totally disconnected from the rest of one's weight and strength. By analyzing the ways that young girls and women are trained *not* to take up the space around them, *not* to use the capacity of their whole body when engaging in physical activity, and *not* to fully project their physical intentions onto the world around them, Young describes the tensions inherent in experiencing one's body both as a thing and as a capacity for action, both as passive object and as active subject. "According to Merleau-Ponty, for the body to exist as a transcendent presence to the world and the immediate enactment of intentions, it cannot exist as an *object*. As subject, the body is referred not onto itself, but onto the world's possibilities. . . . The three contradictory modalities of feminine bodily existence . . . have their root, however, in the fact that for feminine existence the body frequently is both subject and object for itself at the same time and in reference to the same act."[25]

This very tension, which has also been articulated by art historians as the tension between looking and being looked at, gives us another perspective on the central paradox of women's bodybuilding competitions in which women's muscles function not as a product of physical intention, but rather as a new style of spectacle. At first sight, dancers such as Lecavalier and the women in Streb/Ringside would seem to have escaped this condition of ambiguous transcendence. After all, not only are their bodies incredibly built-up, but these women also use those muscles to accomplish extraordinary physical acts. Yet at the same time, the tension between experiencing the body as a thing and as a capacity for action (as an object as well as a source of agency) that Young describes as a critical underlying component of female bodily comportment is still embedded in their physical being-in-the-world. In spite of their strength and physical prowess, these women often move in an oddly distanced, object-like manner, often giving one the impression that they are manic, self-propelled rag dolls.

Let us return now to *Infante, C'est Destroy*, the dance with which I began this whole discussion, in order to review Lecavalier's dancing within the framework of Young's insights about the female body's being-in-the-gendered-world. Although Lecavalier is clearly the main figure onstage, ironically, her dancing presence doesn't create a performative subjectivity. It is true that Lecavalier's dancing is awesome (I would guess that Lecavalier has more developed muscles than her male counterparts—but since the men are invariably dressed in buttoned-up shirts, long pants, and jackets, one can only speculate), but there is also a distractingly manic edge to her movement, which can easily translate into just another representation of female hysteria. Even though Lecavalier is the keystone of the spectacle, even though she is dancing the hardest, breathing and sweating the hardest, she still exhibits the existential ambiguity Young identifies as a trait of female bodily comportment. A close reading of her movement will help us to discover why.[26]

Infante, C'est Destroy begins with a drum solo. The pounding drum is soon joined by a squealing guitar as the lights fade up on Lecavalier and her partner standing still. Even in this brief moment of stillness, Lecavalier's stance is far less relaxed and weighted than that of her male counterpart. Like a racehorse who is too anxious at the gate, Lecavalier is drawing all her energy into her body. Because she is so bound up, her first movements seem like mini explosions, hair and limbs flying like bits of shrapnel all over the place. The music is pushing her to a frenetic pace such that she always seems to take off and land on either side of the downbeat. This creates a slightly frustrating sense of her never quite being there with the music. Her movement is not just fast, it seems rushed, almost driven by an outside force. This manic quality in her dancing has a lot to do with the fact that she rarely releases her weight into the floor.

Even when she is not engaging in full-body activities such as vaulting or rolling across the stage, even when she is sitting on top of her partner who is sprawled out on the floor, something is going on in her body—her head is shaking furiously, her arms are circling or punching the space in front of her, or her feet are doing little tippy-toe steps.

Much of this frenzied, almost chaotic movement seems pointless; it doesn't affect the space around her or her partner's motions, and it rarely has any rhythmic relationship to the music. There are times when she quickly performs a series of arm gestures, something like condensed semaphores, that seem to enact some sort of mysterious ritualized act. Yet those gestures never expand beyond a very limited space around her body, making them into bizarrely private acts. Lecavalier's movements rarely extend beyond her own limited reach space to affect the stage space, the theatrical space of the world around her. For instance, when she does an arabesque, her leg abruptly kicks up behind her body and then drops back with no spatial intention. Her movement never extends through the space, and her gestures often refer back onto her own body, even when she is grabbing or pulling her partner. It is as if she reaches out only to retract into herself. This is particularly striking given the enormous stage on which *Infante, C'est Destroy* was performed at FIND. I would identify much of Lecavalier's dancing as a prime example of Young's "discontinuous unity," particularly in terms of her use of space and weight. Her body tends to move as a series of disconnected parts. Often, an arm thrown behind her body doesn't motivate a turn in that direction, or even a windup to turn in another direction, but rather is simply thrown out and then flops back wherever it lands. It seems as if Lecavalier loses connection with her limbs once they are launched. Because she lets go of any spatial intention in her movement, her dancing can take on a brutal, almost masochistic quality. After a while, she seems to be just throwing her body up in the air, not particularly caring where it lands.

There are exceptions, of course. In a trio with the two other women, there is a much more lyrical quality to her dancing. Their partnering has a more relaxed, almost embracing feel about it, and there is none of the sense of rough competitiveness that underlies Lecavalier's duets with men. Likewise, the enormous video of Lecavalier naked, falling in slow motion, has a peaceful, almost religiously ecstatic quality to it. Still, at the end of this seventy-five-minute spectacle, I had a very conflicted sense of Lecavalier's (not to mention Lock's) whole attitude toward her body. On the one hand, I was astounded by the daring and physical audacity of her movement and wondered if I could ever train to be tight enough and strong enough to do similar feats. On the other hand, I realized the sheer vulnerability of her body put under that kind of physical stress. During one performance of *Infante, C'est Destroy*, Lecavalier reportedly dislocated her hip, but only stopped dancing once the spectacle was over. This disturbing sense of disconnection with regard to her physicality is alluded to in an interview in which Lecavalier is quoted as saying, "to me, all dance is violent to the body . . . dancers are always pushing their bodies to do excessive things."[27]

By analyzing her actual physical movements as well as her position within the spectacle as a whole, I am arguing for a more complex awareness of how dance operates as a form of representation. I believe it is important not only to look at the narrative, iconographic gestures, symbolic images, and social relationships within the choreography, but also to recognize how meaning is literally embodied in the dancer's physicality. As mysterious as it may seem to the audience, I believe a performer's theatrical persona is grounded in the phenomenological realities of weight, space, and movement intentionality—her literal being-in-the-world. While we may not be entirely conscious of these elements within a performance, they undoubtedly affect how we perceive the dancing as well as the dancers. What is intriguing in the example of Lecavalier's dancing is the way that her visible musculature and powerful dancing on the one hand, and her gendered use of space and weight on the other, contradict one another within Lock's rock spectacle. While her built-up body radically challenges a conventionally feminine body or movement style, Lecavalier's disconnected intentionality reinforces her traditionally gendered role within the spectacle. Because Lecavalier's dancing produces these physical attributes simultaneously, her theatrical presence remains an enigma, at once refusing and enacting the bodily codes of gender.

La La La Human Steps and Streb/Ringside are two of the more visible companies working in a genre of contemporary dance that privileges a fast, explosive, and intense physicality. This work, which is the backbone of companies as different in their aesthetic aims as the Stephen Petronio Dance Company, Bebe Miller Dance, or Contraband, draws on a physical training that includes dance technique (both modern and ballet), Contact Improvisation, and fitness conditioning. For me, some of the more intriguing examples of this kind of physicality take place within an alternative dance environment—the so-called "downtown" dance scene in New York City. Here, we see women such as Yoshiko Chuma, Yvonne Meier, and Jennifer Monson (to mention only a few), who use this kind of fierce dancing not in order to display their muscles and dancing stamina, but rather as a physical basis for their improvisatory and choreographic explorations. In the smaller and more informal venues in which these women often perform (St. Mark's Place, Judson Church, Movement Research, P.S.122, The Knitting Factory), the physical strength of their bodies is at once visible in their movement (they don't generally wear body-hugging or body-revealing garb), and yet framed in a manner very different from companies such as La La La Human Steps or Streb/Ringside.

Finn's Shed, by Jennifer Monson, begins with a duet between Monson and John Jasperse. Jasperse runs full tilt across the space, turns and runs back— smack into Monson. They flip one another and then Jasperse slides away, only to get tackled by Monson as she flies horizontally through the air. In some ways, the beginning rough-and-tumble energy of this duet is similar to the kind of whipped-around-the-space pounce-and-smash dancing that is the signature of Lecavalier's partnering. There is a lot of horizontal catapulting of bodies across the space in which one partner catches and then the other returns the favor. Sometimes after a beautiful catch, a partner will simply let go and drop the other dancer splat on the floor. At times affectionate, at times combative, Monson and Jasperse come together and then separate as if they can't really figure out what they want from each other.

There are, however, some essential differences between their dancing and that of La La La Human Steps. In contrast to Lecavalier's discontinuous intentionality and bound, fragmented movements, Monson's dancing usually has a very clear and directed energy. At first, her movement style seems casual, almost random in the way she throws her limbs and head around. But a closer look at her dancing shows how refined her movement impulses are, how she gathers her center before she launches across the space, first seeing a spot on the floor before diving there. When she lands, even if it is only for a split second, Monson releases her weight into the floor with an exhale. This ability to place and release her torso supports the erratic, sometimes chaotic flinging of different body parts. Then, too, there is such a flow of movement through Monson's body that a gesture initiated in the foot or leg can be seen expanding diagonally out the other arm or her head. Because her whole body is affected by her movement, she seems to ride the currents of the air around her, emphasizing the spatial flow of her dancing rather than directly placing her limbs in a shape. This clarity of weight, spatial intention, and movement flow allow Monson to dance in an explosive, raw manner that is both physically subtle and pleasurably rambunctious. She is strong, but not contained. This gives her dancing a more expansive quality than do the tight, driven movements of Streb/Ringside, for example.

While Monson and Jasperse continue to tackle one another throughout *Finn's Shed*, their relationship evolves from the playful synchronicity of their

Jennifer Monson with John Jasperse in *Finn's Shed*. Photo by Dona Ann McAdams.

roughhousing to a more complex physical connectedness. Instead of immediately dropping out of a catch and moving onto something else, they might choose to remain in physical contact, treasuring that embrace for a moment. Other times, Monson or Jasperse will strategically resist their partner's direction, throwing their body as an obstacle for the other dancer to overcome. What I like best about their duet is the ways in which their physical strength can express vulnerabilty as well as invincibility. In the final moment of the dance, Monson and Jasperse emerge from a series of rolls to kneel across from one another. Here they pause, caught in a moment of profound stillness. Suddenly Jasperse catapults across the space that divides them to land in Monson's arms. Accepting his weight, she lowers his body onto the floor, extending her torso across him as the lights fade.

Monson's dancing, both in her own work and in the choreography of others (I am thinking of her extraordinary performance in Jeremy Nelson's *Rojo del Arrabia*) resists the traditionally gendered body codes for women (particularly women dancers) both in terms of the shape of her physique and in terms of its movement potential. Although she is clearly a very strong and powerful dancer, Monson's muscles are not as striated as those of some contemporary women dancers. The fact that her body doesn't "read" as extremely muscled

Jennifer Monson with Jennifer Lacey in *Finn's Shed*. Photo by Dona Ann McAdams.

provides, I believe, an interesting tension here, for she fits neither into the traditionally gendered image of a lithe feminine dancer nor into its more recent
reconstruction as a sleekly muscled one. Because she can't be easily identified
with these commodified images of women dancers, Monson provides us with
a refreshing example of an alternative physicality. Monson's dancing, unlike
Lecavalier's or Streb's, is not marketed commercially as an extraordinary display of a hyperathletic body or the newest "look" in contemporary dance. Indeed, within the subculture of downtown performance Monson's dancing has
become naturalized, and there are many other women dancers within that
community whose movement style is similar to hers. By not foregrounding
the constructed aspects of her physicality as resistance to a feminized norm,
but rather by simply expanding that norm, Monson is able to evade the commercialization of a new bodily "look"—one that has, I believe, actually limited the choreographic vision of companies such as La La La Human Steps
and Streb/Ringside.

Another aspect of Monson's dancing is important to this discussion. Earlier
in this chapter, I spoke of wanting to look at the process through which bodies
are constructed in order to understand the cultural ideologies that are literally
incorporated into contemporary dance—to look at the meanings sewn into

the neuromusculature of the body. Much of this discussion has been devoted to examining how the ideologies of gender are layered throughout women's bodies and movement styles. Using the examples of Lecavalier's dancing and that of Streb/Ringside, I argued that the development of muscles alone doesn't necessarily give us a female physicality that resists gendered norms. Now I would like to turn to another way of reading these contemporary dancing bodies. Seeing the intensely built-up bodies in La La La Human Steps and Streb/Ringside has always made me reflect on their opposite—the legacy of frail bodies in our culture.

The obsessiveness with which American culture approaches fitness and other forms of body management makes me feel that we are desperately trying to refuse the fundamental experience of the body's inevitable loss. Building muscles creates an illusion of the body's strength, an illusion of stability (which, of course, requires vigilant maintenance). In this sense, I see Lecavalier's and Streb's relentlessly pumped-up movement style as embodying a deep cultural anxiety about the inevitable fragility of human bodies. There is something reassuring each time a dancer mounts an obstacle or completes a difficult task, a sense of satisfaction in how she or he takes charge of the physical situation. Fit and strong, young and daring, these dancers embody the possibility of success, the productive harnessing of physical energy.

But bodies are always eluding control (both physical and political). If the disciplined body has become, as Bordo suggests, a symbol of the "correct attitude," then cultural logic has it that the undisciplined, "weak" body reveals a "wrong attitude." Caught in a self-perpetuating binary of good and evil, the religious right has been trying to represent poverty, AIDS, teenage pregnancy, and the like, as endemic to undisciplined, loose, immoral bodies whose physical extravagances have brought on their own destruction. We need to refuse this binary logic (so prevalent in the rhetoric of the fitness industry as well as the conservative right), which pits fit bodies against frail ones. What I appreciate about Monson's duet with Jasperse is the way her strong, explosive movement does not preclude a softer, more tender dancing. Based on a breath rhythm as well as on the percussive sounds of Zeena Parkins, the dancing in Finn's Shed gives us the opportunity to see not just the extraordinary physical feats in this work, but all the movements around those feats as well. Being able to follow the dancers' experience before and after their leaps and lunges, being able to see how a catch affects their bodies as well as their relationship, makes Finn's Shed much less about the display of the dancers' prowess, and much more about their humanity.

Monson's explosive physicality supports a more profound experience of her being-in-the-world. While certainly linked to the strength of her muscles, Monson's body is not entirely defined by them. When I watch her dancing, I see a continuity, a movement history that bespeaks a future as well. Unlike the dancing in La La La Human Steps or Streb/Ringside, in which the hyper-fit bodies flash across the stage in a flare of immediacy that is always threatening to burn itself out, Monson's dancing is grounded in a way that can accommodate change. Although she is strong and rambunctious now, I can readily imagine her continuing to dance, even as her body begins to register the passage of time.

Moving
Across Difference

Dance

and Disability

In 1838 Théophile Gautier wrote the following sentences to describe the Romantic ballerina Marie Taglioni: "Mlle. Taglioni reminded you of cool and shaded valleys, where a white vision suddenly emerges from the bark of an oak to greet the eyes of a young, surprised, and blushing shepherd; she resembled unmistakably those fairies of Scotland of whom Walter Scott speaks, who roam in the moonlight near the mysterious fountain, with a necklace of dewdrops and golden thread for girdle."[1] Gautier's description of Taglioni's dancing focuses on her grace, delicacy, and lightness, suggesting a sylph-like creature who transcends her own material body to provide a tantalizingly elusive vision of the spectator's desire. The ultimate illusion, of course, is that of a perfect dancing body—one completely unhampered by sweat, pain, or the evidence of any physical negotiation with gravity.

As an expressive discourse comprised of physical movement, dance has traditionally privileged the able body. Generally, dancers are treated with a certain paradoxical awe that is an odd mixture of respect for the physical discipline of daily technique classes, fascination with what is often supposed to be a "natural" gracefulness (but is, of course, a result of intensive physical training), and plain old objectification. Although the "look" of dancers has indeed changed with the political, economic, intellectual, and aesthetic revolutions of the past 150 years of Western culture, the idealized image of the ballerina as well as the voyeurism implicit in the gaze of the balletomane still subtly inform most people's vision of professional dancing. How different, we must ask, is Lock's contemporary vision of his dancer-muse Louise Lecavalier as a punk Joan of Arc from Gautier's fantasy of Taglioni as an elusive fairy? Aren't the structures of representation, the frames surrounding these women's bodies, essentially the same? Yet if even the most powerful, visibly muscular body of a woman dancer can be easily commodified and incorporated into the economy of the male gaze, then what kind of body would it take to fracture this visual contract—a disabled one?

This is a chapter about disability—about the ways in which professional dance has traditionally been structured by an exclusionary mindset that projects a very narrow vision of a dancer as white, female, thin, long-limbed, flexible, able-bodied. This is also a chapter about the growing desire among various dance communities and professional companies to radically revise that paradigm by reenvisioning just what kinds of movements can constitute a dance and, by extension, what kind of body can constitute a dancer. Because oppositional categories always figure the "other" within themselves, this chapter travels across the spectrum of representations of beauty and the grotesque, health and disease, alienation and community, autonomy and interdependence. In the following pages, I discuss performances that very few people have had the opportunity to see, as well as other dances that stand at the very center of contemporary debates about the role of politics and life in art. I look at dancing bodies that range from vigorously virtuosic to practically immobile. By demonstrating how some recent dances deconstruct the polarization of ability and disability, I will challenge the prevailing vision of professional dance that equates physical ability with aesthetic quality. In addition, I explore what kind of viewing gaze is implicit in different groups' aesthetic priorities, and examine the ways in which a traditionally voyeuristic gaze can be both fractured and reconstructed by looking at bodies that radically question the ideal image of a dancer's physique. Although most of my discussion will center on specific dances and the various critical responses to them, I also hope to reveal the complex ways in which the opposition of fit and frail bodies is implicated within many of our dominant cultural paradigms of health and self-determination.

Given that disability signifies the cultural antithesis of the fit, healthy body, what happens when visibly disabled people move into the role of dancer, the very same role that has been historically reserved for the glorification of an ideal body? Does the integration of disabled bodies into contemporary dance result in a disruption of ablist preconceptions about professional dance? Or does the disabled body "transcend" its disability to become a dancer? What is at stake in these questions is not merely the physical definition of a dancer's body, but the larger (metaphysical) structure of dance as a form of representation. When dancers take their place in front of the spotlight, they are often displayed in ways that accentuate the double role of technical prowess and sexual desirability (the latter being implicit in the very fact of a body's visual availability). In contrast, the disabled body is supposed to be covered up or hidden from view, to be compensated for or overcome (either literally or metaphorically) in an attempt to live as "normal" a life as possible. When a disabled dancer enters the stage, he or she stakes claim to a radical space, an unruly location where disparate assumptions collide.

The intersection of dance and disability is an extraordinarily rich site at which to explore the overlapping constructions of the body's physical ability, subjectivity, and cultural visibility. Excavating the social meanings of these constructions is like an archeological dig into the deep psychic fears that disability creates. As Ynestra King puts it in her insightful essay "The Other Body": "Visibly disabled people (like women) in this culture are the scapegoats for resentments of the limitations of organic life."[2] In order to examine ablist preconceptions in the professional dance world, one must confront both the ideological and symbolic meanings that the disabled body holds in our culture, as well as the practical conditions of disability. Once again, we are in the position of having to negotiate between the theatrical representations of dancing bodies and the actuality of their physical experiences. Watching disabled bodies dancing forces us to see with a double vision, and helps us to recognize that while a dance performance is grounded in the physical capacities of a dancer, it is not limited by them.

Although I struggle (and ultimately feel uncomfortable) with the adjective *disabled*, I have come to appreciate the word *disability*, which I sometimes write as *dis/ability*. I have coined this new spelling in order to exaggerate the intellectual precipice implied by this word. The slash, for me, refuses the comfort of a stereotype. It is a symbol that marks a steep ravine, forcing the reader to pull up short and gasp in fear of sliding down it. It also functions as a mirror that reflects one's face as one's mouth tries to pronounce the state on the other side of the marker. Say it. *Dis*/ability. There is a certain snake-like s-s-s-s sound in that prefix which captures so much and yet which can, I believe, be imaginatively reinvented. Think, for instance, of all those other *dis*es that are useful in shaking up the powers that be—*dis*abuse, *dis*agree, *dis*turb, not to mention *dis*arm. In a similar vein, popular culture has inverted the power dynamics of "You are dismissed young lady," by creating the wonderfully apt expression "dissed"—as in "I totally dissed her," or simply "dissed!" spoken with a tight lip and horizontal slash of the hand. Of course, these trangressive semantics are only part of the story. Playfully thinking about the possibilities of the *dis* in disability without acknowledging the bodies that mark that condition is too easy. So while the word *disability* rolls off my tongue with a certain beboppiness, the word *disabled* gets lodged in my throat. In our culture, disabled bodies mark so insistently the fragility of health, beauty, and autonomy that many people experience a distinct physical reaction when they encounter someone with a disability. Although the *dis* in *disability* obviously reflects negative stereotypes, I am wondering if it can be reinvigorated, chosen to name an area of inquiry that might very well end up rearranging people's lives.

The politics of naming are, needless to say, fraught through and through with the politics of identity. Who names whom is a difficult question for most cultural critics attempting to be respectful of the power of language. While, for instance, Nancy Mairs will embrace the term *cripple* in describing herself ("'Cripple' seems to me a clean word, straightforward and precise. . . . I like the accuracy with which it describes my condition"), she would never use the term to describe someone else.[3] In her essay, ironically entitled "On Being a Cripple," Mairs distinguishes among the many terms for disability, bemoaning the abstraction and consequent meaninglessness of their generality.

"Disabled" . . . suggests any incapacity, physical or mental. And I certainly don't like "handicapped," which implies that I have deliberately been put at a disadvantage, by whom I can't imagine (my God is not a Handicapper General). . . . These words seem to me to be moving away from my condition, to be widening the gap between word and reality. Most remote is the recently coined euphemism "differently abled," which partakes of that same semantic hopefulness that transformed countries from "undeveloped" to "underdeveloped," then to "less developed," and finally to "developing" nations. People have continued to starve in those countries during the shift.[4]

With this pointed analogy, Mairs underlines how the politically correct terms ("differently abled" and "physically challenged") very quickly become problematic precisely because they pass over important signifiers of difference. By being so general, they strip difference of all its disruptive power, washing it down to a milktoasty variety of "everybody is different and has challenges," which is a convenient way to simply say "we don't really need to pay attention to your issues." As Barbara Hillyer makes clear in a section on language and naming in her book *Feminism and Disability*, these general terms quickly become politically meaningless. "Such an identification of oneself as basically like everyone else blocks the possibility of a nonassimilationist political analysis."[5] Paradoxically, by embracing the term "crippled," Mairs can claim defi-antly: "As a cripple, I swagger."[6]

Despite their theoretical romance with the body, contemporary cultural critics have paid little attention to issues of dis/ability. I suspect this is because the disabled body insistently refuses to be neatly packaged as metaphor. It is hard to abstract disability, the reality of its status "as is" breaks through the theoretical gloss to confront whomever is writing about it. Although the "absent" body—the body as performative and therefore temporary and transient—has frequently seduced contemporary theorists with its chic ephemerality, few have, as of yet, taken up the disabled body. Their reluctance comes from an unwillingness to touch a body that is neither entirely "present" nor intriguingly "absent," but rather liminal, struggling somewhere between the shores of theoretical surefootedness. This fear is a primal one; the material realities of disability threaten to disrupt not merely cultural representations or theoretical precepts, but ways of living as well. King underscores this liminal quality of dis/ability when she writes: "The very condition of disability provides a vantage point of a certain lived experience in the body, a lifetime of opportunity for the observation of reaction to bodily deviance. It defies categories of 'sickness' and 'health,' 'broken' and 'whole.' It is inbetween."[7]

But feminism ought to engage with the issues of dis/ability, for it seems to me that the body politics that serve as the foundation of much contemporary feminist thought have a lot in common with the political body of dis/ability. In the same way that women have historically been positioned as all body, their subjectivities weighed down with the raw matter of life, disabled bodies (particularly disabled female bodies) are seen as overwhelmingly material entities, unable to transcend the physical specificity of their daily needs. Like the female body, the disabled body is frightening and excessive, always threatening to ooze out of its appropriate containers. In a culture that works so anxiously to control the body's functions, desires, and physical boundaries, the disabled body is immediately positioned as deviant, simply because it is a little messier, or because it takes a little longer and travels a little more circuitously to get to its destination. I believe that feminist work on representation and the disciplinary regimes of the body could very productively inform and, in turn, be reinvigorated by an engagement with dis/ability studies.

Of course, what feminism has to confront in disability studies is the simplistic association of disability with passivity. This was particularly true in the budding women's movement of the seventies, where essentialist notions of what to wear, what to read (no pornography please), how to walk, how to have sex, etc., left little ideological room for the political contradictions involved in the practical lives of disabled feminists. In the introduction to their collection of essays on women with disabilities, Michelle Fine and Adrienne Asch recount an anecdote that is frightening (and all too common) in its peculiar brand of logic. "As one feminist academic said to the non-disabled coauthor of this essay: 'Why study women with disabilities? They reinforce traditional stereotypes of women being dependent, passive, and needy.'"[8] This response strikes me as so completely unimaginative that it actually warrants a closer look. Most feminists would never even think anything comparable about poor or illiterate women who are marginalized in our culture by social disabilities. But women with physical disabilities are readily seen as dysfunctional individuals, rather than as members of a marginalized social class. An interesting study done among college students revealed just how gendered this bias is. Most of the respondents attributed disability in men to accidents, work injuries, or war (it's not their fault, just bad luck), while they attributed disability in women to more internal causes such as diseases, revealing a gendered assumption that disability in women is a result of their own weakness or failure.[9]

Another issue that both feminism and dis/ability have in common is the deconstruction of existing notions of self and autonomy. The foundational political, philosophical, and psychological principles of Western culture are based on theories of individual subjectivity and state sovereignty that are predicated on simplistic ideals of independence and self-sufficiency. Even at the end of the twentieth century with its interdependent networks of information and global capital, we still believe that the primary moment of selfhood is when the child (or young adult) becomes independent from her parents or caretakers. This construction of the self as an autonomous individual has always been problematic for women and for men who are implicated in various threads of interdependence, but it is particularly so for people who need daily physical assistance with their lives.

With the help of writings by many feminists of color and women from developing countries where extended families and community interdependence have not completely eroded, contemporary feminist thought has finally begun to deconstruct this narrow-minded view that true selfhood is synonymous with independence from others, but it has yet to analyze the various ways that our society also conflates subjectivity and physical mobility. American culture was founded on a simplistic equation of selfhood with freedom and physical mobility (the frontier mentality), and I believe that many of the psychic and geographic dislocations of contemporary life can be traced to this deeply embedded notion. Early American modern dance shared with early feminists an interest in dress reform. Isadora Duncan, for instance, championed the belief that intellectual and social, not to mention psychological, freedom was very much related to physical mobility—in this case the freedom from the elaborate restrictions of Victorian apparel. While I absolutely agree that freedom from the physical restraints of fashion was and is important for women, I think that we need to develop a more complex and self-critical discussion of physical freedom in order to recognize that the ability to move—anywhere at anytime—does not necessarily equal a true psychic liberty.

The compromising of the human body before its natural time is tragic. It forces terrible hardship on the individual to whom it occurs. But the added overlay of oppression on the disabled is intimately related to the fear of death, and the acknowledgment of our embeddedness in organic nature. We are finite, contingent, dependent creatures by our very nature; we will all eventually die. We will all experience compromises to our physical integrity. The aspiration to human wholeness is an oppressive idealism.[10]

My personal experiences with dance and disability have made me realize the extent to which one's identity is read through one's body, and have also given me an awareness of how simplistic our cultural definition of dis/ability as physical incapacity really is. Several years ago, I was temporarily yet rather severely disabled when two of my discs ruptured into my spinal cord. Not only did I find it difficult to endure the relentless physical pain, the exhaustion, and the difficulty of getting around, but I also found that the medical personnel who were treating me were particularly unimaginative about who I was and what I could continue to do. Their assumption was that because I was in a wheelchair or using a cane, it was time for me to think about retiring from dance altogether (at the ripe old age of thirty-four!). Although my disability colored my daily experience for quite some time, it never entirely defined who I was—even though most people who met me at that time found it hard to accept that I would still identify myself as a dancer. A year later, when I was facilitating a movement workshop at the "This ability" conference, I was struck (once again) at how simplistically we are trained to read cultural identity from the physical body.[11] When I asked a group of disabled and nondisabled participants to talk about their experiences of their bodies, it became clear that any disabled/nondisabled dichotomy set up on the basis of physical ability quickly fell apart. A number of the participants who seemed able-bodied spoke of their intensely disabling experiences of body image problems (including anorexia and bulimia), as well as sexual and physical abuse. And some of the people with physical limitations spoke of trusting and loving their body as it was. Although an experience of paralysis is more difficult to negotiate in terms of access, it isn't necessarily any more personally disempowering than an experience of a body image disorder, even though only one of these people would be considered "disabled" in our society.

Issues of disability eventually affect everybody's life. Yet even though many of us are familiar with the work of disabled writers, artists, and musicians, physically disabled dancers are still seen as a contradiction in terms. This is because dance, unlike other forms of cultural production such as books or paintings, makes the body visible within the representation itself. Thus when we look at dance with disabled dancers, we are looking at both the choreography and the disability. This insertion of bodies with real physical challenges can be extremely disconcerting to critics and audience members who are committed to an aesthetic of ideal beauty. Cracking the porcelain image of the female dancer as sylph, disabled dancers force the viewer to confront the cultural opposite of the classical body—the grotesque body. In my last chapter, I discussed how the binary logic so prevalent in our cultural discourses about bodies, health, and fitness pits fit bodies against frail ones. In the context of this chapter, that binary is redeployed as the opposition between the classical and the grotesque bodies. I am using the term "grotesque" as Bakhtin invokes it in his analysis of representation within Rabelais. In her discussion of carnival, spectacle, and Bakhtinian theory, Mary Russo identifies these two bodily tropes in the following manner: "The grotesque body is the open, protruding, extended, secreting body, the body of becoming, process, and change. The grotesque body is opposed to the classical body, which is monumental, static, closed and sleek, corresponding to the aspirations of bourgeois individualism; the grotesque body is connected to the rest of the world."[12] I realize, of course, that by using the term "grotesque" within a chapter on dis/ability, I risk invoking old stereotypes of disabled bodies as grotesque bodies. This is certainly not my intention. When I discuss the opposition of classical and grotesque bodies, it is not to describe specific bodies, but rather to call upon cultural constructs that deeply influence our attitudes toward bodies. As I have argued earlier in my discussion of naming and terminology, normalizing the disabled body doesn't serve to break down these dichotomies of social difference, it merely disguises them with an alternative discourse.

In this chapter, I would like to explore the transgressive nature of the "grotesque" body in order to see if and how the disabled body could deconstruct and radically reform the representational structures of dance performances. But, just as all disabilities are not created equal, dances made with disabled dancers are not completely alike. Many of these dances recreate the representational frames of traditional proscenium performances, emphasizing the elements of virtuosity and technical expertise to reaffirm a classical body in spite of its limitations. In contrast, some dances, particularly those influenced by Contact Improvisation, work to break down the very distinctions between the classical and the grotesque body, radically restructuring the traditional frames of dance representation in order to offer another way of seeing dancing bodies. As we shall see, while all dance created on disabled bodies must negotiate the palpable contradictions between the discourses of ideal bodies and those of deviant ones, each piece meets this challenge in a different way, establishing its own aesthetic concerns within the choreography and movement style, as well as within the overall context of the performance itself.

At the start of *Gypsy*, tall and elegant Todd Goodman enters pulling the ends of a long scarf wrapped around the shoulders of his partner, Mary Verdi-Fletcher, gliding behind him. To the Gypsy Kings, he winds her in and out with the scarf. Her bare shoulders tingle with the ecstasy of performing. She flings back her head with trusting abandon as he dips her deeply backward. Holding the fabric she glides like a skater, alternately releasing and regaining control. At the climax he swoops her up in her chair and whirls her around. Did I mention that Verdi-Fletcher dances in her wheelchair?[13]

This is Gus Solomons's description of a romantic duet that was one of the first choreographic ventures of Cleveland Ballet Dancing Wheels, a professional dance company comprising dancers on legs and dancers in wheelchairs. Essentially a pas de deux for legs and wheels, *Gypsy* extends the aesthetic heritage of nineteenth-century Romantic ballet in several intriguing new directions. Like a traditional balletic duet, *Gypsy* is built on an illusion of grace provided by the fluid movements and physics of partnering. The use of the fabric in conjunction with the wheels gives the movement a continuous quality that is difficult to achieve on legs. When Solomons describes Verdi-Fletcher's dancing as "gliding," he is not simply using a metaphor; rather he is transcribing the physical reality of her movement. Whether they are physically touching or connected by their silken umbilical cord, the dancers in this pas de deux partner one another with a combination of the delicacy of ballet and the mystery of tango.

Solomons is an African-American dance critic and independent choreographer who has been involved in the contemporary dance scene since his days dancing for Merce Cunningham in the 1970s. An active member of the Dance Critics Association, he is a dance critic who has spoken eloquently about the need to include diverse communities within our definitions of mainstream dance. And yet Solomons, like many other liberal cultural critics and arts reviewers, sets up a peculiar rhetoric in the above passage that tries to deny difference. His remark, "Did I mention that Verdi-Fletcher dances in her wheelchair?" suggests that the presence of a dancer in a wheelchair is merely an incidental detail that hardly interrupts the seamless flow of the romantic pas de deux. In assuming that disability does *not* make a (big) difference, this writer is, in fact, limiting the (real) difference that dis/ability can make in radically refiguring how we look at, conceive of, and organize bodies in the twenty-first century. Why, for instance, does Solomons begin with a description of Goodman's able body as "tall and elegant," and then fail to describe Verdi-Fletcher's body at all? Why do most articles on Verdi-Fletcher's seminal dance company spend so much time celebrating how she has "overcome" her disability to "become" a dancer rather than inquiring how her bodily presence might radically refigure the very category of dancer itself?

The answers to these questions lie not only in an examination of the critical reception of *Gypsy* and other choreographic ventures by Cleveland Ballet Dancing Wheels, but also in an analysis of the ways in which this company paradoxically acknowledges and then covers over the difference that dis/ability makes. In the section that follows, I articulate the contradictions embedded within this company's differing aesthetic and social priorities; I argue that while their outreach work has laid important groundwork for the structural inclusion of people with disabilities in dance training programs and performance venues, the conservative aesthetic that guides much of Cleveland Ballet Dancing Wheels' performance work paradoxically reinforces, rather than disrupts, the negative connotations of disability.

Dancing Wheels began as a joint adventure between Mary Verdi-Fletcher, who was born with spina bifida and now uses a wheelchair, and David Brewster, the husband of a friend who enjoyed social dancing as much as Mary did. In those heady days of "disco fever" they mostly competed in various social dance competitions. Soon, however, the notion of a dance company of dancers with and without disabilities crystalized. In 1980 Verdi-Fletcher founded Dancing Wheels and began concentrating on outreach and audience development, doing lecture-demonstrations at community centers and performances in schools and nursing homes. In 1990, Verdi-Fletcher and her (then) associate director Todd Goodman (who dances on legs) merged with Cleveland Ballet to form the present company, Cleveland Ballet Dancing Wheels. In its present form, however, Dancing Wheels does not perform in the Cleveland Ballet's regular seasons—its primary contributions are to Cleveland Ballet's outreach and educational program. Independently, the company collaborates with a number of ballet and modern choreographers, performing their works in various theatrical venues across the country.

The genesis of the company was anecdotally related by Cleveland Ballet's artistic director Dennis Nahat. Nahat recalled meeting Verdi-Fletcher at a reception when Verdi-Fletcher introduced herself as a dancer and told him that she was interested in dancing with the Cleveland Ballet. In the annotated biography of Verdi-Fletcher's dance career that was commissioned for Dancing Wheels' fifteenth anniversary gala, Nahat is quoted as saying: "When I first saw Mary perform, I said 'That is a dancer.' . . . There was no mistake about it. She had the spark, the spirit that makes a dancer."[14] I am interested in pursuing this notion of "spirit" a bit, especially as it is used frequently within the company's own press literature. For instance, in the elaborate press packet assembled for a media event to celebrate the collaboration with Invacare Corporation's "Action Technology" (a line of wheelchairs designed for extra ease and mobility), there is a picture of the company with the caption "A Victory of Spirit over Body" underneath.

I find this notion of a dancing "spirit" that transcends the limitations of a disabled body actually rather troubling. Although it seems, at first, to signal liberatory language—one should not be "confined" by social definitions of identity based on bodily attributes (of race, gender, ability, etc.)—this rhetoric is actually based on ablist notions of overcoming physical handicaps (the "supercrip" theory) in order to become a "real" dancer, one whose "spirit" doesn't let the limitations of her body get in the way. Given that dancers' bodies are generally on display in a performance, this commitment to "spirit over body" risks covering over or erasing disabled bodies altogether. Just how do we represent spirit—smiling faces, joyful lifts into the air? The publicity photograph of the company on the same page gives us one example of the visual downplaying of disabled bodies. In this studio shot, the three dancers in wheelchairs are artistically surrounded by the able-bodied dancers in such a way that we can barely see the wheelchairs at all; in fact, Verdi-Fletcher is raised up and closely flanked by four men so that she looks as if she is standing in the third row. But what is most striking about this publicity shot is the way in which the ballerina sitting on the right has her long, slender legs extended across the bottom of the picture. The effect, oddly enough, is to fetishize these working legs while at the same time making the "other" mobility—the wheels—invisible. Now I am not suggesting that this photo was deliberately set up to minimize the visual representation of disability. But this example shows us that unless we consciously construct new images and ways of imaging the disabled body, we will inevitably end up reproducing an ablist aesthetic. Although the text

Cleveland Ballet Dancing Wheels. Company photo by Al Fuchs.

jubilantly claims its identity, "Greetings from Cleveland Ballet Dancing Wheels," the picture normalizes the "difference" in bodies, reassuring prospective presenters and the press that they won't see anything too uncomfortable.

The first sentence of Cleveland Ballet Dancing Wheels' mission statement claims that the company works to "Promote the collaboration and artistic talents of dancers with and without disabilities while demonstrating the diversity of dance and the abilities of artists with physical challenges."[15] This is truly an important mission. With their extensive outreach and educational programs, which include teaching dance classes to dancers with disabilities and presenting lecture-demonstrations in local schools and community centers as well as their performance work, Dancing Wheels has increased the visibility of differently abled dancers. Indeed, Mary Verdi-Fletcher is a powerful role model for aspiring young dancers on wheels. In a typical article documenting how Verdi-Fletcher's work has inspired young girls to fulfill their dream of dancing, Steve Wright reports that "Melissa Holbrook and a few hundred of her schoolmates at Brown Elementary learned yesterday that you don't need your legs to dance and that wheelchair users can be ballerinas." The short feature ends by quoting Verdi-Fletcher as remarking that "her dance partners have 'found it was much easier to drag a woman around on wheels than on heels.'"[16] While I appreciate the wonderful role model of cultural ambassador in which Verdi-Fletcher clearly excels, I am curious about the seemingly uncritical stance that she and the company seem to have toward representations of women and images of dis/ability. Certainly Cleveland Ballet Dancing Wheels has increased the visibility of dancers with various disabilities—but, we must ask, visible in what way, and at whose expense? For as long as the representational basis for their work is steeped in the ideological values of classic dance and formalist aesthetics (complete with the fetishization of "line"), their attempts to include dancers on wheels can very quickly get recast within the same old patronizing terms of abled and disabled bodies.[17]

Flashback (1992) is a choreographic collaboration between Tom Evert Dance and Dancing Wheels, and has been performed throughout Ohio as well as at the Marymount Manhattan Theater in New York City. This dance is a series of short vignettes creating a loose narrative that retraces time from the first scene celebrating adult love to the last section, which represents childhood play. The dancing idiom is a cross between classical technique and naturalistic acting, and each section is danced by both dancers on legs and dancers in wheelchairs. Mary Verdi-Fletcher is the only one of the wheelchair dancers, however, who is really physically disabled—the others "play the part" for the purposes of the story line. Although this dance was meant to deliver the message that disabled performers can be integrated into mainstream dance, a structural movement analysis reveals that each section, in fact, reinscribes the *d i s* of dis/ability, marking the "lack" of mobile legs rather than exploring the movement possibilities inherent in various kinds of bodies.

In the beginning of the dance, the dancers present themselves to the audience, moving in unison around the stage. The three dancers on legs weave among the dancers in wheelchairs, lending a hand here and there to swing their partner in an arcing circle on the floor. The physical relationship quickly becomes unequal, however, with the dancers on legs directing and motivating the movement of the wheelchairs while the dancers on wheels follow but never actually initiate any movement with their partners. The dancers on wheels perform a series of classically-based arm gestures that parallel those of the dancers on legs who, however, usually extend the movement through their torsos and into an arabesque. Often, the dancers on wheels are used like static architectural devices to frame the dancers on legs, who are busy presenting the "real" full-bodied dancing in the center of the stage.

Two duets follow this section, the first of which is a romantic waltz—wheelchair style. This section has some of the most imaginative use of wheelchair choreography, there being no dancers on legs to guide the wheelchairs through the space. One such instance is when the two dancers on wheels, Verdi-Fletcher and Nick Carlisle, approach one another with enough momentum to swing one another around in a circle. The choreographic significance of this duet is quickly undercut, however, when the two dancers on legs, Todd Goodman and Susanna Weingarten de Evert, enter the stage to perform their duet —a Latin tango, complete with seductive looks, a low-cut dress, and physically intimate partnering. The implication is clear: dancers on wheels can be sweetly romantic, but the sexy, exciting dancing is reserved for those with legs.

The next section begins with a melodramatic transition in which the male dancer on wheels arises like a ghost from his chair and leaves the stage as another male dancer takes his place. Suddenly, the time and place have shifted and we see an "invalid" and his perky nurse cavorting around the stage. This particular section strikes me as one of the most ideologically peculiar moments of the dance, for it seems to invoke all the worst stereotypes of disability in a completely uncritical manner. The man in the wheelchair is now clearly a "victim" of some accident. The nurse figure treats him like an infant, wiping his mouth and pushing him cheerfully around the stage. Sometimes she runs ahead, clapping her hands in approval when he follows her. Typically, it is she who directs all the movement action; she is the one who touches him, teasingly sits on him, and yet admonishes him with a slap of her hand when he reaches out to touch her in response.

Flashback was the beginning of Cleveland Ballet Dancing Wheels' collaborations with various choreographers. In the summer of 1992, Dancing Wheels sponsored a choreographic workshop to encourage Ohio choreographers to create works for a mixed group of dancers with and without disabilities. The week-long event culminated in a showing of their works-in-progress. This was the start of an ongoing series of workshops that has been very influential in exposing local choreographers to wheelchair-based movement possibilities.[18] Then, in 1994, the resident choreographer Todd Goodman (whose aesthetic was firmly grounded in the world of ballet and musical theater) left. He was replaced by Sabatino Verlezza, a choreographer from New York who worked with the company during the 1993 Celebration of Arts and Access.[19]

Verlezza's background in modern dance brings a welcome shift of physical vocabulary to Dancing Wheels. In August 1995, Cleveland Ballet Dancing Wheels presented a gala benefit performance at the Cleveland Playhouse's State Theater. The program opened with a reconstruction of a dance choreographed in 1959 by May O'Donnell, with whom Verlezza danced for many years. Originally a member of the Martha Graham dance company, O'Donnell has developed a choreographic style more reminiscent of Doris Humphrey and early modern dance's expressive, communal style of movement. In its use of space, fall and recovery, and breath rhythms, *Dance Energies* evoked Humphrey's great modern epic *New Dance*.

Although within his group pieces Verlezza often choreographs a central theme for dancers with legs, leaving the dancers on wheels to provide an architectural backdrop (a process that works against the democratic principles of the company's stated claims), he has begun to experiment with much more exciting movement for the wheelchair dancers. Whereas most of Dancing Wheels' previous choreography involved dancers on legs leading or swinging dancers on wheels around the stage, in the present repertory there is at least some effort to explore momentum and other movement possibilities unique to the wheelchairs. The premiere of *1420 MHZ* was one of the most physically challenging works and provided a very good opportunity to see what extraordinary moves were possible on wheels. The fact that the piece was made for three women on wheels allowed the audience to experience a truly enabling representation of difference without the physical comparisons inevitable when women on wheels dance with men on legs.

Another piece by Verlezza entitled *May Ring* completed the evening's program. I was absolutely stunned by the final image of this dance and I find it hard to believe that neither Verdi-Fletcher nor Verlezza was aware of how this image might read to some of their audience members. *May Ring* ends with a long fade as Verlezza lifts Verdi-Fletcher, arms spread wide and face beaming, out of her wheelchair and high above his head. This is clearly meant to be a final transcendent moment. Yet its unavoidably sexist and ablist implications—reinforced by the fact that Verlezza dances on legs and Verdi-Fletcher dances on wheels—deeply disappointed me. Like Disney narratives and pop songs of my youth that promised salvation through love—this image portrays Verlezza as a prince charming, squiring Verdi-Fletcher out of her wheelchair in order to make her into a "real" woman. Now, it is possible to argue that this image is, in fact, a deconstruction of the ballerina's role, a way of winking to the audience to say that, yes, a disabled woman can also fulfill that popular image. But the rest of the work doesn't support this interpretation. Verdi-Fletcher's smiling, childlike presence suggests little personal agency, much less the sense of defiance or chutzpah it would take to pull off this deconstruction.

In her essay "The Other Body," King describes a disabled woman whom she sees on her way to work each day. "She can barely move. She has a pretty face, and tiny legs she could not possibly walk on. Yet she wears black lace stockings and spike high heels. . . . That she could 'flaunt' her sexual being violates the code of acceptable appearance for a disabled woman."[20] What appeals to King about this woman's sartorial display is the way that she at once refuses her cultural position as an asexual being and deconstructs the icons of feminine sexuality (who can really walk in those spike heels anyway?). Watching Verdi-Fletcher in the final moments of *May Ring* brings us face to face with the contradictions involved in being positioned as both a classical dancer (at once sexualized and objectified) and a disabled woman (an asexual child who needs help). Yet instead of one position bringing tension to or fracturing the other (as in King's example of the disabled woman with high heels and black lace stockings), Verdi-Fletcher seems here to be embracing a position that is doubly disempowering.

In the time since this performance, I have been searching for the reasons why, in the midst of an enormous publicity campaign that seeks to present Mary Verdi-Fletcher as an extraordinary woman who has overcome the challenges of spina bifida to realize her dream of becoming a professional dancer, she would allow herself to be presented in such a fashion. In retrospect, I think that this desire to position herself in the spotlight has everything to do with the powerfully seductive image of the Romantic ballerina as an unattainable sylph. It seems to me that when Verdi-Fletcher closes her eyes and dreams about becoming a dancer, she is still envisioning a sugarplum fairy. Although she has successfully opened up the field of professional dance to dancers on wheels, Verdi-Fletcher hasn't challenged the myth of the sylph yet. Despite its recent forays into modern dance, Dancing Wheels still seems very much attached to a classical ideology of the "perfect" body.

Mary Verdi-Fletcher is a dancer and, like many other dancers, both disabled and nondisabled, she has internalized an aesthetic of beauty, grace, and line that, if not centered on a completely mobile body, is nonetheless beholden to an idealized body image. There are very few professions where the struggle to maintain a "perfect" (or at least near-perfect) body has taken up as much psychic and physical struggle as in the dance field. With few exceptions, this is true whether one's preferred technique is classical ballet, American modern dance, Bharata Natyam, or a form of African-American dance. Even though the styles and look of bodies favored by different dance cultures may allow for some degree of variation (for instance, the director of Urban Bush Women, Jawole Willa Jo Zollar, talks about the freedom to have and to move one's butt in African dance as being wonderfully liberating after years of being told to tuck it in in modern dance classes), most professional dance is still inundated by body image and weight issues. Even companies such as the Bill T. Jones and Arnie Zane Dance Company, who pride themselves on the diversity of their dancers, rarely have much variation among the women dancers (all of whom are quite slim). Any time a dancer's body is not completely svelte, the press usually picks up on it. In fact, the discourse of weight and dieting in dance is so pervasive (especially, but certainly not exclusively for women) that we often don't even register it anymore. I am constantly amazed at dancers who have consciously deconstructed traditional images of female dancers in their choreographic work and yet still complain of their extra weight, wrinkles, gray hair, or sagging whatevers. As a body on display, the dancer is subject to the regulating gaze of the choreographer and the public, but neither of these gazes is quite as debilitating or oppressive as the gaze that meets its own image in the mirror.

In the past twenty years, much has been written about the ways in which the dance profession has engendered an unhealthy atmosphere of intensive dieting, exercising, and drug use to acquire and keep an unnaturally thin body. This is particularly true of classical ballet schools and companies. Dr. L. M. Vincent's seminal book *Competing with the Sylph: Dancers and the Pursuit of the Ideal Body Form* (1979) is filled with oral histories of the extreme diets and fasts that girls go through to stave off the physiological changes their bodies are going through.[21] Although less visible than mobility challenges, body image problems and the resultant eating disorders constitute one of the broadest issues of dis/ability within dance. Books such as Suzanne Gordon's *Off Balance: The Real World of Ballet*, Christy Adair's *Women and Dance*, and autobiographical accounts by the likes of New York City Ballet star Gelsey Kirkland (a particularly gruesome tale of addiction and self-hatred), document the full range of horrors that girls and women will subject themselves to in their pursuit of the ideal dancing body.[22] While modern and contemporary dance forms, as well as dance traditions from some other cultures, may have loosened the tyranny of thinness, they have often replaced it with new expectations concerning the visibly muscled body. In fact, it is the rare professional dancer today who does not have well-sculpted biceps.

"[J]ust as society creates an ideal of beauty which is oppressive for us all, it creates an ideal model of the physically perfect person who is not beset with weakness, loss, or pain. . . . The disabled (and aging) woman poses a symbolic threat by reminding us how tenuous that model, 'the myth of the perfect body,' really is. . . ."[23] In her essay "The Myth of the Perfect Body," Roberta Galler suggests that disabled women use the "symbolic threat" that their bodies pose to the reigning ideologies of beauty, health, and femininity in order to disrupt those oppressive ideals. Galler writes that "disabled (and aging) women are coming out; we are beginning to examine our issues publicly, forcing other women to address not only the issues of disability but to reexamine their attitudes towards their own limitations and lack of perfection, towards oppressive myths, standards, and social conditions which affect us all."[24] This "coming out" of sorts includes mainstreaming in the schools, attending conferences, engaging in visible political acts, and writing. One of the most compelling contemporary essayists I have read recently is Nancy Mairs, whose autobiographical writings document the complexities of living with a degenerative disease (she has multiple sclerosis) and the dual forces of her growing self-esteem and awareness of her identity as a writer in the midst of a gradual loss of neurological control. In articulating her life, Mairs also articulates the ongoing negotiations between her physical experiences and their complete lack of public representation.[25] For instance, Mairs once asked an advertising agent why he never used disabled people in his detergent and cereal commercials. He replied that no one wanted to give the public the idea that these products were "just for the handicapped." His answer, Mairs decides, "masked a deeper and more anxious rationale: to depict disabled people in the ordinary activities of daily life is to admit that there is something ordinary about disability itself, that it may enter anybody's life."[26]

Indeed, dis/ability is finally beginning to enter the public consciousness as the 1990 Americans with Disabilities Act (ADA) forces more and more institutions to make their spaces accessible.[27] Ironically, however, just as the independent living movement gains momentum and disabled people are becoming (somewhat) more visible, American culture is emphasizing with a passion heretofore unimagined the need for physical and bodily control.[28] As King makes clear in her essay "The Other Body," this fetishization of control marks the disabled body as the social antithesis—a body out of control. "It is no longer enough to be thin; one must have ubiquitous muscle definition, nothing loose, flabby, or ill defined, no fuzzy boundaries. And of course, there's the importance of control. Control over aging, bodily processes, weight, fertility, muscle tone, skin quality, and movement. Disabled women, regardless of how thin, are without full bodily control."[29]

This issue of control is, I am convinced, key to understanding not only the specific issues of prejudice against the disabled, but also the larger symbolic place that dis/ability holds in our culture's psychic imagination. In dance, this contrast between the classical and grotesque bodies is often framed in terms of physical control and technical virtuosity. Although the dancing body is moving and, in this sense, is always changing and in flux, the choreography or movement style can emphasize images resonant of the classical body. For instance, the statuesque poses of ballet are clear icons of the classical body. So too, however, are the dancers in some modern and contemporary companies that privilege an abstract body, such as those coolly elegant ones performing with the Merce Cunningham Dance Company these days. Based as it is in the live body, dance is rife with the cultural anxiety that the grotesque body will erupt (unexpectedly) through the image of the classical body, shattering the illusion of ease and grace by the disruptive presence of fleshy experience—heavy breathing, sweat, technical mistakes, physical injury, even evidence of a dancer's age or mortality.

The disruptive force represented by even the mere *thought* of seeing disabled, ailing, or dying bodies on a dance stage can be gauged by the tremendous controversy surrounding Arlene Croce's response to Bill T. Jones's epic work on terminal illness *Still/Here*. In a gesture certain to secure her a place in the annals of the so-called "culture wars," Croce (a dance critic for *The New Yorker*) claimed that she could not review a dance that contained the videotaped images of dying people. In her vituperative essay attacking "victim art" entitled "Discussing the Undiscussable," Croce slams "overweight dancers," "old dancers," "dancers with sickled feet," as well as "dancers with physical deformities who appear nightly in roles requiring beauty of line."[30] Railing against any politicized art that foregrounds the bodily identity of the artist ("Dissed blacks, abused women, or disfranchised homosexuals"), she laments the demise of theater as she knows it. "In theatre, one chooses what one will be. The cast members of *Still/Here*—the sick people whom Jones has signed up—have no choice other than to be sick."[31] The implication here is that the only bodies worth watching are those bodies that signify "choice," a code word for bodies that conform to idealized standards of health, fitness, and beauty. In this peculiar brand of logic, bodies marked by difference (does one "choose" race, height, sexuality?) have no choice—their deviance at once defines and marginalizes them.

Croce's tirade had its genesis, I believe, in an earlier moment in 1989 when Jones carried Demian Acquavella, a company member so physically ravaged by AIDS that he could barely stand, onstage during a performance of *D-Man in the Waters*. This dance was dedicated to Acquavella (the epigraph in the program is a line from Jenny Holzer, "In a dream you saw a way to survive and you were full of joy"), and Jones supported Acquavella as he performed the arm gestures of what was to have been his solo in the dance. Although the dance was hailed as a brilliant synthesis of expressive and virtuosic dancing with a formally structured musical score (Mendelssohn's Octet in E for Strings), the critical establishment had mixed reactions to this last gesture, suggesting it was either emotional manipulation or flagrant self-promotion. For instance, at the end of an otherwise laudatory review, Marcia Siegel writes, "I think Jones has confused realism here with autobiography. . . . With Acquavella's participation, *D-Man in the Waters* sacrifices acute comment for immediate catharsis."[32] Like Croce's critical tirade, Siegel's comments reflect a deep fear that the emotional impact of the "real" (read grotesque) body will get in the way of a more intellectual appreciation of Jones's choreographic composition. As my chapter attests, however, I believe that the disruption of the real that disability symbolizes can provoke us to think differently about the relationship between representation and the actual history of bodies.

I remember seeing this performance at the Joyce Theater in New York City and being amazed at the stunning differences between the smooth, quick, powerful dancing of Arthur Aviles (who won a Bessie award for his dancing in this work) and the spasmodic gestures of Acquavella's upper body (he was suffering from milopathy, an AIDS-related condition that affects the nervous system). Watching his frail body struggle among all the glowing, healthy, virtuosic bodies of his fellow company members made me realize how deeply disability and the grotesque body are at once embedded (and repressed) in dance. Looking back at my journal comments about this performance, I noticed that after describing the dances I wrote: "God, it must be intense to dance in that company now. Art and Life." Like the 1989 version of *D-Man in the Waters* and *Still/Here*, much contemporary dance plays evocatively with the tension between art and life—between the classical and the grotesque body.[33]

Since dance in the West has traditionally privileged an able, contained, virtuosic body, it is small wonder that a number of dance companies with disabled and nondisabled dancers work very hard to foreground the classical body, emphasizing that *all* their dancers' bodies are rigorously trained and technically in control. This integration of disabled bodies within an artform that has made an icon of the statuesque (and sculpted) body provides us with a wonderful opportunity to investigate the cultural dialogue between the classical and the grotesque body. This dialogue takes place anytime live bodies appear onstage, of course, but the fact that it is consciously articulated within the publicity, audience reaction, and critical appraisal of integrated dance groups, gives us the opportunity to trace the web of contradictory discourses about the body within dance.

How the disabled body gets positioned in terms of a classical discourse of technique and virtuosity is not unaffected by gender. Gender is inscribed very differently on a disabled body, and there has been a great deal written concerning the way disability can emasculate men (whose gendered identities are often contingent on displays of autonomy, independence, and strength), as well as desexualize women. Yet the social power that we accord representations of male bodies seems to give disabled men dancers (with a few exceptions) more freedom to display their bodies in dance. My own observations and research suggest that disabled men dancers can evoke the virtuosic, technically amazing body (even, as we shall see, without legs), and yet they also are able to deconstruct that classical body, allowing the audience to see their bodies in a different light. As we have seen in the case of Verdi-Fletcher and Cleveland Ballet Dancing Wheels, disabled women are more apt to hold onto the image of a classical female dancer as graceful, elegant, strong, and beautiful. In the section that follows, I will look at various dance groups whose work has, in different ways, revolutionized notions of ability in contemporary dance. Both Candoco (with the disabled male body) and Light Motion (with the disabled female body) have established new images of physical virtuosity and technical excellence—exploding assumptions that virtuosic dancing requires four working limbs. In addition, there is a growing form of mixed-ability dancing coming out of the Contact Improvisation community that embraces a thoroughly different aesthetic point of view. While Candoco and Light Motion redefine virtuosity in dance, Contact Improvisation redefines the body in dance, opening up the possibility that we can look at the dancing body as a body in process, a body *becoming*. This attention to the ever-changing flux of bodies and the open-endedness of the improvisation refocuses the audience's gaze, helping us to see the disabled body on its own terms.

Candoco is a professional British dance company that evolved from conversations between Celeste Dandeker, a former dancer with the London Contemporary Dance Theater who was paralyzed as a result of a spinal injury incurred while performing, and Adam Benjamin, a dancer who was then teaching at the Heaffey Centre in London, a mixed-abilities recreation center connected to ASPIRE (The Association for Spinal Injury Research, Rehabilitation, and Reintegration). In 1991, these two dancers began a small dance class for disabled and nondisabled dancers. Since then, Benjamin and Dandeker have established a professional company that includes eight dancers and an extensive repertoire of works by some of the most interesting experimental choreographers in England today. Candoco has received various awards in recognition for its work and the company was selected for BBC's Dance for Camera series. Introducing the company's philosophy to the press and the general public, artistic director Adam Benjamin has chosen to redefine the term *integration*. In his manifesto of sorts about the company's history and goals, "In search of integrity," Benjamin writes:

Time and again one sees the use, or misuse of this word "integration" to describe a group or activity that has opened itself up to include people with disabilities. To integrate a group of people in this way of course implies a norm into which they need to be fitted. If however, you're using that word, integrate, from the Latin integratus, it forces you to acknowledge that they are already an integral part of the whole, even if you haven't found them a place yet.[34]

Although Benjamin's philosophy is quite radical in many ways and although Candoco has commissioned some very intriguing choreography that doesn't just "accommodate" the disabled dancers but, as we shall see, recasts cultural perceptions about an "able" physicality, Benjamin is still committed to classical elements of technical virtuosity. For Benjamin, true integration means insisting on high standards of professional excellence in order to create interesting choreographic works for *all* the dancers in the company. He criticizes companies "in which highly trained dancers 'dance circles round' those with disabilities who share the stage but little else, in which there has been no real attempt on the part of the choreographer to enable the performer to communicate. . . . Worse still are dances in which trained, able bodied dancers drift inconsequentially, as if embarassed by their own skills, used instead to merely ferry about the bemused occupants of wheelchairs."[35] Recognizing the need to create their own style of dancing that will accommodate different physical possibilities, the dancers in Candoco are constantly trying out new ways of using momentum, working on a variety of levels including the floor, and coordinating legs and wheels. In a review of the fall 1992 London season, Chris de Marigny registers his own astonishment with Candoco's work. "Indeed *all* the

Candoco in *Cross Your Heart*. Photo by Chris Nash.

dancers perform with amazing skill. This is rendered possible by the extraordinary choreographic solutions which have been invented to allow these people with very different disabilities to create the most startling and beautiful images. New concepts of falling, leaning, and supporting have been created to make both lyrical and at other times energetic work."[36] Reading the press discussions of Candoco's first few seasons, there can be no doubt that this company has stretched people's notions of what is possible in mixed-ability dance companies. Yet because it relies on one very exceptional disabled dancer to break down the public's preconceptions about disability, Candoco sometimes recreates (unwittingly) new distinctions between the classical (virtuosic) and grotesque (passive) bodies within the company.

Victoria Marks was one of the first choreographers to work with Candoco (she was a member of their first class at the Heaffey Center, creating "The Edge of the Forest" for them in 1991), and it is her choreography that is showcased in Margaret Williams's dance film for BBC, *Outside In*. A lyrical film that interweaves surreal pastoral landscapes with the urbane suspended rhythms of tango and the beat of world music, *Outside In* begins with an extended kiss that is passed from one company member to another. The camera lingers on each face, registering everyone's delight in receiving the kiss and allowing the viewer to see how each kiss is transformed en route to the next person. A jumpcut transports the action to a cavernous space in which a single empty wheelchair rolls into the camera's focus. The company then quickly assembles and reassembles, creating a maze of chalk patterns on the floor. This is the first time the viewer sees the full bodies and individual styles of locomotion. One of the most striking is David Toole's ability to careen across the space with his arms. Toole is one of three disabled dancers, but he is the only one who moves easily in and out of his wheelchair. Toole has no legs. Instead, he relies on his strong arms to walk. Ironically, the fact that Toole has no lower body gives him an incredible freedom of movement. His presence is wonderfully quixotic and he can practically bounce from his chair to the floor and back up again within the blink of an eye.

Toole's abilities as a dancer are remarkable—and amply remarked on. Indeed, Toole's dancing is often the subject of extended discussions within reviews and preview articles about Candoco. Adjectives such as "amazing," "incredible," "stupefying" are liberally sprinkled throughout descriptions of his dancing. For instance, in an article in *Ballet International* that reviews the performances of several British dance companies during the spring 1993 season, Toole's dancing is the central focus of the short section on Candoco. "David Toole is a man with no legs who possesses more grace and presence than most dancers can even dream of. . . . Toole commands the stage with an athleticism that borders on the miraculous."[37] This language of astonishment reflects both an evangelistic awakening (yes, a disabled man can swagger!) and traces of a freak-show voyeurism (see the amazing feats of the man with no legs!). David Toole's virtuosic dancing comes at a price—a physical price. Recently, Toole, on the advice of his doctors, had to quit dancing. His extraordinary mobility is predicated on his ability to support and carry his entire body weight on his arms, allowing him to walk, run, or even skip across the stage. These astonishing feats, unfortunately, are actually destroying his arms and shoulders. Because of his status as a virtuosic dancer, however, Toole would find it hard to continue performing in a way that would not hurt his body (such as in a wheelchair).[38]

Interestingly enough, one of the only articles to address self-consciously the issue of the gaze we use to watch a body like Toole's was written by a French reviewer. In the May 1994 issue of *Les Saisons de la Danse*, Delphine Goater wrote a short review of a Candoco concert that risks asking some uncomfortable questions. One of the first things to strike me about this piece was the way the French language has yet to accommodate politically correct terminology. For instance, the able-bodied dancers are described as *valide* (meaning both valid and healthy). Then, too, there was the unabashed frankness with which Goater asked: "Does one look at the handicapped dancer with pity, with admiration for his performance, or as if he were an artist who is only part whole? Isn't there an element of voyeurism or curiosity here?"[39] Goater's questions call forth the dangers of looking at this kind of work, the possibility that the grotesque body might reassert itself as spectacle, but then she quickly assures her readers that Toole's performance is "stunning and beautiful."

Although the medium of film is notorious for its voyeuristic gaze and spectacle-making tendencies, and although Toole is one of the most visible dancers in *Outside In*, the combination of skillful cinematography and inventive choreography in this film actually directs our gaze away from the extraordinary sight of Toole's body to the interactive contexts of his dancing. Even when he is moving by himself, Toole is always in dialogue with another person's movements. For instance, in the second scene, after the group has left the space, one woman remains, stepping among the circular patterns created by the wheelchairs. We see her choosing an interesting pattern and improvising with it—a skip step here, a shimmey-shimmey there. That she is translating the pattern of the wheels onto her body only becomes fully clear when the camera jumps to Toole, who is approaching a similar task—that of translating cheeky Arthur Murray's learn-to-dance footprints onto his own body. At first he seems to hesitate, running his fingers across the black outlines of a shoe. But then he looks directly at the camera and, squaring his shoulders with a determined look, he launches into a dashing rendition of the tango. This solo leads, after a brief tango sequence with the full company, into an extended duet with Sue Smith. The usual negotiation of desire in a tango is replaced here by the respectful negotiation of level changes. From the moment Smith climbs aboard Toole's chair, to the last shot of them rolling away, the choreography refuses the implicit ideology of standing upright by placing most of the movement on the ground. The cinematography follows suit, filming them both at eye (that is to say ground) level. The camera's ability to shift viewpoints so seamlessly provides one of the most ingenious ways of breaking up (by literally breaking down) an ablist gaze—the one that is forever overlooking people who aren't standing (up) in front of its nose.

While the mobility of the camera itself allows for wonderful new ways of viewing dancers, the medium of film tends to reinforce images of the classical body by making everybody look so good. In *Outside In* we lose the experiential impact of breathing, the sound of thuds and falls, the sweat and physical evidence (hair out of place, costumes messed up, etc.) of this very kinesthetic dancing. This is particularly true for the women dancers, who all look exceed-

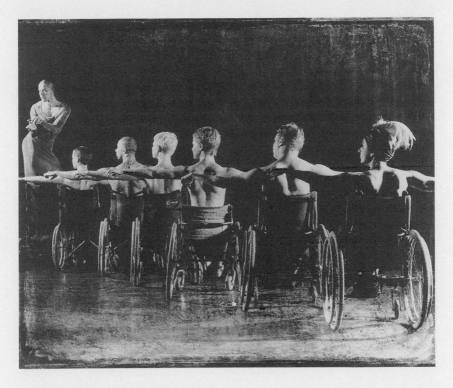

Candoco in *Cross Your Heart*. Photo by Chris Nash.

ingly beautiful throughout the video. Then, too, given the innovative choreography of the earlier section, I was surprised by the mundaneness and passivity of the wheelchair choreography in the next part in which we see the able bodied dancers assist, roll, and tilt the chairs while Jonathan French and Celeste Dandeker perform a series of decorative arm movements in them. The marked difference between Toole's dancing and that of Dandeker and French struck me as reinforcing a notion that being in a wheelchair is physically less interesting than being outside one. Ironically enough, even though one is a man and the other is a woman, both of these dancers get defined within the context of the film as much more passive and feminized than Toole. Although *Outside In* liberates our notions of physical difference by giving us the opportunity to see different bodies in action, it has not sufficiently fractured the iconographic codes in which the wheelchair signifies dis/ability. To see how a wheelchair can effectively become part of the dancing body, we must turn to the work of another company, Light Motion.

Charlene Curtiss was a competitive gymnast and sports enthusiast when, at age seventeen, she was injured on a faulty set of uneven parallel bars. At first, Curtiss resisted the stigma of a wheelchair and struggled around with braces and crutches. Seeing the incredible possibilities of movement available to wheelchair users during a national wheelchair competition, however, she changed her attitude. In 1988, Curtiss established Light Motion to "develop the artistic expression of both disabled and nondisabled artists working together to enhance community awareness of disability issues through the arts." Today, Curtiss teaches and performs as a wheelchair dancer, using the skills she acquired from athletic events, such as the wheelchair slalom, to fashion exciting new ways of moving through space on wheels. In August 1993, Curtiss performed her collaborative duet with Joanne Petroff entitled *The Laughing Game* as a guest artist on the Cleveland Ballet Dancing Wheels gala program.

The Laughing Game begins with two dancers (one on legs and one on wheels) approaching and circling one another, sometimes resting in moments of complementary stillness. After a minute or two, the music's tempo quickens and becomes much more lively, and the dancers respond in kind with their motion. It is in mirroring the rhythmic complexity of the music that the choreography for wheels begins to get really interesting. Using techniques that she learned from the wheelchair slalom, Curtiss executes quick percussive changes of direction, deftly shifting from side to side. She can also spin like an iceskater and stop on a dime. Sometimes the wheelchair choreography is visually more intriguing than the choreography for legs, but most of the time the dancers' partnering complements the physical or rhythmic emphasis of the other. For instance, when Curtiss begins to pick up momentum at one point, Petroff needs to really throw her weight in counterbalance just to keep her partner from flying off the stage. Seeing Petroff use her whole physicality in such a functional and nondecorative manner was both visually refreshing and kinesthetically exciting for me. So, too, was the moment when Curtiss wheeled over a prone Petroff. Later in *The Laughing Game*, the dancers echo the percussive dialogue of the music. In this section, Curtiss makes her chair strut in syncopation with Petroff's own high stepping, showing us how the chair, known for its smooth gliding and spinning capacity, can also claim a rhythm of its own.

Curtiss's dancing is different from other wheelchair dancing that I have seen. Because Curtiss works collaboratively on the choreography, she has been able to craft consciously the representation of dis/ability that is presented within the dancing. For Curtiss, "It's important that the nondisabled person doesn't try to take the disabled person through the moves. You are dancing with somebody with a disability, but you have to dance with them as themselves. . . .

Charlene Curtiss and Joanne Petroff in *The Laughing Game*. Photo by Richard Roth.

You don't pull me through a pirouette. You let me pull myself through the pirouette."[40] What is interesting to me in her performance is how Curtiss claims the chair as an extension of her own body. The chair becomes more than just a device to facilitate getting from here to there. Rather, it is a part of her, expressive of her personality and movement style. This shift is accomplished because of the way that Curtiss can integrate her wheelchair into the musicality of her own body. Wheelchairs, even when gliding across the floor, can seem very static and disembodied, but Curtiss uses hers to match the rhythms of her upper body, rising in a demi-wheelie to step enthusiastically into the downbeat. The fact that Curtiss can bebop and groove with her wheelchair revises the cultural significance of the chair, expanding its legibility as a signal of the handicapped into a sign of embodiment.

Although companies such as Can*do*co and Light Motion are producing work that does not cover over disability, but rather uses the difference in physical ability to create new and inventive choreography, I feel that much of their work is still informed by an ethos that reinstates the classical body within the disabled one. Although embodied differently, cultural conceptions of grace, speed, strength, agility, and control nonetheless structure these companies' aesthetics. Thus, while all the groups that integrate disabled and nondisabled dancers have surely broadened the cultural imagination about who can become a dancer, they have not, to my mind, fully deconstructed the privileging of ability within dance. That more radical cultural work is currently taking place within the Contact Improvisation community.

Giving a coherent description of Contact Improvisation is a tricky business, for the form has grown exponentially over time and has traveled through many countries and dance communities. Although it was developed in the seventies, Contact Improvisation has recognizable roots in the social and aesthetic revolutions of the sixties. Contact at once embraces the casual, individualistic, improvisatory ethos of social dancing in addition to the experimentation with pedestrian and task-like movement favored by early postmodern dance groups such as the Judson Church Dance Theater. Resisting both the idealized body of ballet and the dramatically expressive body of modern dance, Contact seeks to create what Cynthia Novack calls a "responsive" body, one based in the physical exchange of weight.[41] Unlike many genres of dance that stress the need to control one's movement (with admonitions to pull up, tighten, and place the body), the physical training of Contact emphasizes the release of the body's weight into the floor or into a partner's body. In Contact, the experience of internal sensations and the flow of the movement between two bodies is more important than specific shapes or formal positions. Dancers learn to move with a consciousness of the physical communication implicit within the dancing. Curt Siddall, an early exponent of Contact Improvisation, describes the form as a combination of kinesthetic forces: "Contact Improvisation is a movement form, improvisational in nature, involving the two bodies in contact. Impulses, weight, and momentum are communicated through a point of physical contact that continually rolls across and around the bodies of the dancers."[42]

But human bodies, especially bodies in physical contact with one another, are difficult to see *only* in terms of physical counterbalance, weight, and momentum. By interpreting the body as both literal and metaphoric, Contact exposes the interconnectedness of social, physical, and aesthetic concerns. Indeed, an important part of Contact Improvisation today is a willingness to allow the physical metaphors and narratives of love, power, and competition to evolve from the original emphasis on the workings of a physical interaction. On first seeing Contact, people often wonder whether this is, in fact, professional dancing or rather a recreational or therapeutic form. Gone are the formal lines of much classical dance. Gone are the traditional approaches to choreography and the conventions of the proscenium stage. In their place is an improvisational movement form based on the expressive communication involved when two people begin to share their weight and physical support. Instead of privileging an ideal type of body or movement style, Contact Improvisation privileges a willingness to take physical and emotional risks, producing a certain psychic disorientation in which the seemingly stable categories of able and disabled become dislodged.

It is Contact Improvisation that provides the physical groundwork for a duet between Charlene Curtiss and Bruce Curtis, a dancer from San Francisco. Bruce Curtis is a quadriplegic dancer who has been involved with Contact Improvisation since the 1980s, when he began dancing with veteran Contacter Alan Ptashek. Bruce teaches dance and has become well known as a regular facilitator of workshops such as the DanceAbility event held annually in Eugene, Oregon. Produced by Joint Forces and run by Alito Alessi, this event has become a model for similar dance workshops all over the world. As Steve Paxton tersely put it in his essay reporting on the 1991 DanceAbility workshop, Bruce "is accepted as a performer, invited as a teacher. Have we heard of a quadriplegic dancer-teacher before? No we have not."[43]

The improvised duet between Bruce and Charlene begins in classic Contact style with both dancers circling around one another, getting a sense of each other's energy and movement preferences. (In or out of the wheelchair, that is the question.) At first they keep to their own kinespheres, but then Charlene stretches an arm over toward Bruce, who responds by leaning his head into her shoulder. After this brief moment of weight sharing, they circle and twirl around one another until Charlene wheels right up behind Bruce, who leans his whole body back, tilting his chair into Charlene's lap. This moment provokes a physical exchange of weight back and forth that leads by degrees onto the floor. Bruce, whose dance experience is predominantly Contact-based, seems to be more willing to put himself in awkward positions, or place his body's weight across his partner. In contrast, Charlene seems to want to keep the relationship visual, and she subtly shifts her body so that she can maintain an eye to eye (rather than body to body) contact. After several minutes on the floor, Charlene returns to the more easeful mobility provided by her chair, at one point circling around and around Bruce, pulling him into a floor spin. The physical negotiation of spatial levels and momentum necessary when Charlene is on wheels and Bruce is on the floor provides some of the most interesting interactions of their duet. It also gives us an example of two very differently disabled dancers, disrupting the classic able-bodied/disabled binary even further. This sight (site) of two disabled dancers working together is a radical vision and it is made possible, I believe, by the aesthetic and physical refigurings available within Contact Improvisation.

As I noted earlier, Contact Improvisation focuses on the physical relationship of one body to another, emphasizing the kinesthetic sensations and physics of weight and momentum rather than the visual picture of bodily shape within the stage space. In this way, Contact fosters an attention to the dancers' ongoing experience rather than positing a need to fit into an idealized image. Although it has developed, over its twenty-five-year history, a professional elite of renowned teachers and virtuosic dancers, Contact Improvisation is still primarily a casual, folk dance form, relying on its practioners to spread the word and the dance. There is no one centralized institution that licenses, administers, certifies, or oversees the dissemination of this dance form. Instead, there are a variety of healthy communication networks in place, including jams, workshops, conferences, and the biannual journal *Contact Quarterly*. This open structure has allowed Contact Improvisation to grow in many different directions. During the time that I have been involved in dancing and teaching the form, I have seen Contact change its course several times, but the most dramatic shift occurred in the late eighties, when, at the height of a period of incredible virtuosity (in which everyone seemed to be flying at high speeds on one another's shoulders), there was a sudden shift of interest to exploring the physical exchange between people with very different kinds of abilities—a sea change that resulted in a very different priority in the dancing. It would be futile to attempt to explain all the reasons for this remarkable shift. I believe that it comes from a variety of historical factors, including the cultural moment of increased awareness of disability in the arts, as well as the desire in Contact Improvisation to refuse the known, the easy habit, the well-traveled path. Although it has resurged within different communities and with a new sense of timeliness, this focus has taken Contact Improvisation full cycle back to its earliest democratic roots.

Dis/ability in professional dance has often been a code for one type of disability—namely the paralysis of the lower body. Yet in Contact-based gatherings such as the annual DanceAbility workshop and the Breitenbush Jam, the dancers have a much wider range of disabilities, including visual impairments, deafness, and neurological conditions such as cerebral palsy. Paxton creates an apt metaphor for this mélange of talents when he writes: "A group including various disabilities is like a United Nations of the senses. Instructions must be translated into specifics appropriate for those on legs, wheels, crutches, and must be signed for the deaf. Demonstrations must be verbalized for those who can't see, which is in itself a translating skill, because English is not a very flexible language in terms of the body."[44]

My first experience with this work occurred in the spring of 1992 when I and my (then) five-month-old daughter went to the annual Breitenbush dance jam. Held in a hot springs retreat in Oregon, the Breitenbush Jam is not designed specifically for people with physical disabilities as the DanceAbility workshops are, so I take it to be a measure of the success of true integration within the Contact community that people with various movement styles and physical abilities come to participate as dancers. At the beginning of the jam, while we were introducing ourselves to the group, Bruce Curtis, who was facilitating this particular exercise, suggested that we go around in the circle to give each dancer an opportunity to talk about his or her own physical needs and desires for the week of nonstop dancing. Bruce was speaking from the point of view that lots of people have special needs—not just the most obviously "disabled" ones. This awareness of ability as a continuum and not as an either/or situation allowed everyone present to speak without the stigma of necessarily categorizing oneself as abled or disabled solely on the basis of physical capacity. For instance, my own special need was for some help in taking care of my baby so that I could get some dancing in. At one point, Emery Blackwell, a dancer with cerebral palsy, came to my rescue when he strapped her onto his front and wheeled her around outside on his motorized cart.

Since that jam, I have had many more experiences dancing with people (including children) who are physically disabled. Yet it would be disingenuous to suggest that my first dancing with Emery or Bruce was just like doing Contact with anybody else. It wasn't—a fact that had more to do with my perceptions than with their physicalities. At first, I was scared of crushing Emery's body. After seeing him dance with other people more familiar with him, I recognized that he was up for some pretty feisty dancing, and gradually I began to trust our physical communication enough to be able to release the internal alarm in my head that kept reminding me I was dancing with someone with a disability (i.e., a fragile body). My ability to move into a different dancing relationship with Emery was less a result of Contact Improvisation's open acceptance of any body, however, than of its training (both physical and psychic), which gave me the willingness to feel intensely awkward and uncomfortable. The issue was not whether I was dancing with a classical body or not, but whether I could release the classical expectations of my own body. Dancing with Emery was disorienting for me because I had to give up my expectations. Fortunately, the training in disorientation that is fundamental to Contact helped me recreate my body in response to his. As I move from my experiences as a dancer to my position as a critic, the question that remains for me is: does Contact Improvisation reorganize our viewing priorities in quite the same way?

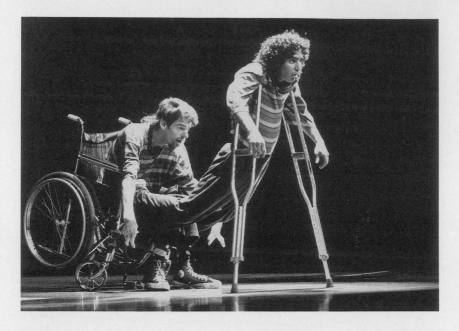

Alito Alessi and Emery Blackwell in *Wheels of Fortune*. Photo by Edis Jurcys.

Emery Blackwell and Alito Alessi both live in Eugene, Oregon, a city specifically designed to be wheelchair accessible. Blackwell was the president of
OIL (Oregonians for Independent Living) until he resigned in order to devote
himself to dance. Alessi, a veteran Contacter who has had various experiences
with physical disabilities (including an accident that severed the tendons on
one ankle), has been coordinating the DanceAbility workshops in Eugene for
the last five years. In addition to their participation in this kind of forum, Blackwell and Alessi have been dancing together for the past eight years, creating
both choreographic works such as their duet *Wheels of Fortune* and improvisational duets like the one I saw during a performance at Breitenbush Jam.

Blackwell and Alessi's duet begins with Alessi rolling around on the floor
and Blackwell rolling around the periphery of the performance space in a
wheelchair. Their eyes are focused on one another, creating a connection that
gives their separate rolling motions a certain synchrony of purpose. After several circles of the space, Blackwell stops his wheelchair, all the while looking at
his partner. The intensity of his gaze is reflected in the constant vibrations of
movement impulses in his head and hands, and his stare draws Alessi closer to
him. Blackwell offers Alessi a hand and initiates a series of weight exchanges

that begin with Alessi gently leaning away from Blackwell's center of weight, and ends with him riding upside down on Blackwell's lap. Later, Blackwell half slides, half wriggles out of his chair and walks on his knees over to Alessi. Arms outstretched, the two men mirror one another until an erratic impulse brings Blackwell and Alessi to the floor. They are rolling in tandem across the floor when all of a sudden Blackwell's movement frequency fires up and his body literally begins to bounce with excess energy. Alessi responds in kind and the two men briefly engage in a good-natured rough and tumble wrestling match. After a while they become exhausted and begin to settle down, slowly rolling side by side out of the performance space.

Earlier I argued that precisely because the disabled body is culturally coded as "grotesque," many integrated dance groups emphasize the "classical" dimensions of the disabled body's movements—the grace of a wheelchair's gliding, the strength and agility of people's upper bodies, etc. What intrigues me about Blackwell's dancing in the above duet is the fact that his movement at first evokes images of the grotesque and then leads our eyes through the spectacle of his body into the experience of his particular physicality. Paxton once wrote a detailed description of Blackwell's dancing that reveals just how much the viewer becomes aware of both the internal motivations and the external consequences of Blackwell's dancing.

Emery has said that to get his arm raised above his head requires about 20 seconds of imaging to accomplish. Extension and contraction impulses in his muscles fire frequently and unpredictably, and he must somehow select the right impulses consciously, or produce for himself a movement image of the correct quality to get the arm to respond as he wants. We observers can get entranced with what he is doing with his mind. More objectively, we can see that as he tries he excites his motor impulses and the random firing happens with more vigor. His dancing has a built-in Catch-22. And we feel the quandary and see that he is pitched against his nervous system and wins, with effort and a kind of mechanism in his mind we able-bodied have not had to learn. His facility with them allows us to feel them subtly in our own minds.[45]

Steve Paxton is considered by many people to be the father of Contact Improvisation, for it was his workshop and performance at Oberlin College in 1972 that first sparked the experimentations that later became this dance form. Given Paxton's engagement with Contact for twenty-five years, it makes sense that he would be an expert witness to Blackwell's dancing. Indeed, Paxton's description of Blackwell's movement captures the way in which Contact Improvisation focuses on the *becoming*—the improvisational process of evolving that never really reaches an endpoint. Contact Improvisation can represent

Alito Alessi and Emery Blackwell in *Wheels of Fortune*. Photo by Edis Jurcys.

the disabled body differently precisely because it doesn't try to recreate the aesthetic frames of a classical body or a traditional dance context. For instance, the proscenium stage of most dance performances creates a visual frame that tends to focus on displays of virtuosity, uses of theatrical space, as well as the presentation of visual lines (such as an arabesque). Contact, on the other hand, refuses this frame by prioritizing the ongoing process—the becoming—of the dancing.[46] Put more simply, the issue here is not *what* the dancers can do, but *how* they do. By thus concentrating on the *becoming* of their dance, Blackwell and Alessi's duet refuses a static representation of dis/ability, pulling the audience in as witness to the ongoing negotiations of their physical experience. It is important to realize that Alessi's dancing, by being responsive but not precious, helps to provide the context for this kind of witnessing engagement as well. In their duet, Alessi and Blackwell are engaged in an improvisational movement dialogue in which both partners are moving and being moved by the other. I find this duet compelling because it demonstrates the extraordinary potential in bringing two people with very different physical abilities together to share in one another's motion. In this space between social dancing, combat, and physical intimacy lies a dance form whose open aesthetic and attentiveness to the flexibility of movement identities can inform and be informed by any body's movement.

We obviously have come very far from Gautier's description of Taglioni, with which I began this chapter. Over the course of mapping the choreographic route from the Romantic ballerina to the disabled Contact dancer—from the classical body to the grotesque one—we seem to have left women behind. With the exception of Charlene Curtiss (who usually performs choreographic rather than improvisational work), I know of few disabled women dancing in the genre of Contact Improvisation. Why aren't there more disabled women active in teaching and performing this work? The question is a tough one, and it may be that there are women out there with whom I am unfamiliar. Yet I believe the answer has something to do with the double jeopardy women (particularly disabled women) put themselves in when they display their bodies without the protective trappings of the classical body's demeanor, costumes, movements, or frames.

Mary Russo begins her essay "Female Grotesques: Carnival and Theory" with a phrase that resonates from her childhood: "She [the other woman] is making a spectacle out of herself."[47] Russo explains what this phrase really means: "For a woman, making a spectacle out of herself had more to do with a kind of inadvertency and loss of boundaries: the possessors of large, aging, and dimpled thighs displayed at the public beach, of overly rouged cheeks, of a voice shrill in laughter, or of a sliding bra strap—a loose, dingy bra strap especially—were at once caught out by fate and blameworthy." What we have here are two contradictory notions of spectacle. "Making a spectacle out of herself" is not, ironically, inviting the voyeuristic gaze (which in dance is usually reserved for representations of the classical body), for that desiring gaze is dependent on a spatial and psychic separation of self and other. The grotesque female body, in contrast, confronts and challenges this gaze. The loss of boundaries that Russo describes as socially reprehensible provokes a fear of contagion, the fear that the visible presence of someone else's "large, aging, and dimpled thighs" will unloose one's own.

The interweavings of representation and bodily experience are as interesting here as they are contradictory. For the grotesque body (which Bakhtin sees embodied in the ancient clay figurines of old, laughing, and pregnant hags) is more likely than not defined as a female body (porous, dripping, sexual) that exceeds its socially defined boundaries (a body out of [state] control). Add disability into this discursive mix, and the intersections are particularly fascinating and complex. For disabled women are doubly defined by their transgressive bodies, blamed for their physical excesses (sagging breasts, big hips) or flaws. Russo's childhood admonition *not* "to make a spectacle out of oneself" is an injunction that most disabled women still feel with unmitigated force.

Incalculable Choreographies

In the fall of 1991, Canadian dancer Marie Chouinard came to Oberlin with her company to perform and teach. While I had seen her perform and had interviewed her about her work, this was my first opportunity actually to dance with her. The experience of taking her workshop inspired me to try to include another—more bodily—source of writing within this chapter on her solo choreography. Scattered throughout this discussion of sexual difference in writing and dancing are italicized passages of personal writing that are meant to wash over the readers, releasing them momentarily from the academic prose of my intellectual arguments. Yet this whispering voice—which evokes my physical responses to dancing, to writing, to my pregnant body, as well as the moments of Chouinard's performances that haunted my imagination—engages the same issues of writing, desire, and the body, albeit in a different manner. Although the sudden appearance of these passages may strike the reader as rather quixotic, this other voice enacts many of the theoretical moves I make in this chapter. By partnering Chouinard's dances with the performative writings of Hélène Cixous and Jacques Derrida, I bring dancing and writing face to face.

Then too, I ask you, what kind of a dance would there be, or would there be one at all, if the sexes were not exchanged according to rhythms that vary considerably? In a quite rigorous sense, the exchange alone could not suffice either, however, because the desire to escape the combinatory itself, to invent incalculable choreographies, would remain.

—**Jacques Derrida**

CHOREOGRAPHING DIFFERENCE

And then if I spoke about a person whom I met and who shook me up, herself being
moved and I moved to see her moved, and she, feeling me moved, being moved in turn,
and whether this person is a she and a he and a he and a she and a shehe and a heshe, I
want to be able not to lie, I don't want to stop her if she trances, I want him, I want her, I
will follow her.   **—Hélène Cixous**

As a dancer and feminist scholar, I am intrigued by these two visions of writing in which sexual identity takes on a certain fluidity of movement. By weav-
ing the language of movement and references to dance throughout their discussions of sexual difference and identity, Jacques Derrida and Hélène Cixous
point to the theoretical possibilities of a form of communication predicated on
the instability of the body and the resultant displacement of meaning. In this
chapter, I want to extend the implications of Derrida's and Cixous's interest in
movement and writing by including another kind of text—that written by
and on the live dancing body of contemporary Canadian performer Marie
Chouinard.[1] For live performance, because it comes *through* the body, but is
not only *of* the body, can problematize theories of meaning and sexual difference in powerful ways. Learning how to read that body in an attempt to understand all the conflicting layers of meaning in physical motion is a complex task
that requires an awareness of the kinesthetic as well as the visual and intellectual implications of dance. I am placing Chouinard's physical choreography
(specifically *Marie Chien Noir*, *S.T.A.B.*, and *La Faune*) in the midst of Cixous's
and Derrida's theoretical "dances" in order to address what I feel is frequently
absent from contemporary theory—an awareness of the material consequences of the live performing body.

This desire to consider the physical body does not stem from a naive belief
in a "natural" or even a "biological" body—quite the contrary. Clearly cultural
values resonate throughout the bodies that constitute them, and often these
structures are physically internalized and thus rendered as "essential" elements of human nature. Dancers, however, can consciously engage in a physical training that seeks to resist oppressive ideologies concerning women and
their bodies in performance, effectively challenging the terms of their own
representation. Because dance is at once social and personal, internal and external, a dancer can both embody and explode gendered images of the body—
simultaneously registering, creating, and subverting cultural conventions.
When Marie Chouinard literally (by taking on the phallus) and figuratively
appropriates Nijinsky's body in her interpretation of his dancing, for instance,
she opens the question of what it means to be a man by refusing to stay in the
role of a woman. By making us aware of her own physical experience while
she refuses the categories of social experience, Chouinard destabilizes the

usual relationships between the body and gender, language and meaning, extending the direction of Derrida's and Cixous's textual choreographies into physical movement.

How do I move between dancing and writing?
My dancing, her writing
her dancing, his writing
this stew of movement and language
Only through the body—my body, as I move
from past performances to present throughts.   And back and forth.
How do I navigate two courses?
Dis/course (whose course? Oh, that stuff.)
The physical course (as in performances coursing through my veins)
Blood Memories

In "Choreographies" Christie McDonald prefaces a series of questions to Derrida about his interest in dissolving sexual difference and the place of "the feminine" in this scheme by quoting Emma Goldman's famous line, "If I can't dance I don't want to be part of your revolution."[2] Throughout this interchange the words "choreography" and "dance"—both feminine nouns in French—continually weave their way into a discussion of feminism and sexual difference. Despite the improvisatory and slightly flippant tone of Derrida's remarks, he repeatedly imbues "the dance" (*la danse*) with an almost sacred vitality. Later in this same passage Derrida is more specific: "[D]ance changes place and above all changes *places*."[3] The revolutionary quality of dancing, then, becomes more than the quick-footedness to move out of the way; it takes on the refined ability to change places without feeling displaced, to move in a way that shifts the meaning of location.

Rolling . . . tumbling . . . spiraling down to and up from the floor, I learn how to locate myself through movement. This means that I must give up a visual focus that insists on seeing the world in focus. I rely, instead, on a combination of peripheral vision, which expands my sight from what is in front of my eyes to what is around me, and a heightened awareness of the floor and gravity. With practice the nausea (the less sexy side of vertigo) disappears and I begin to think of being upside down and inside out not as disorienting but simply as another way of getting one's bearings—in motion.

Throughout much of his interchange with McDonald, Derrida identifies dancing as a "feminine" subversion par excellence. Theoretically, at least, "the feminine" realm is not connected exclusively to the female body (in fact, it often ends up including the male avant-garde—a move that creates its own set of problems) and serves to signify instead anything that is outside, although certainly not unaffected by, dominant structures of power, and that could potentially be subversive or disturbing to that power.[4] This distinction, however, is elusive and, as we see in Derrida's comment, can slip back into a binary paradigm that implicitly connects "the feminine" with women and dance: "The joyous disturbance of certain women's movements, and of some women in particular, has actually brought with it the chance for a certain risky turbulence in the assigning of places within our small European space."[5] While she is resisting, while she is dancing outside of history, woman is also, of course, constructed by that history. Nowhere is this marked more clearly than on her physical body.

Dancing in and around cultural constructions of the female body, she choreographs against the grain of those texts, those histories.
Contredanse. Contredansing. Contredanseuse.

Unwilling to confront the embodied presence of the one who is dancing, Derrida abandons the connection of dancing and women at the end of this improvisatory dialogue. Instead, he traces the word *choreography* back to its etymological root, *khoros*, and refigures dance as a mass chorus of movement:

As I dream . . . I would like to believe in the multiplicity of sexually marked voices. I would like to believe in the masses, this indeterminable number of blended voices, the mobile of non-identified sexual marks whose choreography can carry, divide, multiply the body of each "individual" whether he be classified as "man" or as "woman" according to the criteria of usage.[6]

Deftly darting through McDonald's question about what constitutes "the feminine," Derrida avoids the quagmire implicit in his own theory, which seeks to equate the feminine realm with a subversive stance (or rather, a subversive dance) and the masculine realm with the power of the dominant discourses. By appropriating choreography and dance as deconstructionist tropes—precisely because they are about constant displacement—Derrida attempts to create another category, one constructed in movement, that slips right through sexual difference. While it is tempting to rest a moment in Derrida's dream of a dance that goes beyond gender, envisioning "incalculable choreographies" as a poststructuralist sequel to "Dirty Dancing," popular culture—tempered with a dose of feminism—has infused me with too literal an imagination. The question keeps darting through my head: what do the "incalculable choreographies" actually look like? Whose body is dancing and what is it dancing about?

Here, of course, is the crux of the issue. Despite all this fantastic dancing of words across the page, it would be hard to translate Derrida's vision onto the stage. Real dancing bodies carry the signs of sexual difference in much less ambiguous ways; even movement choruses are often divided by sex. Traditionally, a corps de ballet is all women; when there is a group of men onstage, the sexes are divided spatially. There are, nonetheless, ways in which the gender of the dancer can be worked over, played with, and exceeded in an effort to disrupt these traditional dancing roles and disconcert the audience's reception of that bodily image. While we may know whether it is a he or a she on that stage, the action or theatricality of the performance can place that knowledge in jeopardy. By moving *through* instead of locating her(him)self *in* narrative positions, the dancer is able to step out of meaning before it becomes stabilized.

In this sense, then, dance is a wonderful example of Derridian difference. Based on the motion of live bodies, the dancing "text" is singularly elusive. Any isolated movement or gesture is practically meaningless until it is placed in the context of what went before or after it. But that context is continually shifting in time and space, appearing only to disappear an instant later. In order to make sense of the dancing, the viewer must try to remember the flickering traces of earlier movements at the same time s/he is watching the next series of motions. This ongoing process rarely stops long enough for the connections to catch up, and for this reason dance can be difficult to watch and even more problematic to write about.

Watching: first I unlock the tension in my neck, allowing my skull to rest easefully and loosely on the top vertebrae of my spine. Then I imagine all the pores of my skin opening and expanding so that the movement can literally enter and affect my body.

Writing: I begin with descriptions of the most compelling moments. If a remembered image doesn't take me close enough I repeat the movement or gesture, letting my body help me to verbally articulate what was going on in the dancing.

In the midst of all this poststructuralist profusion, however, is the dancer's physical body, whose movement constructs a presence as well as a continual absence. Derrida leaves no room to discuss the way this presence can be palpable, indeed, powerful, in the midst of its own erasure. As the dancing body evolves from, say, crawling on the floor to standing upright, the cultural meanings usually attached to those actions shift, but at the very moment that these meanings are displaced, another current of meaning is constituted by the very act of moving. What becomes visible, then, is the movement between two moments marked by recognizable images. By dwelling in these moments, dancers can draw the audience's attention to the dancers' own physical reality, pulling our bodies closer to theirs. This process of making (presence) in the midst of unmaking (absence) allows for an intricate layering of visual, kinesthetic, and cultural meanings in which bodies, sexualities, and identities can begin to restage the terms of their alliance. For if sexual difference can be conceived as physical motion rather than a set of stable ideological positions, the resultant narratives of desire might then be choreographed more imaginatively.

Near the beginning of "Mimas, Lune de Saturne," the first segment of the evening-length Marie Chien Noir, *Chouinard travels across a long diagonal from the back to the front of the stage. Crawling low, she first moves like a lizard and then rolls and tumbles and rises with the silent agility of a fox, finally arriving on her feet as she moves closer to the audience. Chouinard looks out toward the spectators, as she takes her place next to a skeleton positioned downstage in a permanent and ironic plié. Shaping her hand like a swan's neck, she extends her arm in a full arc, slowly raising her face to greet the hand-bird, which glides down to her mouth and deeper into her throat. A collective shudder darts through the audience as Chouinard's abdomen contracts convulsively. Turning to stand with her profile to the audience, her swan hand dips down into her interior again, but this time the audience can see the contraction spawn a series of ripples that spread out like water through her body.*[7]

While many of her movements are graceful and sensuous, Chouinard never lets the audience settle back too comfortably in their seats. As soon as we become used to being lulled by the curves and stretches, spirals and suspensions of her dancing, she jerks us out of that contented place by putting a raw and often disturbing edge to her movement. In the sequence I have just described, for example, she creates an edge to her performance (and a certain edginess in the audience) by going too far down into her throat. What may have been an eroticized moment shifts dynamics as she experiences and is apparently willing to engage a very real gag response over which she has no control. At this moment in the performance, Chouinard shatters a classically "beautiful" visual image (and the audience's expected pleasure in watching that image) by insisting that we recognize her own physical experience. Metaphorically, she is also pulling out the space of her insides, that invisible realm of female sexuality, a space that few audience members are able to confront. I suspect it is this enforced intimacy with her somatic experience that brought on the audience's collective shudder.

One of the more radical elements of Chouinard's work, particularly in *Marie Chien Noir*, is her challenge to the representation of feminine desire as being a passive (and silent) desire-to-be-desired, a desire to be someone's "other." The structures of desire exhibited by traditional Western forms of dance such as the Romantic ballet parallel those imposed later by classical cinema. The voyeuristic gaze of the audience, established by the three-pronged gaze of the director, the camera, and the male protagonist in the film, is represented in dance by the looks of the choreographer and the male dancing partner, who literally "presents" the female dancer to the audience's gaze. The solo format that is the basis of Chouinard's performance works against this structure of desire. Since the audience has no male danseur's gaze to introduce the terms of this visual economy, and since there is no implied "other" in the dance to whom she is addressing her performing—and in whose shoes we could place ourselves—we must take a leap of faith and believe that she is performing for us. But since the usual signs that a dancer is performing for an audience—the projected, eccentric (moving outward) movements, the entertaining smiles and easy nods—are missing, the audience is left in the lurch, often wondering if we should be present at all. Over the course of this ninety-minute solo, the stage becomes her space, a self-contained world of reality and fantasy. Even though she places herself on the stage to be viewed, to be consumed (in the high capitalist sense that one pays to see her), her actions elude a facile interpretation, making it difficult for the audience to construct a narrative of desire in which we can participate in the customary manner.

It's dark when Chouinard enters the performance space. She glides slowly across the black floor. A string of twinkling red lights follow her like a luminous tail. Guiding them first into a circle, she slips into the middle. Her body—its whiteness a stark contrast to the black briefs and swimcap she's wearing—glistens in the shadows as she pours oil onto herself and the floor. Then, with the sleepy inertia of a black seal, she launches her body. One small twist is all that it takes to send her gliding peacefully across the dark pool. Again and again we see a small movement expand as her body skates across the shiny black surface.

In Chouinard's performances, there is no safe, aestheticized distance from her sticky physicality. Given the size of most experimental performance spaces, Chouinard's dancing inevitably invades the audience's space. When

Marie Chouinard in *Marie Chien Noir*. Photo by Tom Brazil.

she touches herself, spreads her body on the floor, or drools, her physical experience fills the atmosphere like a dense, mysterious fog. The audience is no
longer positioned on the other, anonymous side of the keyhole. We are right
there, smack in the room, and that exposure forces us to redefine how we are
watching this performance. Her presence forces the audience to recognize
their ability to respond in multiple ways, to take responsibility for meeting her

energy and participating in the event, even if that response is to squirm uncomfortably in one's seat.

Chouinard eschews references to her work as either dance or theater, pre-
ferring instead to call herself a "body artist." In an interview, Chouinard discusses how she might be regarded in another culture as a priestess or a cele-
brant, but that in this society, in order to make "hommages" to the moments
and parts of life she values, she has had to become a performing artist and be
content with presenting her work in the theater. Still attuned to that image of
the *religieuse*, Chouinard consciously works to "hypnotize," fascinate, the audience in the hope of activating our imaginations. She intends to draw the audience into her world and to communicate in a way that is experiential and
communal—as in a religious rite. But the fact that Chouinard works so intensively with investigations of her own (female) body complicates her intention
to make the audience a responsive witness to her performances.

*On another occasion in this same first section, Chouinard is dunking her long hair
in and out of a tub of water. At first crouching by the washtub, she dunks her head
again and again. Rising progressively higher with each repetition, she layers the
visual rhythm of her movements with the aural rhythm of the sounds of sloshing
water. These rhythms subside into the more erratic sounds of dripping water as she
stands and lets the water drain off her hair. Gently folding up her hair in a sensuous
manner evocative of Renoir's paintings of women bathing, she walks over to the
center of the stage and starts to fling her hair in an arc that sweeps back and loops
forward, tracing its trajectory with sprays of water. Her hair sweeps the floor expan-
sively and it seems at first as if she is simply intent on drying it, until the slapping
sounds become more and more insistent. Eventually this slapping on the floor is
picked up by Chouinard's hands and transferred to her body. Keeping a steady
rhythm going, she alternately slaps her chest, arms, and face.*

This moment, like the one where she repeatedly falls and gets up, and like
several others in the piece, straddles a peculiar line. Chouinard is not exactly
beating herself; the energy here is not particularly masochistic. Her body takes
in the slap as it exhales, reducing the pain and producing another rhythmic
sound with her breath. At the same time that there is something brutal to
what she is doing, there is also a feeling of the body being awakened and re-
freshed, like diving into a cold Maine pond on a hot day. Breathing throughout, her body does not build up any tension during this episode of rhythmic
slapping, and this release allows Chouinard to emerge from this moment right
into some very luscious, lyrical, and flowing dancing.

In a panel discussion by the recipients of Calgary's Olympic Arts Festival

Modern Dance Commissions, Chouinard discusses what makes her passionate about dance. "It is always a discovery. Maybe the audience thinks it knows the idea we are proposing but, for me, when I am dancing on stage I am doing something that is unknown. . . . When I dance, my body becomes a laboratory for experiences . . . physical, mystical and other kinds. By working with the body you can make openings for the flowing of life."[8] Physical and visible—visible in her own physicality—Chouinard dances at once for herself and for an audience. Her performance is thus both encoded in the structure of its own representation and continually—kinesthetically—exceeding that structure. At times her body on stage is so clear, so classically beautiful, so much a part of our cultural repertoire of "woman," that the image of her body takes over the audience's consciousness.[9] At other times, when the movements of her dancing body exceed the boundaries of her skin and extend out to affect the audience *kinesthetically*, we can actually participate in her embodied experience. No longer confined to an image of "woman" or even contained within the limits of her own skin, her body spills out into the audience. This close amorphousness of Chouinard's performing body is often described as creature-like or "otherworldly."[10] Considering the fact that Chouinard reveals so much of and about her body on stage, one might think that she would be seen as the female dancer par excellence—a "real" woman, with both the sexist and feminist connotations of that word. But the combination of eccentric, nonnarrative sequences in Chouinard's dances with the terrifying and sometimes messy closeness of her bodily functions situates Chouinard outside of the safe, traditional depictions of the female body. Given our interests in movement and language, we might then ask: How can this dancing body enter the writing—in motion?

In *The Newly Born Woman* and "Coming to Writing," Hélène Cixous brings the metaphorics of physicality into writing.[11] Movement, for Cixous, starts with the breath, that moving upward and outward of a writing voice.

Writing was in the air around me. Always close, intoxicating, invisible, inaccessible. . . . "Writing" seized me, gripped me, around the diaphragm, between the stomach and the chest, a blast dilated my lungs and I stopped breathing. Suddenly I was filled with a turbulence that knocked the wind out of me and inspired me to wild acts. "Write." When I say "writing" seized me, it wasn't a sentence that had managed to seduce me, there was absolutely nothing written, not a letter, not a line. But in the depths of the flesh, the attack. Pushed. Not penetrated. Invested. Set in motion.[12]

Cixous's insistence on the physicality of the writing body, especially her focus on metaphors of birth and maternity (blood and milk), seems to imply a direct relationship between the female body and "feminine writing." Because Cixous imbues her presentation of somatic textuality with her notion of the feminine, many feminist scholars, particularly in the Anglo-American tradition, react strongly to what they perceive to be the essentialist overtones of her project.[13] It is true that Cixous takes what Diana Fuss, in her concise survey of the "essentialist/constructivist" debate in feminist theory, calls "the risk of essence."[14] At times, for instance, Cixous portrays the "feminine" in writing as a "truthful" voice that reflects the presence of the body. And if, as she repeatedly declares, "*In body/Still more*: woman is body more than man is,"[15] then the figure on the other side of the equals mark is usually a woman. It is important to note that, for Cixous, a bodily presence in writing is not necessarily limited to women. It is just that the evangelistic force of her writing in these works is aimed at encouraging women to reverse the dynamics of an oppressive discourse that claims women are *only* their bodies (and therefore shouldn't hold public office, etc.). Although she frequently writes in mystical language that slips away from a historical grounding, Cixous is mindful of the ways that social ideologies influence the somatic and erotic textuality of writing bodies. Often, however, Cixous is writing *from* a historical positioning of women and men in Western political and intellectual history *toward* the possibility of a utopian moment in which the cultural ideologies that structure sexual difference are radically transformed. "And let us imagine a real liberation of sexuality, that is to say, a transformation of each one's relationship to his or her body (and to the other body), an approximation to the vast, material, organic, sensuous universe that we are. This cannot be accomplished, of course, without political transformations that are equally radical. (Imagine!)"[16]

I was eight and one-half months pregnant when Marie Chouinard came to perform and give a workshop. I was planning to sit out and just observe, but I couldn't. After watching her dancing for so long, I had to try it on my body. We started with a small bouncing motion and audible breaths that came from deep inside our abdomens. She pointed to her stomach and told us not to pretend that it was empty (as many dancers are wont to do), but to realize its fullness, to take time to feel the activity and energy inside that part of our bodies.

"Release the muscles around your anus," she instructed us.

This attention to the center of the body, her imagery and movement sequences seemed especially designed for me—for someone with so much extra activity inside her belly. Dancing with, instead of in spite of, my pregnancy was pleasurable and deeply absorbing. I realized that this kind of internal attentiveness created much of the intense and yet distanced quality of her dancing presence.

In their book *The Newly Born Woman*—which is set up, interestingly enough, as an authorial *pas de deux*—Catherine Clément and Hélène Cixous evoke two distinct visions of a dancing woman. Clément's solo essay ("The Guilty One") speaks of the feminine role as that of the sorceress or the hysteric, the dancing image of a madwoman whirling ferociously in a tarantella. Circling, circling and never going anywhere, Clément's vision of this mad dancer exemplifies a classic psychoanalytic model of the hysterical woman who displays her transgression—her desire for more from the world, the desire to move in it—in a fit of dancing that releases her emotions but also insures her eventual reincorporation into the web of society. In this scene the madwoman's dancing, while certainly a frightening representation of woman's sexuality, also serves to exorcise her madness (she literally dances it out), and she returns to the group exhausted and subdued. Cixous's own written solo ("Sorties") is inspired, in part, by this mad dancing woman who dares to get up and dance her passion. But Cixous's dancer is not fated to sit down again. "Unleashed and raging . . . she arises, she approaches, she lifts up, she reaches, covers over, washes a shore, flows embracing the cliff's least undulation, already she is another, arising again."[17] Filled with an explosive, expansive energy (the word "sortie" suggests a pushing out, an outburst, an escape), this newly born woman jumps over historical and social restraints to explore the dancing pleasures of her changing sexuality: "She doesn't hold still, she overflows."[18]

To read Cixous only in terms of her political pragmatism is to limit severely the radical potential of her intervention in the very process of women's inscription in the world—the way their bodies are written onto a cultural slate. In one sense, Cixous joins Derrida in positioning women (by invoking "the feminine") as outside of and therefore subversive to Western metaphysics. But rather than simply relegating women to "other" status (as Derrida seems to do), Cixous explores the sources of that otherness in the female body. This body, however, is neither completely "natural" nor "textual." In fact, it refuses the very logic of those categories. "A body 'read,' finished? A book—a decaying carcass? Stench and falsity. The flesh is writing, and writing is never read: it always remains to be read, studied, sought, invented."[19] Written over and writing (on and for) itself, this body is engaged in a constant process of splintering and deferring. Here, the body meets the page as a mirror meets another mirror, always already reflecting back the inscription of the other. "Life becomes text starting out from my body. I am already text. History, love, violence, time, work, desire inscribe it in my body."[20] Keeping the body present within texts, Cixous stages the "whole of reality worked upon my flesh" in a written performance that moves through words and into dance.

Recently, I've begun to talk while moving. The subject of this dancing discourse could be almost anything—a news item, a letter from a friend, an article that I'm working on. I've found this new performative discourse curiously captivating. In motion, my body can stop the flow of a thought or sentence and insist that I notice some phrase, idea, or even a silence. My body catches this moment in movement and repeats it, or enlarges it, until it expands into my verbal focus. Flushed and energized after this kind of work, I sometimes feel as if I've reached through to the other side of hysteria—where language and body weave their way in and out of one another, facilitating (instead of blocking) the expressive quality of that "other" discourse.

Following Cixous's writing is like being on a roller coaster of images, speeding through dense active descriptions with verbs flying every which way, trying to catch up with that newly born woman who is always just slipping out of sight around the next bend. The cyclical timing of transitional phrases that continually loop back over the previous ones—traveling over, through, across, and around—creates a breathy abundance of language that spills over its own meaning. The repetitious rhythm of her words and their incessant movement back and forth shape a writing presence that is analogous in many ways to Chouinard's performing presence in *Marie Chien Noir*.

She doesn't "speak," she throws her trembling body into the air, she lets herself go, she flies, she goes completely into her voice, she vitally defends the "logic" of her discourse with her body; her flesh speaks true . . . she conveys meaning with her body. She *inscribes* what she is saying because she does not deny unconscious drives the unmanageable part they play in speech.[21]

Her dance is solid, concrete actions; her movement suggests design, even writing; the *voice* surges. Out of her movements, often drawn from bodily functions, emerges a new body language which shatters the traditional notion of dance.[22]

While these two passages come from different historical moments and geographic places—"Sorties" was originally published in France in 1975 and Chouinard's press packet was published ten years later in Montreal—and express different artistic impulses, they both speak of the relationship between body and voice in terms of an embodied language that explodes tidy separations of the physical from the intellectual. These movement images reflect back on a body that spills over, continually exceeding the culture that seeks to contain it. One physical manifestation of that transgression is the voice. For both Cixous and Chouinard, the voice is a meeting of body and discourse. Yet that voice is not an exclusively private or internal calling. Swelling far beyond the body that produces it, the voice emanates into the public domain. Indeed, Cixous seems to be speaking for Chouinard when she writes:

Voice! That, too, is launching forth and effusion without return. Exclamation, cry, breathlessness, yell, vomit, music. . . . And that is how she writes, as one throws a voice—forward, into the void. . . . Woman must write her body, must make up the unimpeded tongue that bursts partitions, classes and rhetorics, orders and codes, must inundate, run through, go beyond the discourse.[23]

The edge in Chouinard's dancing, which I discussed earlier, takes on another form in "Mimas, Lune de Saturne." This time the edge is the sound of her voice: her calling, her chanting, her screeching. In the middle of this dance Chouinard again comes forward to face the audience. Looking out with a blank expression, she drops to her hands and knees and waits with her mouth open until enough saliva collects to start dribbling out. She sucks it back up into her mouth and darts back a few feet to repeat the whole procedure. Finally backed into a corner, she begins a walking journey that starts as a lullaby and ends as a fierce war dance. Bent over and swinging her upper body like a pendulum, her arms making a circle that frames her head, she hums a song as she sways from side to side. The soothing sound becomes more urgent as her stepping becomes more insistent and percussive. The stamping pattern takes over her body and crescendos into a driving rhythm. Chouinard lifts her upper body, clenches her hands into fists, and stares vehemently off into the distance. Her voice starts calling fiercely like a pack of angry crows, and her body explodes in fits and starts of motion.

Abruptly, she drops that driven energy and walks over to the washtub. A moment's respite of silence and the sound of her hands in the water gives way to her voice. Chouinard seats herself comfortably on one leg, slips one and then the other sleeve of her shirt off her shoulder and slides her hand down her pants. Her head cradled in one arm, she closes her eyes as if to listen to a song inside herself. A deep, light tremor begins in her breathing. Swelling along with her pleasure, these undertones break out into a vibrato of chants and cries that steer my attention away from the visual spectacle of a woman masturbating, toward another, imagined, one of an archaic mourning ritual.

Incalculable Choreographies

The voice is the sound of the body in motion. Contrary to popular opinion, dance is not a "silent" artform. Most people find it difficult to dance without an audible breath, and vocal sounds can help the dancer achieve various qualities of movement. The voice is like another limb, stretching out into the space of the performance.

Over the course of a discussion concerning her use of vocal sounds in performance, Chouinard described her feelings about the human voice. Frustrated by the narrow limits of our usual monotone speech and feeling as if the traditional notes on a musical scale did not allow for a full expression of her individual voice, Chouinard chooses to explore instead the vocalization of her own body's movements and pleasures. In this way, as in the song of orgasm in "Mimas, Lune de Saturne," she feels she finds a voice that expresses the uniqueness of her somatic experience. Vibrating through the air, Chouinard's voice gives the audience a palpable kinesthetic experience of her body. Yet while her breath clearly generates the chanting, these sounds seem to turn around and repossess her. This cyclical looping out of her voice into the performance space and then back into her interior body creates a fascinating and important disjunction. Rather than affirming the voyeuristic potential of the scene, her eerie voice slices through that objectifying gaze, once again pulling the audience away from a comfortable state of passive watching.

For Derrida, voice suggests a metaphorics of "presence," which he sees as an outdated remnant of Western metaphysics. In this philosophical tradition, vocal expression is seen as the transcendent signifier of an authentic self—as if somehow one's voice always does what one wants it to—as if the voice is, in fact, consonant with the self. Eschewing voice in favor of writing, Derrida points to the deferral or suspension of direct reference in written texts. Ironically, he describes this textual free play as the "performativity" of writing. I doubt Derrida has ever seen Marie Chouinard; nor, I suspect, has he spent much time actually listening to the human voice. The fleshy presence of the voice in performance often exceeds or counters the body that sponsors it. And certainly in the above example, the voice pulls away from, instead of reinforcing or unifying, a "coherent" image of "a woman dancer." What we see in Chouinard's performance is the same kind of "performativity" that for Derrida imbues writing, but we see it through a live body and voice. Herein lies a crucial difference for feminist theory.

In her book *Thinking Fragments*, Jane Flax critiques Derrida for not including any discussion of the material condition of discourse in his discussion of sexual difference and writing. "What is still 'absent' (forbidden) is the in-corporation of 'women' *qua* embodied, desiring, and concrete and differentiated being(s) *within* culture, language, ruling, or thinking *on our own terms* and not as man's 'other,' 'Object of desire,' or linguistic construct."[24] The reluctance on the part of many poststructuralists to deal critically and phenomenologically with the live female body is a fear, I suspect, of being too weighed down with a kind of essentialist mass. This fear (which many feminists also share) is based on an oppressive image of the body as a sticky blob of unconscious matter that tends to burp, fart, or get its menstrual period at the most inconvenient and embarrassing moments. But simplistic biologism obviously doesn't begin to account for the many ways in which our bodies structure our consciousness. Looking at live dance performances and analyzing how those performers use their articulate bodies (and voices) helps us to reexamine the discussions of physicality and sexual identity so critical to contemporary feminist thought. In performance, women can consciously, creatively confront what Mary Ann Doane calls the "double bind" of representation. "On the one hand, there is a danger in grounding a politics on a conceptualization of the body because the body has always been the site of women's oppression, posited as the final and undeniable guarantee of a difference and a lack; but, on the other hand, there is a potential gain as well—it is precisely because the body has been a major site of oppression that perhaps it must be the site of the battle to be waged."[25] Chouinard continues to wage that battle in her 1986 dance *S.T.A.B. (Space, Time and Beyond)*.

Naked, her body painted red and her face painted white, Chouinard emerges from the wings onto a vast, darkened, unadorned stage. Each step she makes resounds with a clank of her tin shoes. Enclosed within an aviator's helmet that sprouts a long white tube curving down to the floor, her head seems heavy and slightly detached. Her movements are much less fluid than in Marie Chien Noir. *Close, almost bound to the body, her movements are cautious and jerky, as if she is feeling out a new environment, testing the quality of the space around her. Soon the microphone attached to the helmet is amplifying her breathing as her body twists and turns. The microphone modulates her voice and the sound that is projected out into the theater seems to come from deep inside her throat. Almost all of her motion is concentrated in her central torso, which twitches and convulses like an amphibian about to regurgitate a meal. Often Chouinard will stand in one spot as the contractions of her body send up a harrowing series of screeching, gulping, growling sounds that explode out to boomerang back into her body, where they sponsor a new cycle of convulsions.*

The cumulative effect of this twenty-minute solo is, well, weird. The no-man's-land of the stage space and its otherwordly lighting effects gives Choui-

Marie Chouinard in *S.T.A.B. (Space, Time and Beyond)*. Photo by Louise Oligny.

nard's presence on stage a mystical, almost possessed, materiality. Gradually increasing in intensity and frequency throughout the course of her dance, Chouinard's vocalizations begin to echo themselves in an ongoing, layered conversation. Then, after a last loud emission of these peculiar bodily sounds has faded out, Chouinard calmly takes off her headpiece and stands holding the white tube next to her as the lights dim in a very long fade.

What intrigues me in *S.T.A.B.* is the way that the embodied languages of movement and voice work in tandem to create an opportunity for what Derrida identified as "a certain risky turbulence" in the representation of the female dancing body. Specifically, I am interested in how Chouinard's voice and movement create an ambiguous image in which it is unclear whether the vocal sounds are motivating the movement or the movement is forcing the body to speak. The technological frame of *S.T.A.B.* further enhances those peculiar moments by giving this image a slight shift in synchrony produced by the voice's amplification. As Doane documents in her article "The Voice in the Cinema: The Articulation of Body and Space," advances in filmic sound technology have allowed cinema to present an image (what she calls the "fantasmic" body) whose visual and vocal movements create a convincing embodied presence on the screen. Through the use of synchronous dialogue and the addition of various "natural" room sounds, the filmic soundtrack is "married" to the image to reinforce the blissful unity of illusion that is the backbone of traditional film. The sound enacts—makes real—the space framed by the story. Even the voice from off the screen (voice-off) belongs to a character situated in a space that is presumed to be just beyond the camera's focus. In this way, Doane argues, the voice is always tied to a visible (or imagined) body: "The voice-off is always 'submitted to the destiny of the body.'"[26]

Breaking this blissful unity, however, is another use of vocal sound in film, the interior monologue, which employs the voice to display "what is inaccessible to the image, what exceeds the visible; the 'inner life' of the character."[27] Doane calls this a "disembodied" voice and discusses the subversive potential in its position outside a representation of the body. "It is its radical otherness with respect to the diegesis which endows this voice with a certain authority. . . . It is precisely because the voice is not localizable, because it cannot be yoked to a body, that it is capable of interpreting the image, producing its truth."[28] Presumably, then, this authority of the voice-over in the interior monologue could be used to present a fuller picture of a female character. Escaping the image of her body, which is caught and held as an object-to-be-viewed in the apparatus of filmmaking, her voice could conceivably move with a great deal more freedom, commenting on the "truth" of the image.

Unfortunately, as Kaja Silverman demonstrates in the *The Acoustic Mirror: The Female Voice in Psychoanalysis and Cinema*, the female voice may be even less her own than her body. In traditional film, these voice-overs are what Silverman calls "thick with body"—desperate, breathing heavily, screaming, or about to die. The mechanisms of unity that Doane discussed in her article work, for Silverman, to resubmerge the female voice within the female body.

In Silverman's analysis, for a voice to be "thick with body" is not (as it is for Cixous and Chouinard) liberating. Quite the contrary: Hollywood film in this light most often presents the female embodied voice as a nonlinguistic, nondiscursive black hole.

In a chapter on feminist cinema, Silverman discusses the representation of the female body and the place of her voice in experimental film. Silverman contrasts the work of women like Bette Gordon, Yvonne Rainer, Patricia Gruben, and Sally Potter, who try in their films to disengage the female voice from the image of her body, with the "embodied" writing of *"écriture féminine,"* specifically the work of Luce Irigaray. In doing so, she sets up what is in my opinion an unnecessarily narrow field of choice: a fatally embodied voice ("only at the price of its own impoverishment and entrapment"[29]), or a tragically disembodied one. Over the course of a careful intertexual analysis of Irigaray's work and that of experimental feminist filmmakers, Silverman argues convincingly for the potential of representing a female subject through the skillful use of the disembodied voice. While she criticizes Irigaray's conflation of a discursive "writing the body" with real female bodies, Silverman seems to be recommending a deflation of the female subject down to her disembodied voice. What I object to most strongly, and why I see Chouinard's *S.T.A.B.* as a way out of this feminist maze of voice and body, is the sense that there is no freedom of movement in between the poles of a "silent" body and a bodiless voice—an implication that suggests that, when it comes to the female body, every choreography is somehow already calculated.

"Thick with body," Chouinard's voice in *S.T.A.B.* serves as an extension of her body. Although it "exceeds the visible" and does turn the body inside out (her voice comes from inside and is projected out), it is not exactly an interior monologue, as the audience can plainly see the body that engenders the voice. The struggles of the body to produce the peculiar modulations of Chouinard's voice and the slight lapse of time between her speaking and its projection through the sound system create a rupture or an edge that makes the stage image strange. Her voice hangs in the space between being fully embodied and being completely disembodied because the sounds don't seem to come "naturally" from her body. They don't even sound like what we might expect her voice to sound like. Distorted by her inhaling and exhaling while she talks, her voice roars in a throaty vibration not easily described either as feminine or masculine. In the midst of a performance completely predicated on the dialogue between the body and the voice, the effect of this slight echo is powerful indeed.

Suspended between her breath and its vocal amplification, Chouinard occupies a curious space in *S.T.A.B.* Aurally close yet visually distanced, her body drifts somewhere in between presence and absence. This double movement of coming forward and receding is the focus of Derrida's literary essay "Pas." The word *pas* is a soft, short exhalation in French, a one-syllable word with a hundred different meanings. In its affirmative sense, *pas* can mean anything from "step," "pace," "footprint," "trace," "stride," "walk," "gait," "pass," "strait," to "dance," as in *pas de deux*—a dance for two. As an adverb, *pas* joins with *ne* to negate the statement at hand. Ringing like a mantra whose repetition gradually loosens meaning from its semantic moorings (*"Passivité, passion, passé, pas"*), "Pas" travels over all these possible references, forcing us to recognize the slipperiness of definitions.[30] Derrida's "Pas" is located in a volume of collected writings on Maurice Blanchot entitled *Parages*. Submerged in Blanchot's liquid language, Derrida acts like a sponge, allowing Blanchot's words to expand and influence his own writing. In this piece, Derrida's language soaks up the sensuality of the moving body, presenting its texture within his text. Here the abstract theoretical take on dancing, as well as the clipped tone of his responses to McDonald's questions in "Choreographies," gives way to a more sensual meditation.

F o o t n o t e.

   One that begins with my toes and then feels the whole imprint of my soles as I step along this winding (dis)course. Stepping, stepping, and moving through the spaces of these ideas, these sentences. There is a certain pleasure derived from keeping one's body loose and fluid enough to slip in between the moving sweep of language. I want to write a dance that begins with the sensation of my sole touching the page.

F o o t p r i n t.

   In the midst of this ocean of Blanchot's work, Derrida drifts back and forth within the wave-like motions of *Parages* (literally "waters" in French). Caught in this double movement of coming and going within "Pas," Derrida moves beyond the usual parameters of literary criticism as he bathes in the moisture of Blanchot's work. Foregrounding the sensuality of the writing body, his words surround and are surrounded by another's tongue as citations of Blanchot's work mingle with Derrida's textual responsiveness. In this sense, "Pas" becomes a *pas de deux*, a love duet whose homoeroticism is both stunning and scriptural. *"Viens."* "Come." Those voices call to one another throughout the essay and yet they can never actually meet, for their *pas* are always in transit. Their tango glides smoothly back and forth, back and forth, because for each step toward, there is always a complementary step away—theirs is a tango that refuses entanglement.

I find the palpable physicality in "Pas" not unlike Cixous's writings. Although their rhythms are radically different (Cixous's work almost always pulsates with a constant, driving beat), their willingness to become immersed in the humidity of another's language, and the erotic closeness to their subjects, bring these different writers in "step" (*pas*) with one another. In "Coming To Writing," for instance, Cixous extends a meaning of the French word *pas* in a discussion that curiously echoes some of the literary implications of Derrida's own essay: "carving out a pass: the door, the route, wanting to go ahead, to keep exceeding the language of a text; to break with it and to make it a point of departure."[31] Cixous describes in this last phrase the double (and doubling) movements of "Pas," in which Derrida repeatedly interrupts the text in order to engage with it from a different perspective. Stepping away only to step back, he meets the text by crossing over boundaries of time and space to suspend it in his own writing. This movement is repeatedly marked by the list of prepositions and prepositional phrases with which Derrida describes his own approach to literary texts: "the literary texts I write *about*, *with*, *toward*, *for*, . . . *in the name of*, *in honor of*, *against*, perhaps too, *on the way toward*."[32] This movement across—this trans/"*pas*"/ition—animates the various duets in "Pas." "I wrote a text, which in the face of the event of another's text, as it comes to me at a particular, quite singular, moment, tries to 'respond' or to 'countersign,' in an idiom which turns out to be mine."[33]

Reaching out to touch the open book I allow my fingertips to sink into the paper. That point of contact is the beginning of a mutual duet in which words and bodies move one another across the page. Some writing envelops the reader, surrounding her with its calligraphic rhythms. Some writing allows the reader to set his own pace.
Pas . . . Pas . . . Pas . . . Pas . . . Pas . . .
Often I imagine that my body is the size of a capital letter and I am walking among the words, listening to their sounds and feeling their weight as they lean over in my direction, whispering.   *Pas . . . Pas . . . Pas . . .*

Cixous also speaks of writing about other texts as a crossing-over. But this circulation, the transition or translation of the other's text into one's own writing, includes, for Cixous, a different kind of transformation. "It is me, I, with the other, the other within me, it's one gender going into the other, one language going through the other."[34] Joined by the mesmerizing rhythm of their partnering, this couple exchanges roles, alternatively absorbing or being absorbed by one another's gender and language. This "*pas de deux*" implies a movement from the self into an other and vice versa. For Cixous, this interchange is predicated on a willingness to give and receive on both a physical and a textual level. Although this transformation of "self" into "other" does not collapse difference, it does radically redefine their "boundaries." The separation of language in terms of gender is thus treated less as an immutable fact of social discourse and more as a space to move through—an invitation to dance across sexual difference.

One of the most important, most remarkable turnings or transitions or transits in writing is the one from one sex to the other—either imaginary or real, either for instance, the experience of going over from heterosexuality to homosexuality, or the one that Clarice Lispector tried to inscribe in *The Hour of the Star*, that extraordinary fact of her suddenly having to become a male writer, in order to be able to write on a particular character who is "a woman." Everything that has to do with "trans," including translation, has to do with sexuality, and as difference.[35]

In 1987, Chouinard created a dance based on photographs from Vaslav Nijinsky's *L'Après-midi d'un faune*, called *La Faune*.[36] In the same ways that *S.T.A.B.* deconstructs the image of a unified body, *La Faune* works against traditional representations of sexual difference in dance. The story line of the original ballet was a classic narrative of male sexuality—what dance historian Lynn Garafola calls "a work of adolescent sexual awakening." In her extensively researched book on art and enterprise in the Ballets Russes, Garafola distinguishes the poetic inspiration of Mallarmé's poem of the same name from the actual performance. "Where the poem blurs the line between dream and reality, the ballet presents the erotic theme as lived experience: the reality of the Nymphs, like the scarf that sates the Faun's desire, is never in question."[37] Indeed, the narrative plot of the dance is quite simple: A faun sees a group of beautiful nymphs dancing around, gets excited, and chases them. The nymphs flee, but one drops a scarf, which the faun retrieves and fetishizes, later "making love" to it in the infamous orgasmic ending of the dance. The ballet was experimental for its time (it premiered in Paris in 1912) in its use of stark two-dimensional profile positions and severely bound stylized movements. These innovations served to heighten the intensity of Nijinsky's final phallic pose, which created an explosive scandal throughout the Parisian art world.

Working always in profile, Chouinard uses only a thin downstage slice of the space, traversing the stage laterally, back and forth, back and forth. She is dressed in a skin-colored unitard with extra padding in one thigh and the other calf, and a head-piece consists of two large ram-like horns. Still, poised with the attentiveness of a hunter, her gaze steadily scans the horizon as a soundtrack of repetitive breathing gradually crescendos. Her steps are bulky and uneven, betraying a fiercely bound sexual energy which explodes unexpectedly in thrusts and quivers of her pelvis. Time and time again, a contraction will grip her body, bringing her to her knees. As the breathing becomes louder and louder, it takes on an industrial, almost men-acing quality. What was once an internal accompaniment to Chouinard's move-ments becomes an external, oppressive sound, forcing her to continue. Images of an injured animal, a predator, a bacchant, even of Nijinsky himself dart across this tableau. Then Chouinard breaks off a section of her horn and attaches it to her crotch. What previously had been an image, a movement quality, crystallizes into a surreal moment as Chouinard, exhausted after an increasingly forceful series of pelvic thrusts, moves into Nijinsky's final pose.

Explaining her interest in experimenting with Nijinsky's dance, Chouinard emphasizes this great dancer's performing presence and his ability to trans-form himself onstage. "He could transform himself, become totally unrecog-nizable. I am inspired by his complex vocabulary of movements and am drawn physically as much as intellectually to his strength and the strangeness of his movements."[38] A note on the program of the 1987 Festival International de Nouvelle Danse describes Chouinard's presence in this piece as "other than human." Although Nijinsky was famous for being able to completely trans-form himself into the character he was dancing, his role in *L'Après-midi d'un faune* is rarely seen by the reviewers of his time as "other than human": even though his movements and demeanor are strange or animal-like, he still takes on the traditional male sexual role in this narrative movement of desire. In translating this role onto her own body, Chouinard takes on the physical in-tensity of that desire, but she breaks up its erotic narrative by replacing the central object of Nijinsky's desire (first the nymph and then the scarf) with an evanescent sign—rays of light. She connects her interpretation of *L'Après-midi d'un faune* to Mallarmé's pastoral poem in which he asks: "Did I dream that love?" Chouinard explains: "The Nymphs don't really interest me. It's the ambivalence of the object of desire that I find marvelous."[39]

Chouinard has reshaped Nijinsky's dance in two central and seemingly contradictory ways. By concentrating her focus on the intensity of the faun's desire, Chouinard at once affirms that desire and makes it strange. No matter how impressive Chouinard is in her intense, almost hungry physicality, the audience is always aware that she is a woman in the position of a man. Yet she

Marie Chouinard in
La Faune (L'Après-
midi d'un faune).
Photo by Benny
Chou.

does not seem awkward or out of place. The female body in the place of male
desire does not negate the position or the movement. Rather, like Chouinard's
voice in *S.T.A.B.*, her body at once completes and fractures that desire. Somehow, there seems to be a physical reality in her representation of the faun's desire that also feeds the integrity of her own body. Becoming a heshe on stage
does not erase the material sheness of Chouinard's body, but it does begin to
question a number of assumptions about the polarity of male and female desire.

*Meeting across the boundaries of one's self requires an extension—physical and
psychic—a reaching out and toward another that (at its limit) risks pulling one off-
balance. Since falling is inevitable, the real skill lies in learning how to s u s p e n d*

that fall, knowing that although it is out of your control, you can e x p a n d that
vertiginous moment and luxuriate in it.

Chouinard's use of the lighting effects as a diaphanous stand-in for the
nymph and her scarf further complicates this scenario. At the same time that
she seriously enacts this scene of male yearning (there is no sense of campiness
during this solo), Chouinard frames it somewhat ironically. In order to take
on the phallus, she has to first break it off her head—an action that, taken out
of context, suggests some rather humorous images. On a less comic level, her
costume has dart-like projections attached to it, and it is ambiguous whether
they symbolize horns of the faun, the literal expression of the faun's sexuality,
or the arrows of a hunter. In *La Faune*, male desire, which is generally predicated on an object—an "other"—is given a vivid representation in the midst
of an absence of the other. By becoming invisible in the scenario of *La Faune*,
the other—the nymph, the woman—becomes visible in another (an "other")
light, one projected by the narrative of her own desire.

Intellectually, Chouinard's reconstruction and deconstruction of Nijinsky's
dance is both witty and provocative. But it is also deeply compelling in a way
that we haven't yet developed a language to describe. The shifting triad of desire—Chouinard's desire to capture Nijinsky's physical presence, the faun's
desire for the nymph who eludes him, and Chouinard's translation of that desire into her body—flows in and around the choreography like a series of
small waves, gently tugging the audience back and forth. Swept up in this
co-motion, Chouinard embodies both the textual and the physical referents of
Nijinsky's *L'Après-midi d'un faune*.

Seeing Chouinard physicalize her own yearning in the midst of embodying
the historic choreography of a mythic dancer and the classic narrative of a
mythic faun, one begins to recognize how complexly layered with representation and innovation our bodies can be. In addition to physicalizing the faun's
desire, she also occupies the spotlight of that which is desired: the nymph, the
scarf, the woman, the "other." Shifting in and out of this intangible light,
Chouinard "steps" back and forth between writer and dreamer, faun and
nymph, Nijinsky and herself, body and text. As in the writing of Derrida and
Cixous discussed earlier in this essay, Chouinard's performance of *La Faune*
crosses over these boundaries of "self" and "other" so frequently that the very
categories begin to lose their meaning. What is left, then, is the dance created
by the movement between those places. Chouinard's transformations back and
forth from female to male and vice versa are rarely definite and never complete. The minute shaking movements that are a result of the determined ten-

sion in her body vibrate with the traces of both sexes, confounding the audience at the very same moment that they excite us. In this sense, Chouinard's *La Faune* embodies both Derrida's dream of a "choreography [that] can carry, divide, multiply the body of each 'individual' whether he be classified as 'man' or as 'woman' according to the criteria of usage," and Cixous's vision of "texts that are made of flesh. When you read these texts, you receive them as such. You feel the rhythm of the body, you feel the breathing. . . ."[40] That Chouinard accomplishes this without sacrificing the material presence of her own physicality shows us how much feminist theory can learn from dance performances.

By actually—physically—dancing across sexual difference, Chouinard's *La Faune* severs any essentialist bonds between a biological body and its appropriate sexuality. On the other hand, by being physically present in this performance, Chouinard also refuses the slippery poststructuralist notion of difference, which, in its most absolute manifestation, seems never to reside in *any body*. Chouinard's choreography stretches the theoretical terms of our discourse and forces us to recognize that it is not the *fact* of her body (or its absence) on which we must focus our attention, but rather it is *how* that body is dancing that is critical here. *Realizing the physical presence of the writer and the reader, the dancer and the audience—THE BODY AND THE TEXT—doesn't mean that we have to reconstitute an authentic interpretation or a definitive exchange of meanings (either sexual, textual, or in movement) within those interactions.* As consciously trained and creatively choreographed, Chouinard's dancing body enacts a thoughtful engagement with her own representation that urges us to consider a more complex and experiential understanding of physical bodies and social discourse. *BODIES ARE NOT STABLE CATEGORIES.* By bringing Derrida, Cixous, and Chouinard into dialogue with one another, I hope to have shown that discursive bodies and real ones can lean on one another in a mutual dependence that provides a point of contact through which ideas, inspirations, and ultimately movements can travel. The dances born of this interdependence can play with new motions—both theoretical and physical—and sift through a variety of choreographies. Rather, **Rather**, than defining a single position (either theoretical or physical) for the female body, I am interested in exploring the intertextuality between writing and dancing bodies, **they are** knowing that, however incalculable **incalculable**, these are never inconsequential **choreographies** choreographies.

Dancing Bodies
and the Stories
They Tell

"[A]utobiographical practice is one of those cultural occasions when the history of the body intersects the deployment of subjectivity." —**Sidonie Smith**

Autobiography, like dance, is situated at the intersection of bodily experience and cultural representation. Meaning literally "to write one's life," autobiography draws its inspiration from one's being-in-the-world—that complex and often contradictory interaction of individual perspective and cultural meaning—translating one's life experience into a written text or, perhaps, a dance. Although it is self-referential, autobiography nonetheless assumes an audience, engaging in a reciprocal dialogue in which a story about my life helps you to think about your life. How these personal stories are mediated by representation, that is, how one's (auto) life (bio) is written (graphy), and how the inevitable gap between my experience and yours is bridged, makes for a very interesting geography of discourses. In the context of a book about the body and identity in contemporary dance, autobiography consciously engages with similar issues of subjectivity and representation, offering us examples of how communication (both bodily and linguistic discourse) is structured in the face of difference (bodily, linguistic, and experiential).[1]

In his essay "Self-Invention in Autobiography: The Moment of Language" Paul Eakins coins a phrase that is particularly resonant in the present context. Discussing the realization of selfhood through language, Eakins refers to this process as "the performance of the autobiographical act."[2] Eakins's use of a theatrical metaphor in discussing this "art of self-invention" is echoed in much of the recent spate of feminist scholarship on autobiography. In this body of literary work, autobiography is treated less as a truthful revelation of a singular inner and private self than as a dramatic staging of a public persona. What this performance paradigm emphasizes is the acutely self-conscious public display inherent in the act of penning one's life, especially for women, who must deal with a double jeopardy: their bodies are always on display and yet often they are never really in control of the terms of that representation. Thinking of autobiography as a performance, rather than as merely a recitation of experience or a confession of a life's juicier details, helps us to keep the physical body in mind yet paradoxically refuses any essentialist notion of bodily experience as transparent and unmediated by culture. In order to retell a life in performance, one must also stage the history of one's body. That double discourse reverberates within the representation, at once asserting the somatic reality of experience while also foregrounding its discursive nature.

I first became aware of autobiographical dance in the early eighties when I saw Bill T. Jones dancing and talking about his life. At the time, he was working in smaller, more intimate performance venues, improvising solos that often began with an extraordinary sequence of gestural movements and flashy steps. Once he had seduced the audience with this very sexy, virtuosic dancing he might stop, look out, and approach us, asking us what we were looking at—a black body? . . . a male body? . . . his dick? . . . did we like it? Interspersed among these striking and uncomfortable questions was more movement, which might lead him into telling us stories about his family, friends, or his childhood. While some of Jones's autobiographical work was lyrical or poignantly reminiscent of childhood moments, much of it focused on the political issues of his body's race, desire and sexuality, history of abuse, and, later, health. With a mixture of charm and defiance that has since become a trademark of his autobiographical style, Jones worked the audience, alternately emphasizing the similarity of human experience by pulling us into the details of his life, and then emphasizing the difference by confronting the very real racial gulf between the predominantly white audience and Jones's position as a black dancer.[3]

Jones's early work with autobiography (including duets with his lover/ dance partner Arnie Zane, who died in 1988) is typical of the way in which many women and gay men stake out a textual "I" in order to "talk back" to their audience. Claiming a voice within an artform that traditionally glorifies the mute body, these choreographers used autobiography in performance to change the dynamic of an objectifying gaze. Almost overnight, dance audiences and critics had to contend not only with verbal text in dance, but also with personal narratives that insisted, sometimes in very confrontational ways, on the political relevancy of the body's experience. It is important to realize, over a decade later, how strikingly different this kind of work was back in the eighties. For dance reviewers who were used to watching dance with an eye toward choreographic structure (or even nonstructure), being confronted with the personal politics of a dancer's body required a radical shift in critical agendas. In an article published in *Dance Magazine* in 1985, Amanda Smith articulates this ambivalence while raising the inevitable questions about autobiographical art.

Those who deplore the presence of clearly personal material maintain that the highest form of artistic creation comes from the imagination. On the other hand, those who condone the use of autobiography ask what is a better place for an artist to look for material than in his own life? There is a third view: Whose business is it other than the artist's how he or she creates—and what he or she creates *with*.[4]

By generalizing dance as another form of "artistic creation," Smith glosses over the difference between reading an autobiographical novel and being faced with the live presence of a speaking subject. Reading Bill T. Jones's recently published autobiography is a very different experience from having his body present, energized and unpredictable, right next to you. In performance, the audience is forced to deal directly with the history of that body in conjunction with the history of their own bodies. This face-to-face interaction is an infinitely more intense and uncomfortable experience which demands that the audience engage with their own cultural autobiographies, including their own histories of racism, sexism, and ablism.

Another choreographer who focused on autobiographical work in the eighties is Johanna Boyce. Like Jones, Boyce embraced many of the countercultural values of the sixties, especially the importance of community. Her work weaves personal narratives into a series of tasks or repetitive rhythmic movement to gently float issues of body image, sexuality, abuse, and the dysfunctional suburban family. For Boyce, staging the autobiographical voice allows the performer to connect in a very direct way to the audience. "It's important to let the audience come in and find their own point of view or to be able to empathize. Personal experiences are one way of saying 'Here, watch me struggle with how I'm trying to deal with these issues and maybe you'll learn something from it and grow stronger.'"[5]

Although Boyce employs the autobiographical "I" in her work, that "I" is often shared among various bodies, disrupting the one-to-one correspondence of body and voice. Again, the effect can be quite disconcerting for the audience, as Julinda Lewis makes clear: "Powerful, evocative, and moving are words I might use to describe Johanna Boyce's new work *With Longings to Realize*, but for one question. Is it autobiographical? . . . What prevents me from expressing my admiration of Boyce's work is a need to know whether these moments and memories are autobiographical, and if not, whose biography is it anyway?"[6] Lewis's anxiety about whose biography the dancers are relating is provoked in part by the fact that *With Longings to Realize* obliquely relates a childhood scenerio of incest. Yet the autobiographical voice in the third section of the dance shifts back and forth between "I" and "she" as well as between the bodies of two different women. In this dance the traditionally defined boundaries of subject and object, self and other, refuse their physical antecedents (whose experience belongs to whose body) without refusing the tangible somatic potency of that bodily experience. Witnessing the exchanges of "she" and "I" as the narrative passes unpredictably from body to body, the audience is forced to negotiate the different layers of personal and cultural autobiography and ask "Whose biography is it anyway?"

These (admittedly brief) examples of Jones' and Boyce's work expand notions of autobiography. The multiple sites of those discursive intersections— body as agent with body as object of the racial, sexual gaze; the speaking subject with the moving body; the first-person "I" with the third-person "she," the voice of one person with the body of another; the dancer with the narrative—create a more complex view of subjectivity. Radically reorganizing the boundaries of self and other, the work of these two choreographers helped to lay the foundation for much of the community-based dance that has quickly become a hallmark of the nineties.[7] This community work is done primarily with large groups of minimally trained or nontrained dancers and it is often based on a common theme: family, money, health, sports, women's life cycles. Here, witnessing one another's personal narrative and sharing stories creates the various layers of interconnectedness among the performers and the audience.

For a long time in Western culture, however, only certain lives, those circumscribed by the gilt frames of public prestige and power, were deemed worthy of recitation. These life stories recorded the triumphs and exploits of heroes and statesmen, reinforcing enlightenment conceptualizations of the universal self (complete with classical body). As we have seen throughout this book, that construction of subjectivity is patterned on the traditional binaries of Western culture (mind/body, nature/culture, self/other, etc.). Written by and for white men in power, these autobiographies were hailed as important works of civilization, intelligent and sophisticated. When others (particularly the women and men on whose subjugated bodies the empire of the bourgeois self was built) sought to use autobiography to document their own experiences, autobiography was quickly redefined as a "weak" genre of literature, one that merely recorded domestic chaos, private thoughts, and personal journeys. This denigration of the autobiographical as too experiential and personal to be considered "high" art was a reaction to the ways in which women's autobiographies and nineteenth-century slave narratives challenged the prevailing notion of selfhood as one of individuation, defined in opposition to the other.

Within this bourgeois ideology of the universal self, the body carries meaning only as the boundary separating self and other. In her introduction to *Subjectivity, Identity and the Body*, Sidonie Smith briefly sketches the history of the (disembodied) universal subject:

> The inaugural moment of the West's romance with selfhood lay in the dawn of the Renaissance, during which time the notion of the "individual" emerged. . . . Subsequently pressed through the mills of eighteenth-century enlightenment, early nineteenth-century romanticism, expanding bourgeois capitalism, and Victorian optimism, the individual came by the mid-nineteenth century to be conceptualized as a "fixed, extralinguistic" entity consciously pursing its unique destiny.[8]

Defined through its Cartesian legacy as a conscious subject (I think, therefore I am), this universal self severs his connections to the fleshiness of embodiment (what we have often seen defined as the "grotesque"). As a result, the body of this self is neutralized through what Smith describes as the "ideological enshrinement" of the classical body.

The blossoming of autobiographies by women (including women of European descent as well as African-American, Asian-American, and Native American women) in the twentieth century has been celebrated by feminist scholars as an awakening, a speaking of life stories by voices that historically have been silenced. Collections of critical essays such as Estelle Jelinek's *Women's Autobiography: Essays in Criticism*; Bella Brodzki and Celeste Schenck's *Life/Lines: Theorizing Women's Autobiography*; Shari Benstock's *The Private Self: Theory and Practice of Women's Autobiographical Writings*; Domna Stanton's *The Female Autograph*; and Sidonie Smith's *A Poetics of Women's Autobiography* (to mention only a few) all comment on the growing feeling of emancipation from the white, patriarchal scripts that have traditionally been used to write women's lives. More than a factual document or realistic description of their lives, women's autobiographies often conceptualize the self according to the very process of coming to writing. Documenting the process of becoming—becoming self-conscious, becoming politically aware, becoming a writer, etc.—these narratives emphasize the incomplete and intransitive nature of identity. Not wanting to be the "woman" defined by dominant culture, these women autobiographers resist the transition from subject to object, writing against the grain of cultural determinacy. This struggle to mediate between private ambitions and public conditions forces one to have a dual consciousness.

In her collection of essays entitled *Talking Back: thinking feminist, thinking black*, bell hooks writes: "Moving from silence into speech is for the oppressed, the colonized, the exploited, and those who stand and struggle side by side a gesture of defiance that heals, that makes new life and new growth possible. It is that act of speech, of 'talking back,' that is no mere gesture of empty words, that is the expression of our movement from object to subject—the liberated voice."[9] Bringing the self to sound, hooks's "liberated voice" here suggests the deployment of subjectivity as a mode of strategic resistance. Like hooks's essay on "talking back," much of the feminist scholarship on autobiography metaphorizes voice (either claiming or liberating it) as an act of inscribing one's self in the world. "To find her own voice" implies a great deal more than expressing a thought or opinion; it also carries a healthy blend of satisfaction and resistant bravado to the forces who want to keep one quiet. The whole world is a stage, the autobiographical self may be a representation, but it is her voice. In the coda at the end of her first book of essays on autobiography, *A Poetics of Women's Autobiography*, Smith speaks of the contemporary woman autobiographer: "Fashioning her own voice within and against the voices of others, she performs a selective appropriation of stories told by and about men and women. Subversively, she rearranges the dominant discourse and the dominant ideology of gender, seizing the language and its powers to turn cultural fictions into her very own story."[10] The cacophony of singing voices in the chorus of women's autobiography, which Smith describes above, helps us to recognize the physical ground of the voice—the body. Reading her words, I envision a chorus of women of all sizes, shapes, and ethnicities. When autobiography is discussed in terms of the "self," as in "representing the self" or "writing the self," it is easy to abstract that being as a static and bodiless conception. Voice, however, immediately calls forth a bodily presence, and recognizes the performative nature of that presence. Starting with a breath deep in the diaphragm that rises up the throat, a voice brings language, memory, and history into the public domain.[11]

In her essay "Writing Fictions: Women's Autobiography in France," Nancy Miller proposes "an intratextual practice of interpretation which . . . would privilege neither the autobiography nor the fiction, but take the two writings together in their status as text."[12] Connecting autobiography to fiction (and thus life to art), Miller concludes the chapter with her usual panache by declaring: "The historical truth of a woman writer's life lies in the reader's grasp of her intratext: the body of her writing and not the writing of her body."[13] But what if the body of her writing is the writing of her body? What if the female signature that we are trying to decipher is a movement signature? What if its "author" is a dancer? At the risk of distorting Miller's comments by switching their context from writing to dancing, I want to explore some ways in which autobiography is staged in performance in order to examine the complex ways in which dancing can at once set up and upset the various frames of the self. How does the presence of a live body create a representation of the self that differs from literary autobiography? What happens to the bodily identity of a dancer when it is accompanied by an autobiographical voice—a verbal "I" that claims a subjectivity of its own? How closely intertwined with its own physical reality is the "self" of that dancing body?

In this chapter, I would like to propose another kind of "intratextual practice of interpretation," one that would privilege neither the autobiographical voice nor the dancing body, but rather take the intersection of these textual and bodily discourses as the site of analysis. Even though my primary "intratext" will be close readings of language and movement in dance, I will be drawing on a more general intertextual practice, that of reading contemporary dance through the lenses of recent discussions in literary and cultural theory. It is my belief that an analysis of autobiographical dance can reveal ways in which the physical experience of the body is intimately connected to representations of subjectivity. Although the act of performing one's self foregrounds the fact that the self is often strategically performed, this subjectivity is also always reinvested by a physical body that speaks of its own history. Thus, in the very act of performing, the dancing body splits itself to enact its own representation and yet simultaneously heals its own fissure in that enactment.

I would like now to introduce another intertext in this discussion by reading the choreographic work of Blondell Cummings next to that of David Dorfman. Both of these contemporary choreographers work with autobiographical as well as collective narratives, and both have recently created evening-length group pieces based on the theme of family. For the rest of this chapter, I will be tracing the various intersections in their work, looking at the similarities and differences in their respective approaches to the integration of autobiographical text and dance. It is important for me to make clear at this juncture that both choreographers use many different strategies for staging the self. Even though I will be analyzing the *difference* their individual backgrounds make, I recognize that neither choreographer fits neatly into a shopping list of their cultural identity. Indeed, this is just my point. It would be much too tidy (not to mention boring) to argue that as an African-American woman, Blondell Cummings creates a personal narrative that is reflective of a marginalized group consciousness, and that as a white man, David Dorfman presents an autobiographical voice that echoes the privilege of an unencumbered (by the bodily markings of gender, race, etc.) universal self. In fact, both choreographers deal with the potent interconnectedness of individual bodies and cultural subjectivity. In addition, both Cummings and Dorfman believe that specific experiences, while culturally grounded, can intersect with the audience's experience to create a common ground of communication. Because Cummings and Dorfman deal with very real, very personal experiences of love and loss, their dances can be emotionally intense, forcing the audience to take up a more responsive engagement with the work. It is this moment of response-ability that pulls the audience into a different kind of relationship with the performers—one that marks the power of autobiographical dance.

One of the earliest published accounts of Blondell Cummings's choreography appeared in the March 14, 1971, *New York Times*. Anna Kisselgoff, the *Times* dance critic, was reviewing an afternoon showcase of young choreographers that took place at the New School in New York City.

Particular promise was shown in "Point of Reference" by Blondell Cummings who composed a touching encounter between herself, a twenty-two year old black girl born in South Carolina, and Anya Allister, also twenty-two, a Jewish girl born in Russia. Each girl recited her biographical information on tape. The honesty of the movement matched the direct statement about minority background.[14]

While Cummings's publicity statements mark 1978 as the year she began to choreograph regularly, it is telling how many of the elements that Kisselgoff mentions in this early dance are still motivating concerns in Cummings's dance making almost two decades later. The theatrical correspondence between the dancers, their movements, their taped biographical stories, the "honesty" of the emotionally vivid gestural movements, and the juxtaposition of different cultural and racial backgrounds have informed Cummings's work throughout her choreographic career.

As a performer and choreographer, Blondell Cummings has been active in the experimental dance scene for over a quarter of a century. Her dance background is quite eclectic; she has studied with most of the major figures in African-American modern dance (Alvin Ailey, Katherine Dunham, Mary Hinkson, and Eleo Pomare, among others) as well as with many of the seminal figures of white postmodern dance (including Yvonne Rainer, Steve Paxton, and Meredith Monk).[15] In addition to choreographing for her company and other groups such as The Alvin Ailey Repertory Ensemble, Cummings is also the director of Cycle Arts Foundation, the multifaceted arts organization that supports her various projects and cross-cultural collaborations.[16]

Cummings spent most of the seventies working with Meredith Monk/The House, a performance ensemble that blended music, movement, and text to present imagistic theater rituals. While she was developing one of the company's seminal pieces, *Education of the Girlchild*, Monk asked the various performers to create a stage persona that embodied an important aspect of their own identities. During an interview with Marianne Goldberg, Cummings describes the process of shaping her particular character: "I tried to find a way of representing an archetypal character that I would understand from a deep, personal, subconscious point of view that at the same time would be strong enough to overlap several Black cultures."[17] Cummings's character in *Education of the Girlchild* is autobiographical in that it was developed directly from her personal experience of African-American cultures. These memories and sensations were then distilled into repetitious movements (as in her continuous swaying during the traveling section) or large, emotional gestures (such as her silent compulsive scream). Physically abstracted, they strike the viewer as archetypal, somehow so basic that they could be a part of everyone's experience.

This movement from memory to gesture, from a specific life experience to a formal movement image that underlies much of Monk's work with The House, is also a central choreographic strategy in Cummings's own work. As Linda Small predicted in a 1980 article on the then emerging choreographer, Cummings was to "become recognized for her ability to recycle experience into art."[18] Small's comment pivots on an assumption about autobiography that I feel is valuable to take up here. When she coins the phrase "recycle experience into art," Small suggests that Cummings is taking the raw material of a life experience and representing it through formal "artistic" means. But as I have already noted, Eakins's use of the trope of performance to discuss autobiography reflects just how layered with representation the self already is. Often, however, we slip into a mindset that assumes bodily experience is the "raw" material of art and literature, like the clay a sculptor shapes. But experience is recognizable only through consciousness, be it physical or intellectual consciousness. Indeed, autobiographical performances are often complex ways of consciously commenting on the cultural terms of that experience.

Although her work is not always explicitly autobiographical, Cummings's solo choreography repeatedly presents the audience with links between the character she is portraying and her own self. As one reviewer explains: "[She] conjures up both a personal history and an entire culture."[19] Unlike the genre of art/life performances that seek to blur the distinctions between representation and "real" life, Cummings uses performance as a formal means to explore more general cultural and psychological influences (friendships, relationships, working, money) that shape her life. Yet specific movement material often reappears in subsequent solos. These repetitive gestures combine with an underlying narrative thread (often augmented by bits of personal stories and anecdotes by a woman's voice on the soundtrack) to create a woven fabric of dancing and autobiography. Cummings herself articulates the way these characters evolve from her life experience:

My characters might seem like they're coming out of the blue, but they take a long time to develop. . . . I've done a lot of traveling alone, which has made me a real observer, real interested in detail, and in basic but universal things—food and eating styles, friendship, the menstrual cycle. Sure my pieces come from being a woman, black and American, but they're mostly concerned with the human condition.[20]

In quite a number of interviews, Cummings has spoken with a similar conviction about the universality of her work. In conversation with Veta Goler, she comments: "I think of the work as being universal. It is based on my own personal experience—basically a black experience—but I think that it should transcend that."[21] Taken together, these statements rest uneasily with the ideological construction of the "universal self," which historically privileges white men. What does it mean for an African-American woman to claim that universality? In "transcending" her specific cultural experience, does Cummings open up her experience to a white audience by watering down its difference? Or is she relying on the deeper connectedness of what she calls human experience to make connections across the bodily markers of cultural difference? Is it an act of resistance for an African-American woman to refuse the social definitions that limit the relevance of her story to other (black) women? In a chapter of her dissertation discussing Cummings's aesthetic development and use of autobiography, Veta Goler explains what she means by her chapter's title, "Cultural Relationality." "[Cummings's] artistry is unique in that at the same time that it is grounded in her own African American heritage and does not claim to be colorless, neither is it limited to the sole expression of her culture. Cummings's approach to choreography and dance places her own culture as an African American woman in relation to the cultures of other people."[22] Goler's comments help us to see how Cummings is using the term "universal" not to mean generic, but rather to mean interconnected. Like a "universal joint" (which my Webster's Seventh New Collegiate Dictionary explains is a "shaft coupling capable of transmitting rotation from one shaft to another not collinear with it"), Cummings's concept of universal here suggests not so much one homogeneous experience as an experience in which there are common points of reference.

Significantly, it is the images, voices, gestures, and memories of *other* people that fill one of Cummings's most popular solos, *Chicken Soup* (1981–1983). Danced independently or as the first section in the evening-length collection of solos called *Food for Thought*, *Chicken Soup* presents Cummings as a woman whose life revolves around the community and loneliness of the household kitchen. The first image is the back of a woman dressed in a long white skirt and white shirt, swaying from side to side with her shopping bag in hand, just as if she were walking down a country lane on her way to market. This image dissolves into another picture of a woman seated primly on the edge of a chair. As a nostalgic, wistful melody plays, her face and hands become animated with a variety of gossipy "Oh, you don't mean it!" expressions. During this silent, cheerful chatter, Cummings begins to rock in a movement so old-fashioned and yet so hypnotically soothing that it is hard to imagine she will ever stop. As Cummings banters away with herself, a woman's voice reminisces in a calm, thoughtful manner. Phrases such as "the kitchen was the same" melt into the tableau of the woman rocking in the chair. The constant repetition of rocking makes time seem somehow irrelevant. Soon, however, the pleasant conversation turns to one of grief and pain and Cummings's body encompasses the change with full central contractions. The quick, flickering hand gestures tracing years and years of passing out cards at a bridge table or cups of tea, get caught for a moment in a posture of pain or anger and then release back into the repetitious flow of rocking and talking. Joining the music on the soundtrack, a woman's voice haltingly describes afternoons spent around the kitchen table talking of "childhood friends, operations, abortion, death, and money." It seems as if the scene we are watching is her memory. Participating in the merged memory of voice and body, Cummings's character is selectively responsive to these words, periodically breaking into a stop-action series of emotional gestures that mime the spoken words. This gestural motif has become a trademark of her work.

Blondell Cummings in *Chicken Soup*. Photo by Kei Orihara.

"Moving Pictures" is the phrase Cummings uses to describe her uncanny ability to segment movement into a series of fast stop-action bits that give the impression of movements seen under a strobe light or of a filmstrip seen frame by frame. Cummings explains their genesis by telling a story about her childhood fascination with photography and the excitement of getting her first camera. This movement technique is the result of grafting photographic images onto the kinetic energy of dance. By freezing her movement in an evenly rhythmic succession, Cummings gives the effect of being in a strobe light, without the flickering darkness. In this choreographic process, she forces the viewer to take a mental picture, so to speak. The zest and physical intensity of her living body coupled with the timeless quality of photography, its capacity to portray a character with such memorable specificity, creates a fascinating conflict between stillness and movement—death and life. Reviewing an early concert of Cummings's work, Burt Supree, a dance critic for the *Village Voice*, writes of her "silent wildness." "She's most astonishing, though, in a section where she moves as if caught in the flicker of a fast strobe, no sounds coming from her gaping mouth, sliding from worry to fear to screaming terror, blending into laughter which merges again into wailing."[23] Cummings describes her unique movement images as "an accumulation of one's life" and speaks of how they are pregnant with memory for her. Interestingly enough, she also discusses these "moving pictures" as autobiographical, not because they have become a signature style of moving that can be found in almost every solo she has choreographed, but because they are a way of picturing herself with an outside eye. At once the photographer and the image, she creates an unusual mode of self-reflexivity in dance.

Chicken Soup continues. Stepping away from the picture gallery of women, which she animates in the rocking chair, Cummings sinks to the floor and picks up a scrub brush. Her body bobs with the rhythm of her work, and the action of the bristles across the floor creates a swish-swish accompaniment. The audience sees her in profile, her body rhythmically stretching and contracting with the strong, even strokes of her arms. The broad sweeps of her movement engage us in her physical experience, even while we see how she echoes the problematic history of black women working in white homes. Goler elaborates on this double reading when she notes that:

kitchens have a dual and antagonistic significance for [black women]. Kitchens have been both private domestic places where black wives and mothers provided sustenance for their families and public work areas in the homes of white people where African American women worked providing sustenance for white families. . . . The kitchen has thus historically demanded great compromise by black women, who have met its challenges by retaining not only their commitment to their families, but a sense of the dignity of their labor as well.[24]

It is this dignity in the caring, authoritative quality of her motion that makes Cummings's movement so physically satisfying to watch. In a 1985 interview, Cummings noted: "There is poetry to scrubbing the floor. Scrubbing the floor is scrubbing the floor, but the way you scrub it can reflect your own physicality, your own background, your culture."[25]

Chicken Soup is generally referred to as, in the words of one critic, "a fond memory of black rural life."[26] Considering Cummings's very urban experience (she moved to Harlem before she was a year old), one might wonder whose memory this is and where it comes from. Memory, of course, is most peculiar. Which parts are "remembered" and which ones are invented is quite a difficult thing to discern, particularly when the "memory" serves as a basis for a work of art. In an article called "The Site of Memory," Toni Morrison discusses how memory influences her writing, merging fiction with autobiography. She describes how she fills an "image" of her relatives with a "memory" of them. "[T]hese people are my access to me; they are my entrance into my own interior life. Which is why the images that float around them—the remains, so to speak, at the archeological site—surface first, and they surface so vividly and so compellingly that I acknowledge them as my route to a reconstruction of a world, to an exploration of an interior life that was not written and to the revelation of a kind of truth."[27] I think that memory serves a similar purpose for Cummings in *Chicken Soup* by allowing her to connect to women in her history and to participate in their worlds. Seeing her gossip in a chair or shake a skillet, I feel as if this is the first time as well as the hundredth time Cummings has gone back inside these images to merge past and present, dancing bits of stories from all these women's lives.

When Cummings introduced *Chicken Soup* during an informal lecture-demonstration at Franklin and Marshall College in the fall of 1987, she spoke of her interest in food and how she could guess someone's characteristics just by looking in their refrigerator. Cummings described *Chicken Soup* as a solo about women—many different women—who use food to nourish and connect to other people. Her intention was to make a dance that spanned a variety of cultures—Jewish, African-American, Italian—and that desire is reflected in her choice of texts, which include a piece by Grace Paley as well as a recipe from *The Settlement Cookbook*. In fact, however, when Cummings presented the work on television in the "Alive from Off Center" program during the summer of 1988, the cover of the *New York Times* "Television" section announced her work as a vision of "traditional roles of black women in America."[28] A curiously intrusive interference by the television producer had Cummings performing the dance in a generic Formica kitchen, wearing a housedress and a flowered apron. The effect, especially for someone who had seen the solo in a theater space, with no set and white costuming, is quite bizarre. The tacky television realism stages a very narrow definition of "traditional roles of black women in America," removing the wonderful ambivalence of Cummings's earlier version of this dance. Unlike the stage portrayal of this solo, where it is unclear whose memories she is dancing, the television production reduces this woman to a generic two-dimensional figure who is trapped in the specific context of her own spic-'n'-span kitchen.

Doubly inscribed (by the culture) as black and as a woman, Cummings must confront these multiple identities as she places her self-representation on the public stage. It would be as simplistic to assume that elementary addition— black plus woman equals black woman—creates a specific and singular identity as it would be to assume that Cummings can erase the signs of these social categories in her dancing. The publicity for this television show underscored how *Chicken Soup* is read as exploring a specifically black heritage. This insistence on viewing the dance only within one cultural tradition, the one referenced by her race, disturbs Cummings. In an interview, she spoke of wanting to sound a resonant note in everyone's background—to create a common memory.

What happens for me is that it [the sense of familiarity] stops when you start saying that you see me as a black person in the chair because then it might stop your ability to have it go back into your own background. Because if you see it as black and you're not black, then it seems to me you will not allow yourself the same liberty to identify with that character and then you start bringing all the references to a black person and why that makes that black.[29]

The issues of identification that Cummings touches on in this statement are rife with complexity. Self versus other, difference versus sameness, individuality versus community are indicative of polarities deeply rooted in this culture's social, political, and religious epistemologies. Cummings is caught in this sticky web of identifications, for although she claims she wants to create a "universal" image of a woman that anyone could relate to, she has also described with tears in her eyes the moving and self-affirming experience of dancing *Chicken Soup* for a predominantly black audience in the "Dance Black America" series at the Brooklyn Academy of Music. "Doing *Chicken Soup* was exciting. The opera house was packed. To do nontraditional dance and have black people say 'I truly understand' was wonderful. I thought, 'So this is what it's all about.' If I never have another moment like this again, it's been worth all the working."[30]

Cummings's relationship to the performance of her African-American identity shifts with the context of her performing. In other words, when there is a positive connection to be made, as in the Dance Black America program, when the condition of being black is expansive and not limiting, Cummings embraces the strategic essentialism of that identity. Within an evening-length dance program focused on the many varieties of dance forms coming out of the African-American heritage, Cummings's solo could be seen as encompassing one aspect of that multidimensional experience. But when she is touring or guest teaching at academic institutions around the country and the audience is predominantly white, Cummings seeks to transcend that category of difference, because she believes it will limit the audience's responsiveness to her work.

In her essay "Women's Autobiographical Selves: Theory and Practice," Susan Friedman critiques certain theoretical models of autobiography that are predicated on a singular self. "[T]he individual concept of the autobiographical self . . . raises serious theoretical problems for critics who recognize that the self, self-creation, and self-consciousness are profoundly different for women, minorities, and many non-Western peoples."[31] Because they are isolated and alienated from the powerful sense of "self" in a white patriarchal society, women and minorities, Friedman asserts, need to approach autobiography as a way of building another kind of identity with the raw materials of "interdependence" and "community." This sense of defining a selfhood in relationship to others is a concept that is strikingly absent from earlier visions of the autobiographical self. Friedman cites a variety of sources, from Nancy Chodorow on developmental identity to Regina Blackburn on African-American women's autobiography, that attest to and explain the "collective consciousness" of a "merged" identity of "the shared and the unique."[32] Although the dual consciousness discussed here originally arises negatively from a sense of marginalization or a feeling of oppression, it acquires power by connecting the individual to a group identity. It is important to realize, though, that this groupness is not a sameness. Zora Neale Hurston ironically illuminates this interconnection of "the shared and the unique" in a comment from her autobiographical work, *Dust Tracks on a Road*.

I maintain that I have been a Negro three times—a Negro baby, a Negro girl and a Negro woman. Still, if you have received no clear cut impression of what the Negro in America is like, then you are in the same place with me. There is no *The Negro* here. Our lives are so diversified, internal attitudes so varied, appearances and capabilities so different, that there is no possible classification so catholic that it will cover us all except My people! My people![33]

In Hurston's work, that group identity, while foundational, is nonetheless deconstructed, figured as evolving and therefore always in motion. This diacritical relationship to the markings of identity does not preclude a sense of selfhood, however; it simply re-presents it as a process rather than a product. As

Trinh T. Minh-ha so eloquently phrases the issue: "The challenge of the hyphenated reality lies in the hyphen itself: the *becoming* Asian-American; the realm inbetween, where predetermined rules cannot fully apply."[34]

Cummings, like many artists of color, is struggling to find a way to articulate the multicultural tapestry that informs her work. As I argued earlier, I believe that her use of the terms "universal" and "transcend" is very different from that of the feminist theorists whose work on autobiography has influenced my own thinking about autobiography. In these theories, the universal self transcends all racial, sexual, and class differences to assume that every subjectivity is made in his image—that his readers share (at least ideologically) the privilege of *not* having to account for their difference. But when Cummings uses these terms, she is turning assumptions of privilege upside down. I believe that Cummings doesn't want to cover over the fact of her difference as much as she wants to expand the commonality of certain human experiences beyond that difference. However, the fact that many critics still see *Chicken Soup* as about African-American women rather than as more general in scope, suggests that despite Cummings's efforts, the politics of the gaze that marks the white male body as universal and the black female body as "other" is quite difficult to dislodge. In order to deconstruct that binary dynamic, we need to explore issues not only of cultural subjectivity among women and minorities (sexual, racial, class, and ability minorities, that is), but also performances that include a parallel investigation by white men of embodied identity and cultural subjectivity. If, as so many theorists are quick to point out, white male identity has traditionally been predicated on a psychic disembodiment, then the body might just be the right place to begin to dismantle that privileged "I." Because of his willingness to cite his body as a locus of history, memory, and pain, Dorfman pierces through an overly self-satisfied demeanor, fundamentally changing the stakes of his (self-)representation.

David Dorfman was raised in a working-class Jewish suburb near Chicago. An athlete (he played baseball and football in high school), he began to take dancing seriously only after having graduated from college with an undergraduate degree in business. At the end of his brief biography in a recent program from a series of May 1996 performances at Dance Theater Workshop, Dorfman writes: "He would like to thank long-time mentors Martha Myers and Daniel Nagrin for taking a chance and rescuing him from counting leisure suits in St. Louis." The humor in this statement doesn't quite cover over the fact that, as a white man, he was expected to enter a very different realm than dance. After graduating from Connecticut College with a Master of Arts degree, Dorfman moved to New York City where he danced with Susan Marshall before establishing his own company in 1985. Although Dorfman's company is best known for its spectacular, rambunctious dancing, it is his autobiographical work that I find most compelling within the context of this book. I should note, however, that I am using the term "autobiographical" very loosely to include not only his solo works that use the autobiographical voice, but also his duets with Dan Froot (three to date), as well as his community pieces, including the latest, *Familiar Movements*, which is about family relationships.

Like Cummings, Dorfman weaves past memories into his present circumstances. And like Cummings, his solo work illuminates human situations and multicultural issues. However, unlike Cummings, whose chosen text wraps around her dancing like a silken shawl, Dorfman's verbal delivery is usually direct and often manic, as if speaking about his life opens a veritable floodgate of emotions. His autobiographical solos use performance strategies very different from those of Cummings's solo work: he publicly and obviously addresses the audience; he almost always faces out when speaking, and he inevitably uses the first-person autobiographical "I." There is no question in the audience's mind that he is performing himself, narrating true details from his life experience. Indeed, it is the immediacy of these experiences that is most often reflected in his performing persona. While Cummings's "Moving Picture" technique of stop-action motion helps her to essentialize the vibrancy of her dancing in timeless, archetypal images of women, Dorfman's frenetic and often bound physicality seizes the present moment to physically reenact a psychic state. Even when his narrative reflects a range of cultural situations and issues concerning love, loss, and survival (moving from the history of the Jewish people to the history of AIDS in America), Dorfman focuses on his personal reactions to these situations, using the first-person narrative to present transformative moments within his life history. Both Dorfman himself and reviewers have likened his verbal delivery to that of performance artist Spalding Gray. In Dorfman's performances, however, the privileged self-centeredness (which, in my opinion, completely defines Gray's work) is fractured by the compositional looping of kinesthetic action and verbal repetition, as well as by the strategic intertwining of the history of his body. Although Dorfman may begin his story in a straightforward manner, the unified subjectivity suggested by his confident "I" at the beginning of the piece unravels by the end, shredded by the "other" in himself.

While there are two people present throughout the dance, *Sleep Story* (1987) is essentially a solo that begins and ends with Dorfman running in place, talking. As he begins his story about visiting a Holocaust memorial in Eastern Europe, however, a tension is set up between his efforts to speak coherently and clearly enough to be understood by the audience and his breathing, which becomes increasingly audible as the dance progresses. To add to this bodily disruption, another dancer periodically slams into him, forcefully knocking him to the ground. This dancer crouches in the shadows next to him throughout the piece, unexpectedly interrupting his story midsentence by tackling him. At first, Dorfman agilely rolls back up to his feet after each attack, continuing the narrative exactly where he left off. Each blow brings in another bruising memory of absence, as his story interweaves a tale of past cultural loss (the Holocaust) with that of his own personal loss (Uncle Bob, his girlfriend) and the respective losses in his artistic and dance communities (his ballet teacher Ernie Pagnano, Willie Smith). As his body becomes physically more distressed, his memories become more entangled with one another. "The next day after that I was told my ballet teacher Ernie had died that Saturday before the Sunday we were at the sculpture." Eventually, these memories become overwhelming: "And I realized that no matter how long the story got there would always be another part yet to be uncovered and I had to find some way to break away, to break the spell, or I'd be telling this story the rest of my life." As if to break the spell, Dorfman gets knocked down more and more frequently, interrupting his history with the violence of each blow. Getting up becomes harder and harder as he segues from the contemporary deaths of his family and friends back to the Holocaust in a desperate litany of "And then I remembered that they weren't sleeping . . . And then I remembered that they aren't sleeping . . . And then I remembered that they weren't sleeping . . . And then I remembered that they aren't sleeping . . . weren't . . . aren't . . ."

Sleep Story hinges on the role of the storyteller as both historian and prophet, a role deeply rooted in Jewish culture. Like one of Isaac Bashevis Singer's characters, Dorfman tries to use the memory of the past to make sense of the present. Abruptly assaulted by each encounter with the past, however, he becomes physically and psychically overwhelmed with the experience of remembering loss. At the end of the dance, his narrative unwinds, his body becomes exhausted and yet running, still running, he marks the possibility of survival. This survival is not really a hopeful one, however, but rather a deadening, monotonous continuation. While *Chicken Soup* pulls at the seams of the subjective "I" by literally incorporating the historical bodies of women into a solo dance that bleeds beyond the tidy boundaries of self and other, *Sleep Story* implodes the stability of the "I" by giving voice to the devastating effect of past and present genocide. In *Chicken Soup*, Cummings becomes the one, becomes the many, bringing memory to life through her dancing body. *Sleep Story*, on the other hand, refuses the nostalgia of memory in the face of present losses. Dorfman's body cannot recreate life out of the devastation of his religious and artistic communities, and he gets caught in the existential treadmill of "weren't sleeping . . . aren't sleeping . . . weren't . . . aren't . . ."

In *Sleep Story*, although his narrative spreads across time and space, Dorfman's body remains in the present. His text consciously recognizes the shared history of Jewish persecution, and through that memory, through the connections to his own bodily history, he remembers (and recounts) the contemporary loss of life as the result of AIDS. This history of absence is evoked through his narrative, which is permeated by the lives and deaths of other people. His body, however, resists these connections. Doggedly getting up again and again to keep on running, Dorfman closes the pores of his skin, physically refusing to deal with the interconnected memories that pour out of his mouth. This is the central contradiction in the work, and it sets up a dramatic tension not only within his performative presence, but also within the audience's bodies. (The sigh of relief when the lights finally go down on this short solo is palpable.)

At the end of her introduction to *Subjectivity, Identity and the Body*, Sidonie Smith lists a series of intriguing questions about the relationship of the writer to her body—questions that I find equally provocative for a study of autobiography in dance.

Whose history of the body is being written? What specific body does the autobiographical subject claim in her text? . . . Does the body drop away as a location of autobiographical identity, or does the speaker insist on its founding identification? What are the implications for subjectivity of the body's positioning? How is the body the performative boundary between inner and outer, the subject and the world? . . . Is the body a source of subversive practice, a potentially emancipatory vehicle for autobiographical practice, or a source of repression and suppressed narrative?[35]

Although Smith must tease out the body from the textual examples that form the basis of her book, in dance that body is already visible. Nonetheless, the question of how a performer claims her or his bodily history is indeed critical in framing the autobiographical subject. In *Chicken Soup* and *Sleep Story*, Cummings and Dorfman create autobiographical works based on emotional moments that resonate among us all. Marking the human continuum of life and death, joy and grief, their bodies become channels for shared experiences. Yet, neither of these pieces actually claims to be the particularized (and contradictory) bodily history of the autobiographical subject. Interestingly enough,

Dancing Bodies and the Stories They Tell

both Cummings and Dorfman have made work that figures much more specifically the material circumstances of their bodies.

In 1986, Cummings created another solo that presents the physical antithesis of the satisfying and solid characters in *Chicken Soup*. It also is marked by
an existential loneliness similar to that of *Sleep Story*. "Blues II" is the last section of a larger work, *Basic Strategies V*, a dance that explores how people deal
with money and work. Although I want to concentrate on the complicated
images in her solo, I will take some time to sketch in the first part of the dance,
for it sets up many of the double readings within her solo. Originally commissioned by Williams College and the Massachusetts Council on the Art and
Humanities, *Basic Strategies V* is a collaboration with the writer Jamaica Kincaid and composer Michael Riesman. In what Cummings terms her process of
"collage," this work layers sets, costumes, music, taped texts, and movement to
create multiple references to self and community. Unlike *Chicken Soup*, however, *Basic Strategies V* uses the texts, sets, and costumes not as background accompaniment for the dancing, but rather as primary elements that create the
basic irony and dramatic tension of the piece.

The remarkable text by Kincaid, who was born in St. John's, Antigua, focuses the dancing in the first group section. The fluid and rhythmic carrying,
pushing, pulling movements are juxtaposed to a story (spoken by a soft woman's voice) that braids a history of her people with a history of an Anglican
colonial cathedral. The slaves built this cathedral for their masters, but now
the descendants of both the slaves and their masters worship there. Noting the
ambiguity of her history, the narrator's liquid voice on the soundtrack loops
back on itself repeatedly: "My history before it was interrupted does not include cathedrals. What my history before it was interrupted includes is no
longer absolutely clear to me. The cathedral is now a part of my history. The
cathedral is now a part of me. The cathedral is now mine."[36] It is never entirely clear how the story of the cathedral relates to the dancing on stage. This
section, subtitled "Blues I," is cast in a cool, blue light with a large, luminous
moon in the background. Dressed in nondescript dance clothes, Cummings's
dancers move back and forth across the stage, low to the ground, squatting or
walking, their movements seeming to serve as background texture for Kincaid's words. Toward the end, a recognizable character of an elder crosses the
stage, gradually growing more and more hunched over with each small, shuffling step.

During a brief interlude, Kincaid's second text begins. Although it is read
by the same smooth voice, this one is much less personal and describes with
encyclopedic detail the habitat, production, and reproduction of the silkworm.

Coming after the storytelling intimacy of the first section, this new factual tone strikes an odd, almost dissonant chord. Reading like an article from *National Geographic*, the information seems tame enough, if somewhat irrelevant. As the interlude finishes and Cummings's solo begins, however, the context changes and the spoken text transforms into a series of metacomments on the politics of colonial enterprise, cheap third-world labor, and the production of Western luxuries.

At the beginning of her solo section, subtitled "Blues II," the lights fade up gradually to reveal a statuesque Cummings wearing a shimmering black evening gown and cape. Slowly raising and lowering a champagne bottle and fluted glass, she turns in a curiously disembodied and vague manner, as if she were a revolving decoration in the middle of the ballroom floor. Her impassive face and glittering dress are reflected in the large mirrors that fan out to either side of her. Functioning as a kind of *huis clos*, these mirrors confine her movements, meeting each change of direction with multiple reflections of her body. Sometimes Cummings moves with proud, grandiose strides, covering the space with a confident territoriality. Other times, she seems possessed, pacing the floor in this prison of mirrors only to meet up with another reflection of the woman she wants—was intended—to become.

On one level, these mirrors function as reflections of common cultural representations of women. Glamorous in the evening gown that connotes a romantic lifestyle and independent income, Cummings's many mirrored figures are visually more enticing than the body they reflect. In a way Cummings seduces the viewers through these images in order to disrupt our visual pleasure and, presumably, the economy that supports it. For instance, in the midst of a waltzy section where she is swirling around the stage, she abruptly drops to her knees and, drawing her skirt over her face, begs for money. This split-second transformation of her body from ease to despair and back again reminds the viewer of the fragility of that seductive world. This early fracture is quickly smoothed over by the romantic music and Cummings's lyrical dancing. But the crack in the illusion widens as slides are projected on a screen above her head. Alternating images of third-world famine refugees with Western signs of wealth and power (e.g., Ralph Lauren advertisements), these slides throw Cummings's whole persona into question. Is she attempting to buy into these white, patriarchal images? Is she happy? Or is this whole scenario a tragic pretense? At this point in the solo, Cummings launches into an energetic stream of repetitive actions that pull her back and forth across the stage. The lively rhythm of her feet and hand gestures soon borders on mania as the tranquillity of the earlier dancing gives way to a literal dis-ease with the

Dancing Bodies and the Stories They Tell

Blondell Cummings. Photo by Cherry Kim.

costume. Eventually, she takes off the black dress and in the closing moments of the dancing she sits on a chair in her underwear, restlessly gesturing and pointing, in an effort to "speak" her tangled emotions.

Seen within the context of Kincaid's texts and the slides, the apparent glamor of Cummings's persona is undercut by the insistent issues of race, class, and gender. The pristine image of self-involvement—the private satisfaction initially projected by the mirrored glittering gown, champagne bottle, and solipsistic dancing—is clouded by the recognition that both idealistic (advertising) and realistic (photojournalism) images pervade the very fabric of our consciousness. Confronted at every turn with the cultural reflections of who she is, the woman in "Blues II" is fragmented into a series of confusing and conflicting images.

Once the gown, with all that it represents, has been taken off near the end of this solo, the persistent question of "Who am I?" remains for the character. Although Cummings intended that this disrobing should suggest a symbolic stripping away of cultural masks to reveal basic human needs and emotions, there is little sense of resolution or closure. Amid the bombardment of media images, the woman without the dress is still tragically searching for a single identity that fits. Restlessly turning her head, or bent over with an extreme expression of pain, she tries on the very same gestures of hugging, talking, and rocking a baby that seemed so solidly soothing in *Chicken Soup*. Yet in this new context, these movements are not quite so comfortable, and the woman onstage flits through a seemingly endless succession of gestural memories until finally the music stops and the lights fade out.

These two solos, *Chicken Soup* and "Blues II," enact a struggle also found in many contemporary women's autobiographies. In *Chicken Soup*, the body is represented as the condition of the self, the place from which memories arise. The still, photographic images of the first tableau and the vague reminiscences of the voice provide a setting suggestive of a women's community. Gestures of rocking a baby, cooking and eating, waving good-bye, and grieving are consciously portrayed in a way that affirms belief in their universality—in the archetypal engagement of women in community. In this dance, the body is opened up very wide and presented as a well of remembering and knowing. In "Blues II," however, the dancing figure is less comfortable with her embodiment. Although some of the movements are similar to *Chicken Soup*, an increasingly restless quality in their motion creates a sense that this female character would like to escape her own skin. Surrounded at every turn by reflections of her body that she is unable to control or escape and that insistently clash with one another, with the slides and with the soundtrack, this woman seeks to disengage her body from these pervasive images by taking off her gown. Yet, black and female, her body has been "written" over in so many ways by these background images of black women in her culture that it is still difficult to find an "original" signature.

The ability to tell one story is missing in "Blues II." The gowned woman in this dance is at once connected to and disconnected from the many narratives suggested by the visual images and Kincaid's texts. Because her body is a figurative screen for the contradictory meanings of these visual images and the powers that control their representation, it is impossible for her to find a convenient identity or a comfortable way of moving. Physically dwarfed by the mirrors and the slides, the woman drifts through this mélange of cultural representations like a ghost through a maze. The mirrors amplify her spatial (and psychological) disorientation, reflecting and fragmenting the visual definition of her self. As a result, her internal physical equilibrium is disrupted and she either floats aimlessly about the stage or rushes frantically from one reflected image to another in a bewildered attempt to find one that looks right. Whether she is physically inert or psychically distraught, the dancing seems to be compelled by a restless searching for a visually and physically satisfying self. Wresting the power of seduction and colonialization from the media images projected above her head, Cummings shows not only the cracks and flaws in these cellophane narratives, but also the possibility of other stories emerging from their gaps. Even when she rejects the "lie" of the dress, even when she takes off the costume of "high" culture, there is no reassuringly "natural" body underneath it all. Her disrobed figure at the end of "Blues II" has refused the fantasy of capitalist consumer culture, but has nothing with which to replace that fantasy, and the dance ends without closure, extending its ambivalence past the final curtain.

Even though "Blues II" is not a factually accurate account of Cummings's life history, and even though she never claims the personal "I" of the narrator's voice-over, this solo still reads, I would argue, autobiographically. Pulled back and forth between the images in the mirror and those of the screen, Cummings's body searches for the right history, the right place, the right movements. Witnessing her discomfort as she fails to find the right fit, the audience must negotiate its own relationship with these images of luxury and poverty, seduction and despair, desire and disease. In a similar manner, Dorfman's solo *Out of Season or Eating Pizza While Watching "Raging Bull"* asks the audience to negotiate its own contradictions as it witnesses his autobiographical recitation. I first saw this solo during the St. Mark's Danspace's December 1992 benefit, "Amazing Grace." Billed as a work-in-progress, this version of *Out of Season* starts as an autobiographical monologue about Dorfman's mother's death and his subsequent weight gain, and quickly unravels into a series of free associations interspersing pop images (disco lives!) with the more jagged-edged truths of interracial relationships, the erotics of homosocial bonding, and the realities of human suffering. Although Dorfman has worked this solo into a mini-epic and has performed it in various venues over the last several years, it remains one of his most challenging works to perform, most likely because it repeatedly positions his body as a visual display.

Dorfman first appears, after having tackled the person who introduced him, walking noisily over to the mike centerstage. He is dressed only in briefs and a jock strap, with a plastic crash helmet on his head and football shoulder pads, kneepads, and several other helmets attached to his hips. This weird outfit makes his large frame look even bulkier, and as he stares unprepossessingly out to the audience, he looks as if he has wandered into the wrong place. "Shall I?" he asks the audience in the tone of the master of ceremonies he has

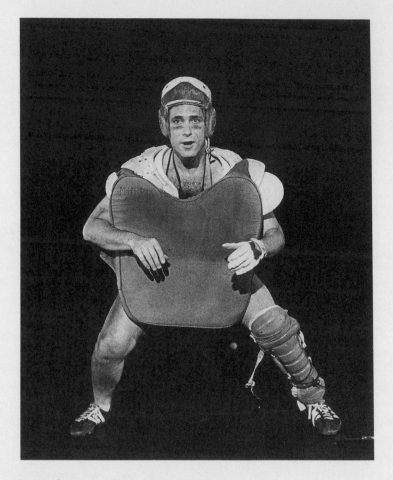

David Dorfman in *Out of Season*. Photo by Tom Brazil.

always wanted to be. As he prepares to become Superman, he pulls the helmet on his waist around to cover his crotch. But the strongman act is limp today, no longer carrying the mythic potency that it once had in the 1950s. Dorfman falters almost before he has begun. "They killed me and I don't even know why," he says with fake innocence, clearly knowing full well why Superman has succumbed. "Is this an omen for the white presumably heterosexual man?" This last statement garners a handful of knowing laughs. Textually it is unclear whether this is simply another "Oh, we are so oppressed" wail of the men's movement, or a serious inquiry into the fragility of white male privilege. His body, however, intersects with this comment, giving the viewer the sense that

Dorfman is not politically innocent here. His tongue-in-cheek tone, sly glances at the audience, and ridiculous outfit clearly offer a parodic commentary on his text. After launching into a battery of drill-like movements that slams his body into the floor and dishevels his armor, Dorfman rises almost apologetically from the ground, adjusts his padding, and steps over to the mike to continue his monologue: "I most enjoy talking to you about the intimate details of my life from behind the microphone."

What follows is an autobiographical sketch of several male friendships, hinting at an erotic undercurrent. Dorfman foregrounds his youthful naiveté ("I wasn't sure what he was asking"), as well as his ambivalence (he repeatedly uses the term "presumably" heterosexual as if to throw that category into question). Of course, Dorfman always reassures his audience that he didn't ever *do* anything with these various men (his identity isn't that much up for grabs), but then he immediately follows this pronouncement of his homosexual chastity with stories of his love for disco and dancing. What's an audience to think? Suddenly we realize that his crotch helmet is much more than a phallic signifier; it becomes, along with the Superman myth and the jock scene, a piece of armor (a chastity cup?) that keeps other men out. Although this section does crack the veneer of the self-assured "I," it does so rather flippantly, glossing over the ambiguity of desire with a reassuring pat of the helmet in question. A deeper fissure is yet to come, however.

Once he has narrated his transformation into a dancer by demonstrating his best disco steps, Dorfman steps out of the limelight to approach the tender subject of weight. "You know, I didn't always look like this . . . I wasn't always so well-equipped . . . I actually used to be a slim and trim and fit dancer, I have the pictures to prove it." By now, Dorfman is back in front of the microphone, his amplified veil of performative security. He continues: "I just lied again. Don't you love those words—slim and trim and fit? I love them so much I could just strangle them." Dorfman proceeds to tell us how he gained weight after an injury that not so coincidentally came soon after the death of his mother. He leaves this issue unexplored, however, and moves into his final litany: I care about your future, I care about your nurture, I care about your nature, I care about your torture . . . I care about your love."

I was profoundly intrigued by this last autobiographical section of the dance because of Dorfman's willingness to address his body image on stage. With few exceptions, this issue has been confined to the province of "hysterical" female performance artists like Karen Finley, and it is significant, I believe, to see white men grapple with the implications of their own embodiment. As we have witnessed throughout the discussions of identity and the body within the context of this book, traditional Western conceptions of the self refuse the specifics of that messy experience of the body. In her book *Volatile Bodies: Towards a Corporeal Feminism*, Elizabeth Grosz turns the tables on these categories by suggesting that "Alterity is the very possibility and process of embodiment."[37] In this solo, Dorfman deconstructs, among others, the contemporary icons of the classical, athletically "fit" body by foregrounding the punishing obsessiveness of masculine competition. But Dorfman is not only willing to "expose" his corporeality, he intentionally frames his body within the fleshiness of his somatic experience. Although his body is not inscribed by the culture in the same way that Cummings's is, Dorfman uses his persona in *Out of Season* to reveal the ways that his body is, in fact, marked by his emotional experiences, including his fledgling homosexual desire and his mother's death. Given that male bodies are culturally constructed as metaphoric battlements, fortresses against any form of invasion (be it disease, emotions, etc.), Dorfman's deliberate unmasking of masculinity (in a wonderful parody of castration anxiety, he literally wears the ultimate mask—the football helmet—on his crotch) transforms the bodily ground of his speaking "I."[38]

It's his body that speaks most profoundly in another solo about death and loss, *Dayenu*. Referring to the Passover song, Dorfman explains its meaning at the beginning of the dance: "After each of the wondrous deeds that the Lord did for the Hebrews in their wanderings, if the Lord had done no more, it would have been enough." But in Dorfman's solo, this grateful sense of "enough" takes on a reverse, militant meaning, for "It's not enough." In an interview with Iris M. Fanger for a profile on his company in the April 1992 *Dance Magazine*, Dorfman relates the origins of the piece, in a text he wrote after witnessing the 1991 "Day without Art" vigil in New York City. Echoing the dance's final litany, he comments: "It's not 'enough' to have a loved one taken away, and it's not 'enough' to get just a certain amount of government funding for AIDS research. . . . I don't want to settle. I want to remember that it's not enough."[39] Although it was motivated, in part, by his frustration with political agendas that allow so many to die, *Dayenu* also touches obliquely upon a personal subtext, the death of his mother. While his speaking voice is generally confined to a public, manifestoesque tone, Dorfman's body in this solo absorbs the softer underbelly of his feelings, representing a hesistancy and vulnerability that creates a very different presence from his speaking self.

Dayenu begins as a warm pool of light gradually surrounds Dorfman, who is upside down in a shoulder stand, his head tilted uncomfortably to one side, his cheek smashed into the floor. He begins speaking: "This is a church. And somewhere in the stained glass windows is a Star of David, and Christmas

David Dorfman in *Dayenu*.
Photo © Beatriz Schiller
1997.

trees. And I'm a David." Among the odd assortment of secular and religious
holidays he mentions Passover and the story of "Dayenu," of how "it would
have been enough" each time. He pauses briefly, and then speaks again: "And
what I'll do now has nothing to do with what I've just said." The audience
chuckles at this last remark, unaware of where he is heading. But an odd quiet
quickly takes a hold of the space as Dorfman rears his head in a silent scream.
He crouches down like an animal, ritualistically facing all four directions,
arching his head back into this silent scream with each new change of facing.
Slowly he closes his mouth and stands up. For the first time, the audience recognizes him as a man dressed in a suit and a tie. That image of poise and assur-
ance never really gels, however, for a current of motion leads him shuffling
frantically, like a young child who is overeager to finish his first recital, across
the space.

Once on the other side of the room, he reaches back, as if trying to recap-
ture something lost. His body seems to get stuck in this peculiar knock-kneed

position, and he is forced to walk back in a stiff, painful manner. His out-stretched hand loses its reason for being there, and yet oddly enough he doesn't drop it. Crumpled, it nonetheless remains stuck out in front of his body, like a molted snakeskin left vacant when the living thing moves on. When he finally arrives back at his original spot, he swings his whole body at once, and then stiffly, bit by bit, brings his arm back to his side. In this striking sequence, the audience can see him leave that other body (his mother's?) and return to his own. Once again, however, his own body has no stability, can't hold up, and immediately he is off, shuffling across the floor. Eventually, he returns to speaking, breaking the poignant silence with "And what I'll say now has everything to do with what I just did."

In *Dayenu*, Dorfman's body carries the narrative beyond a simple illustration of or commentary on his verbal text. Although he still looks directly at the audience while he is speaking, much of the emotional power in *Dayenu* comes during the moments of silence, the places in the dance when what he does next has everything and nothing to do with what he's just said. Part of this dramatic tension comes from the complexity of his own history, the desire to acknowledge his mother while at the same time distancing himself from the devotional faith that structured her existence. In this solo, Dorfman allows the memories and experiences of other people's deaths to affect his own body, accepting the fact that the history of his body includes others.

When Dorfman talks about his autobiographical work, he uses the term "universal" to suggest that, while he deals with the particulars of his life experience, the themes of competition, loss, love, and body image that he touches upon are significant issues in many people's lives. Although Dorfman's social positionality is different from Cummings's, he is acutely aware of issues of difference (his Jewish heritage is undoubtedly a significant factor in this awareness) and shares her sense of the universal as interconnected rather than homogenous. When these choreographers work autobiographically, they are conscious of finding the intersections between their lives and personal issues and those of others. As Cummings makes quite clear in an interview with Veta Goler, the personal content of her work is meant to speak across difference as well.

When I do solo work, I am acting as the voice of the internal self. But that doesn't exclude the fact that that internal self has a desire to share with other internal selves. And that is part of the aesthetic experience that I hope to present, whether I'm doing a solo, which is dealing with the internal voice and the identity of a self, or a group piece, which brings together many people and many individual selves. To me, both are a kind of community, or an act of community. That's what I'm constantly exploring in my work. I'm trying to open out those options for individuals to define their own identities. I'm also exploring my own options. I'm investigating what that is about, as an artist, as a woman, as an African American, as a dog-owner, as a neighbor that lives in my house, on my block, on the upper East Side. These are all different communities, and they're all a part of who I am. Hopefully, in that act of sharing, people get a sense of community, and get to define community in a way that we haven't defined it before.[40]

Autobiography as an act of community. Although on the surface this may seem like a contradiction in terms, in fact, autobiography has long served as an act of community. Giving testimony and bearing witness by recounting one's life experiences has helped marginalized communities hold onto the experience of their own bodies while reclaiming their history. In the next chapter, I explore what happens when this history of a body, which we call autobiography, becomes the history of a people.

Embodying History

Epic Narrative

and Cultural Identity

in African-American Dance

What would it mean to reinscribe history through one's body? What would it mean to recreate the story of a life and the history of a people? How does one rewrite the history of slavery, the history of faith, the history of a past, in order to project the story of our future? How can we reenvision the historical legacies of our time through the eyes of hope and human survival instead of rage and cynicism?

These questions guide my reflections on a genre of contemporary performance that I call the New Epic Dance. Over the past seven years, I have witnessed full evening-length dance/dramas by choreographers as diverse as Garth Fagan, David Rousseve, Jawole Willa Jo Zollar, and Bill T. Jones. These works explore various facets of African-American cultural heritages, refiguring written history in order to embody a tale of the choreographer's own making.[1] I am particularly interested in how these theatrical dances both enact and re-work mythic and historical images of slavery, colonial power, and religious faith within a contemporary parable that allows individual dancers to infuse the story with their own histories and physicalities. Using dance as a metaphor for the physical desire to survive and the metaphysical need to fill that survival with hope, these choreographers have, with the help of their collaborators and companies, created theatrical spectacles that evoke the elegiac as well as the celebratory spirit of a people wedged in between two worlds. In many ways, these epic works remind me of the term that Audre Lorde used to describe her autobiographical work "Zami: A New Spelling of My Name." Grounded in, but not limited to, the historical facts of a people's existence, these epic dance narratives weave what Lorde calls a "biomythography," elaborating visionary sagas of social and personal survival.

The creation of an individual life narrative, the (auto)biography, which I explored in my previous chapter, is expanded in the New Epic Dance to include expressions of cultural identity that call upon mythic and archetypal, as well as historical, images of African-Americans. Works such as Garth Fagan's *Griot New York*, David Rousseve's *Urban Scenes/Creole Dreams*, Urban Bush Women's *Bones and Ash: A Gilda Story*, and Bill T. Jones's *Last Supper at Uncle Tom's Cabin/The Promised Land* focus on the collective survival stories of African peoples in America. Because of their narrative scope, which is to say their desire not only to remember the past and document the present but also to narrate future possibilities, as well as their ambitious integration of dance, song, and theatrical text within a full evening-length performance, these works are clearly epic in scale. There is, of course, a crucial distinction between the traditional Western Homeric epic and these late twentieth-century revisitations of that densely layered form of narrative. Traditional epics tend, generally, to celebrate conquest and the lives of warrior statesmen. By contrast, these contemporary African-American epics celebrate and honor the legacy of a people who have survived conquest; heroism is located not in the defeater, but rather in the spirit of those who have refused to be defeated.

In order to be effectively and potently embodied in performance, history has to be recast, so to speak—situated in a different light and taken up by different bodies. The importance of history here is not the importance of historical fact or artifact; such documents, authorized in the service of white dominance, are rightfully suspect. Rather, history for so many African-Americans is located in the story—in the telling again and again. This retelling of ancestral blood memories is the compelling force behind much of the New Epic Dance. For stories to be historically meaningful, however, they need two things: a sense of truth (which, while it does not need to be static, must be galvanizing); and a sense of community between speakers and listeners, a realization of what is at stake in this exchange of the word. In her essay "The Site of Memory," Toni Morrison draws a distinction between "truth" and "fact."

Therefore the crucial distinction for me is not the difference between fact and fiction, but the distinction between fact and truth. Because facts can exist without human intelligence, but truth cannot. So if I'm looking to find and expose a truth about the interior life of people who didn't write it (which doesn't mean that they didn't have it); if I'm trying to fill in the blanks that the slave narratives left—to part the veil that was so frequently drawn, to implement the stories that I heard—then the approach that's most productive and most trustworthy for me is the recollection that moves from the image to the text. Not from the text to the image.[2]

I believe that this distinction is vital in that it helps us to recognize the spiritual power of what Lorde call "biomythography"—that is, the recreation of history as myth, as tales that embody common ideals. "Truth," as opposed to "fact" gives these (hi)stories an activating spiritual force that is so crucial, particularly in communities faced with the awesome task of rewriting their own subjectivity back into the tales of history. What is important for Morrison is not the primacy of historical text, but the potency of the embodied image. History is written about past events. Stories are told in order to connect the knowledge of the past and hopes for the future with one's experiences of present realities. In this way, history can be refigured as a living continuum rather than as chronologically dated events. This redeployment of history is predicated on a collective consciousness of cultural identity—a sense of self that is connected to a sense of one's people. (This is, needless to say, rarely a conflict-free connection.)

In her chapter on the power of storytelling at the end of *Woman, Native, Other*, Trinh T. Minh-ha begins her discussion of "Truth and Fact: Story and History" with "Let me tell you a story," and goes on to tell her readers a story about remembering, truth, and community. "The story depends upon every one of us to come into being. It needs us all, needs our remembering, understanding, and creating what we have heard together to keep on coming into being. The story of a people. Of us, peoples. Story, history, literature (or religion, philosophy, natural science, ethics)—all in one."[3] Although there are some people who, along with my *American Heritage Dictionary*, still equate truth with fact and "fidelity to an original," many of us recognize that truths need to be creative rather than static. For truth must be the beginning of action, not simply its consequence or fate. Thus Minh-ha continues: "Truth is when it is itself no longer. Diseuse, Thought-Woman, SpiderWoman, griotte, storytalker, fortune-teller, witch. If you have the patience to listen, she will delight in relating it to you. An entire history, an entire vision of the world, a lifetime story. . . . To listen carefully is to preserve. But to preserve is to burn, for understanding means creating."[4] It is this creative element in retelling the story that makes this history—the history of peoples and their stories rather than the history of facts—inherently performative. For the telling has a listener and the listener's reality affects the cadence and the "truth" of the telling. Of course, before the West became so enamored with writing history, epics were oral performances and so their "truths" necessarily evolved as they passed from mouth to mouth through generation and region.

The genre of contemporary African-American performance that I am defining as the New Epic Dance is staged in Jones's and Zollar's work as a collective biomythography. These dance/dramas combine music, dance, and text to present a revised history that plays with the tropes of ironic repetition, reenactment, and reinterpretation. While all the works I have mentioned deserve in-depth discussion, the limitations of time and space, as well as my desire not to treat these important works in a cursory fashion, have prompted me to confine my extended analysis to two works: Bill T. Jones and Arnie Zane Dance Company's *Last Supper at Uncle Tom's Cabin/The Promised Land* (1990), and Urban Bush Women's *Bones and Ash: A Gilda Story* (1995–1996). I have chosen these two performative epics to compare because they provide a very different kind of theatrical experience for the audience, foregrounding the representation of race, memory, and historical experience in ways that ask their viewers to engage with their own historical memories. Although these two works look and feel very different from one another, they are both animated by a visionary sensibility that seeks to reform the legendary evils of greed and the lust for power in order to create a new infrastructure of social interaction. Both works refuse our contemporary cynicism, meeting a fin-de-siècle hopelessness with a conviction that humanity can be reborn. And both works are, I believe, deeply feminist in spirit, if not always in detail. The complex interweaving of oral, danced, and theatrical texts in *Last Supper* and *Bones and Ash* documents our national legacy of interracial hate and gendered and ethnic inequalities. Yet this very bleak history is enriched by personal narratives of love, religious faith, and spiritual transcendence. By reinterpreting classic stories and cultural stereotypes through contemporary dancing bodies, both Jones and Zollar refuse the static doneness of historical documentation, lifting the black and white printing off the page and imbuing it with the ability to move, shift, and, finally, to transform itself.

In this chain and continuum, I am but one link. The story is me, neither me nor mine. It does not really belong to me, and while I feel greatly responsible for it, I also enjoy the irresponsibility of the pleasure obtained through the process of transferring. Pleasure in the copy, pleasure in the reproduction. No repetition can ever be identical, but my story carries with it their stories, their history, and our story repeats itself endlessly despite our persistence in denying it.[5]

These words by Minh-ha begin the story of my telling, my witnessing. For in the context of this book, I am the conduit—the speaker who translates—

these epic performances for a reading public. The dances I have seen have influenced how I think, how I see. Taken in and witnessed through my body, they come alive through my language and my ideas. Unfortunately, most people will not have had the opportunity to see these works for themselves and so my writing may be the only exposure they have to these epic dances. This is, indeed, a great responsibility. Thus I want to be clear about how I, a white, feminist dancer and writer negotiate the position of witness and critic here. My experiences with these works may well be different from other dance writers, particularly African-American dance critics. Yet while I acknowledge the potency of experiences of racism and my privilege in this regard, I do not believe that this difference invalidates my perception, nor do I believe that I can't write about African-American performance in a way that is both cognizant of this difference and informed by a knowledge of that cultural perspective. In other words, while I would never pretend to have an "insider's" viewpoint, neither will I be satisfied with claiming my outside status as a way of refusing responsibility for representing this very important work. Being white is no excuse for not making the effort to learn about and come to understand the complexities and multiple layers of meaning in contemporary African-American epic dance.[6]

In his inspiring book *Negotiating Difference: Race, Gender and the Politics of Positionality*, Michael Awkward takes up the negotiations of power that are inherent in white critics' writing about black texts. Awkward is a professor of English and so his examples come mostly from literature, yet his careful delineation of a critical position that could both register the racial privilege inherent in white criticism and also recognize what he calls the possiblity of "interpretive crossing-over" can provide an important example of conscious criticism for cultural critics involved with any form of cultural production. In his chapter "Negotiations of Power: White Critics, Black Texts, and the Self-Referential Impulse," Awkward analyzes various interpretive positions across the continuum of white criticism of African-American literature. While many white critics still approach African-American literature in purely formal Euro-aesthetic terms, as (to use Houston Baker's term) "superordinate authorities," Awkward argues for the possiblity of other kinds of readings. "I want to emphasize my belief that neither a view of an essential incompatibility between black literature and white critics nor of whites as always already dismissive and unsophisticated in their analyses of the products of the Afro-American imagination is still tenable."[7] Awkward later uses Larry Neal's discussions of white critical practices to suggest the possibility of a "thick" reading that reflects "some understanding of [black] cultural source."[8] For Awkward, race is as much a political ideology and commitment as it is an essential or biological fact.

For Neal, critical competence with respect to Afro-American expressivity is determined not by tribal connections into which one is born; rather, it is gained by academic activity—"by studying"—in the same way that one achieves comprehension of the cultural matrices that inform the work of writers like Joyce, Yeats, and e.e. cummings. Demystifying the process of acquiring an informed knowledge of Afro-American expressivity, Neal insists that the means of access for all critics, regardless, of race, is an energetic investigation of the cultural situation and the emerging critical tradition.[9]

My chapter on African-American epic performance is compelled by the conviction that this work is too important not to deal with, even if that means taking a risk by putting myself in a less comfortable critical position. Because I am a dancer and a theorist who is concerned about the fate of material bodies at the end of the twentieth century, I want to expand Neal's notion of "studying" to include not only book work, but also the physical situatedness of a culture—that is to say, investigating the ways African-American bodies live, move, perform, tell stories, walk, etc. Although issues of racial difference have greatly influenced academic discourse over the past two decades, too often these discussions of "race" or "difference" remain purely abstract, content to stay in the comfort of armchairs and ivory towers. I believe, however, that there is a crucial difference between merely talking about "attention to diversity" and actually committing oneself to a critical and personal engagement that recognizes and connects with the power and variety of African-American expressivity. I quoted Minh-ha earlier because I felt that her elaboration of the continuum and transmission of culture at once recognizes the differences between "I" and "they" ("No repetition can ever be identical") and sees the interconnectedness, the "our" ("but my story carries with it their stories, their history, and our story repeats itself"). It is with a recognition of this difference, in tandem with the belief that this difference can produce a viable critical engagement, that I continue.

*Re*writing, *re*inscribing, *re*creating, *re*envisioning, *re*figuring, *re*framing, *re*incorporating, *re*interpreting, *re*presenting—the reader will no doubt have noticed the frequency with which I have used the prefix *re* so far. This is not merely a poststructuralist tic of mine. The act of going back to take up again —returning, reclaiming, repossessing—this is a strategy that is central to contemporary African-American performance. Adrienne Rich once described this process as "re-vision—the act of looking back, of seeing with fresh eyes, of entering an old text from a new critical direction."[10] Nowhere is this device more provocatively explored than in the first section of Jones's *Last Supper at Uncle Tom's Cabin/The Promised Land*. Here, Jones both reenacts the sentimentalized Christian ethos of salvation embedded in Harriet Beecher Stowe's 1852 novel *Uncle Tom's Cabin*, and deconstructs the racist stereotypes connected to the popularized minstrel versions of that abolitionist story. At once fragmenting and reinventing the tropes of blackface, the family, religious faith, womanhood, slavery, and "Uncle Toms," Jones outlines the ambivalent relationship his dancers have with those historical characters. Employing theatrical devices to foreground the performance of racial and gendered stereotypes, Jones indicates the contradictory closeness and distance—the similarities and the differences—between then and now.

Prompted by the inhumanity of the Fugitive Slave Act of 1850, which required all American citizens (both northern and southern) to return runaway slaves to their legal owners, as well as by her sister-in-law's exhortations to use her literary talents in the service of abolitionism, Harriet Beecher Stowe wrote *Uncle Tom's Cabin* in serial installments for an antislavery newspaper, *The National Era*. In 1852, the novel was published by a small press in Boston, and it proceeded to sell more copies than any other book in the world at that time, excepting the Bible. *Uncle Tom's Cabin* quickly entered the national discourse, as the character of Uncle Tom was taken up by both the North and the South, at once reified as a saint (indeed a veritable black Christ) and villified as a traitor to his race. In a capitalist coup of marketing that would make even Disney proud, the figure of Uncle Tom proliferated within the growing industries of novelty consumerism and commodity culture, not to mention the wildfire of popular performance. Even before the novel was published in its final form, there was already a theatrical version in repertory, and there is speculation that for every one person who read the novel, fifty people saw the play in some form or another. The absence of copyright laws, in addition to the extensive network of small regional and traveling theater companies, paved the way for the hundreds of versions of Stowe's novel that dominated local and national stages over the next half-century. The ubiquity with which versions of *Uncle Tom's Cabin* saturated antebellum America is evoked by Richard Yarborough when he details how:

Not only was a children's version of *Uncle Tom's Cabin* issued in 1853 . . . , but within a year there also appeared "Uncle Tom and Little Eva," a parlor game "played with pawns that represented 'the continual separation and reunion of families.'" In fact, Stowe's best-seller inspired a veritable flood of Uncle Tom poems, songs, dioramas, plates, busts, embossed spoons, painted scarves, engravings, and other miscellaneous memorabilia, leading one wry commentator to observe [that Uncle Tom] became, in his various forms, the most frequently sold slave in American history.[11]

Tracing the various literary and performative histories of *Uncle Tom's Cabin* in antebellem America is a daunting task to say the least, and it is certainly not within the scope of this study to include an extensive analysis of how the character of Uncle Tom changed over the years. Nonetheless, it is important to note that, unlike the folk images that tend to picture an "Uncle Tom" as an old, passive, southern darkie who is perfectly happy serving his white master, Stowe's Uncle Tom is a young, strong, vibrant man who assumes a leadership role within whatever community he finds himself. Although his behavior toward his various masters is shaped by a Christian saintliness and maternal concern for these white souls, it is his final act of resistance to white authority—his refusal to betray another slave—that, in fact, gets him killed, beaten in body but not in spirit. Stowe has been faulted for valorizing Uncle Tom's refusal to betray his master's trust and flee slavery. Nonetheless, the Christian martyrdom of this character needs to be understood within the nineteenth-century economy of domesticity. As a black Christ figure, Stowe's character is male and heroic, but not masculine in the typical sense of that word. Rather than being simply a failure of Stowe's imagination to envision a defiant black man, this characterization can be seen as a deliberate attempt to reinstill traditionally feminine values in an increasingly industrialized and male public sphere. In her book *Sensational Designs: The Cultural Work of American Fiction 1790–1860*, Jane Tompkins argues that "the popular domestic novel of the nineteenth century represents a monumental effort to reorganize culture from the woman's point of view; that this body of work is remarkable for its intellectual complexity, ambition, and resourcefulness; and that, in certain cases it offers a critique of American society far more devastating than any delivered by better-known critics such as Hawthorn and Melville."[12] Although the legacy of Stowe's novel will continue to be debated (as it was at the time), there is no doubt that this story of social evils and private triumphs conquered the public imagination with a force unparalleled in American literature.

Within six months of the novel's publication, there were already several stage adaptations of Stowe's *Uncle Tom's Cabin*, including one by George Aiken, which played in Troy, N.Y., before moving to the National Theater in New York City on July 18, 1853.[13] With its peculiar combination of dramatic plot and blackface, Aiken's production provides an interesting antecedent to Bill T. Jones's reenactment of Stowe's work. Even though it repeated the theatrical convention of having whites in blackface play African-American characters, Aiken's drama was one of the more politically progressive stage renditions of *Uncle Tom's Cabin*. Much like Stowe's novel, Aiken's version was a veritable nineteenth-century tearjerker—what one review called a "pièce de mouchoir"—and its morally "uplifting" story was seen as theatrical fare suitable for families and women as well, so that a whole new series of matinee performances was added to accommodate this new audience.[14] As family entertainment rather than vaudeville, the seriousness of dramatic intent of this play differed radically from other blackface melodramas. The Uncle Tom figure in this production was a white man in blackface, but the actor, G. C. Germon, reportedly struggled to maintain a sense of the theatrical power of the part. By refusing to indulge in the comic buffoonery that usually marked blackface roles, this actor was able to transcend the mode of performance in order to create a realistic persona onstage. One reviewer of the time spoke of Germon's very different performative presence (he was considered a "straight," as opposed to a comic actor). "His very first words, however, showed that a good hand had his part. The accent, a broad and guttural negro accent, but the voice deep and earnest—so earnest, that the first laugh at his nigger words, from the pit, died away into deep stillness."[15]

In his book *Love and Theft: Blackface Minstrelsy and the American Working Class*, Eric Lott argues that the largely Irish working-class audience was moved by this play because they identified their own struggles as new immigrants as a form of economic slavery. Indeed, the local northern sentiment about the institution of slavery in the South radically changed at this time, as the working class became an ideological partner in the abolitionist movement. It is also important to realize that by September 1853, the National Theater, where Aiken's production of *Uncle Tom's Cabin* was playing, had begun to accommodate African-American spectators, a fact that suggests that somehow this staging of Stowe's story was able to cross over to a black audience as well.

Unfortunately, most other productions were less progressive. Indeed, several revised the play's themes so completely that they ended up supporting a proslavery stance. Replacing with images of "contented darkies" the anguish of an economic system based on the selling of black bodies and the cruelty of separating families, these productions took the minstrel tradition to its logical racist conclusion, creating songs and dances that displayed happy, carefree slaves. (In fact, one such burlesque turned Stowe's subtitle, *Life Among the Lowly*, into *Life Among the Happy*.)[16] It was with the plethora of these comic, bastardized versions of *Uncle Tom's Cabin* that the figure of Uncle Tom became increasingly comic, passive, and elderly, paving the way for the contemporary meanings surrounding the figure of "Uncle Tom."

Given the cultural baggage this particular character has acquired over the past 145 years, it seems reasonable to ask why an African-American male choreographer would want to recreate Stowe's narrative onstage. Is it in order to lend a more authentic voice to the story? Is it in order to rewrite the ending of Tom's life, to reject his Christian martyrdom in favor of a more strident rebellion? Or perhaps to reanimate a figure who, although written into existence by a white northern woman, has been repeatedly restaged by both black and white bodies throughout the histories of minstrelsy, regional theater, and Hollywood cinema? Fortunately, Bill T. Jones has been—not uncharacteristically—quite verbal and forthcoming about his artistic process. But the journey from a 1989 entry in his recently published autobiography, *Last Night on Earth*—"I read *Uncle Tom's Cabin*. I find it to be hokum, misinformation. I find it moving, infuriating, beautiful, embarrassing, and important"[17]—to the description one page later of *Last Supper at Uncle Tom's Cabin/The Promised Land*—"It would speak about being human. About how we are the places we have been, the people we have slept with. How we are what we have lost and what we dream for"[18]—requires more than a fleeting summary of Jones's artistic intentions; it requires a close analysis of the complex cycle of referentiality that gives his work such resonance for a contemporary audience.

The first section of Jones's *Last Supper* is staged as a frame within a frame. This scene is played within a two-dimensional backdrop created by hanging a checkered gingham patchwork quilt that opens like a makeshift curtain to reveal a small stage. This "cabin" set simultaneously evokes both the influences of early Americana and the stylized replication of that period as "folk" art. It is on this stage-within-a-stage that we witness a much abbreviated version of Stowe's novel. Like many nineteenth-century theatrical renditions of *Uncle Tom's Cabin*, Jones's take is a series of allegorical vignettes and tableaux that punctuate Tom's narrative of redemptive faith with the equally uplifting and equally melodramatic stories of Eliza and Eva. With the notable exceptions of the narrator (played by Justice Allen), the authoress Stowe (played by Sage Cowles), and the character of Uncle Tom (played by Andréa Smith), most of the other dancers have on masks with highly exaggerated and often grotesque features. For example, the slave trader Haley's mask looks almost comically evil, a cross between a skeleton and a German Expressionist painting. The blackface masks are also cartoonish, especially the figure of "black Sam." However, to simply label these figures stereotypical caricatures, as many reviews of

Bill T. Jones/Arnie Zane and Company in *Last Supper at Uncle Tom's Cabin/The Promised Land*. The Cabin Scene. Photo by Martha Swope, © Time Inc.

the *Last Supper* have done, is to misrepresent the ironic repetition in Jones's staging. For Jones's reenactment of the iconographic features of the minstrel tradition doesn't simply repeat the racist stereotypes that underlie Stowe's novel and run rampant throughout most of the minstrel versions of Uncle Tom's story. Rather, Jones ironically reframes these caricatures in order to create a perspective that at once distances and embraces this legacy of cultural reproductions.

Jones's work reflects the proliferation of meanings implicit in any reclaiming, reinscribing, or rewriting of one's history. In *Love and Theft*, Eric Lott describes the strategy of reclamation in Martin Delany's black nationalist novel *Blake* in terms that also reflect what I think Jones is doing in his version of *Uncle Tom's Cabin*. "*Blake* writes black agency back into history through blackface songs taken 'back' from those who had plundered black cultural practices. Rather than reject the cultural territory whites had occupied by way of minstrelsy, Delany recognizes that occupation as fact and occupies in turn."[19] Throughout his epic narrative of struggle and faith, Jones is employing repetition—but repetition with a crucial difference. Like Lott's description of Delany's work, Jones's redeployment of the minstrel tradition reflects that tradition's hybrid nature while also claiming it as a vehicle through which to re-assert his own historical voice.

For instance, the masks—literally a face on top of a face—foreground the performative nature of stereotypes, forcing the audience to recognize the cli-chéd sentimentality of those images. And yet these two-faced characters oper-ate in a very postmodern fashion, for they split the actor and the character, re-fusing any essentialist notions about who should play whom. Indeed, Jones's use of masks allows him to cast across the performer's own racial, gender, or age groups. Aunt Chloe is played by a white man, Larry Goldhuber, while Si-mon Legree, the monstrous slave owner described in the text as a mean man who prides himself on having a "fist of iron for hittin' niggers," is portrayed by a black man, Justice Allen.

This kind of reframing, refiguring and cross-referencing is most striking in the very first dance sequence when Harry, "a beautiful quadroon boy," is asked to entertain the slave trader by doing the "Jim Crow." Now the "Jim Crow" has a highly complicated history. The term first entered the national discourse in the 1820s with the arrival of T. D. "Daddy" Rice, a white northern performer who popularized a parody of the "dancing darkie" by "blacking up" and performing a syncopated jig. To "jump Jim Crow" quickly became a main attraction in the minstrel shows, and even as African-American per-formers entered that tradition after the Civil War, the caricature remained a staple of minstrelsy. Played ironically by black performers in blackface, the "Jim Crow" is a dance that simultaneously lampoons the white master and caricatures the black slave, at once portraying and ironically displacing racist notions of African-Americans' inherent musicality and natural dance ability.[20]

Although the "Jim Crow" first became known through white performances of black dancing on the minstrel stage, Harriet Beecher Stowe naturalizes this racist portrayal of the black body by placing it on the plantation. In Stowe's novel, the "Jim Crow" dance, performed by the young (and desirable) quad-roon boy Harry, actually sets the dramatic action in play. The book begins with a conversation between the "kindly" (and paternalistic) slave owner Mr. Shelby, who owes money to the not so kindly slave trader Mr. Haley. Their discussion is interrupted by Harry, who enters the scene and is requested by Shelby to entertain Haley by doing the "Jim Crow." Stowe's description of the boy's dance reveals the racist views concerning the dancing black body so prevalent even among the abolitionists of her time. "The boy commenced one of those wild, grotesque songs common among the negroes, in a rich, clear voice, accompanying his singing with many comic evolutions of the hands, feet, and whole body, all in perfect time to the music."[21] It is after seeing Harry dance that Haley wants to buy him, underlining the connection between the performing body's public visibility (that it is always available for the spectator's gaze) and the slave's body's inevitable purchasability (that it is always for sale).

In the "Cabin" section of Jones's *Last Supper* the "Jim Crow" is performed by Sean Curran, a wonderfully accomplished white dancer whose roots in Irish step dancing give him the necessary skills to execute a very good "Jim Crow." Despite its entertaining rhythms and virtuosic footwork, it is difficult to watch this divertissement without confronting the colonialist legacy of this dance. As Jacqueline Shea Murphy makes clear in her essay on Jones's epic, "Unrest and Uncle Tom": "The term 'Jim Crow' itself provides a clear instance of how tightly intertwined African American performance and violent oppression have been in this country. 'Jim Crow' originally named a minstrel song-and-dance act that today one understands to have stereotyped, parodied, and degraded African Americans; the term became synonymous, late in this century, with a system of (sometimes violently enforced) racial segregation."[22] The effect of this contemporary cross-racing of an historically racist image is both curiously disturbing and sensational. Jones's restaging of the "Jim Crow" takes place within Stowe's narrative, but the spectacular element of the scene is emphasized such that he provokes a double critique. In this scene, the audience witnesses the ambiguity of simultaneous entertainment and political confrontation. We see Curran, in blackface mask, aping a minstrel portrayal of "Jim Crow," and yet we also see him doing a very virtuosic solo that demands respect in its own right. By way of his directorial choices, Jones seems to be suggesting that there is absolutely nothing essential about the connection between the sign of "Jim Crow" and its referent in the black body, a move that allows Jones both to criticize the historically racist portrayals of "Jim Crow" and to elaborate on the performative nature of any identity category.

The postmodern flickering in and out of history, race, and identity at play in much of this first section of *Last Supper* is grounded by the powerfully realistic representations of Eliza and Uncle Tom. The Eliza character, for example, is portrayed by a tall, lean, young African-American woman, Andrea Woods. Although the figure of the heroically maternal Eliza is masked in the "Cabin" section, her brief appearance in this section must be realistic enough to foreshadow her magnificent solo in the next scene of the dance. "Eliza on the Ice" is a complex theatrical meditation on the very brief but important moment in Stowe's book where Eliza escapes to freedom with her son by jumping on moving blocks of ice to cross the Ohio River. In his staging of this scene, Jones elaborates on the existential meanings implicit in Eliza's state of liminality—of literally being suspended between two shores—by creating multiple Elizas, variations on a central theme. This section is a good example of how Jones negotiates between deconstructing deterministic essentialist or racist notions about the inextricability of color and identity, and recognizing the historical legacies of such constructions. Jones knows that in order for history to be refigured, it must first be figured in such a way that powerfully evokes the real bodies at stake within the representation.

The "Eliza" section begins in darkness. As the lights rise slowly, they reveal a line of five different Elizas standing one behind the other. The first woman, Andrea Woods, holds the Eliza mask she wore in the first section of the dance. She removes the mask and turns to hand it to the woman behind her, who in turn hands it to the woman behind her. The mask passes through the hands of the four women until it ends up with the Stowe character. As she begins to recite Sojourner Truth's famous "Ain't I a Woman?" speech, the first Eliza (whom Jones has dubbed "the historical Eliza") begins to dance. To the stirring words of Truth's rhetorical questioning ("I have ploughed and planted and gathered into barns and no man could head me! And ain't I a woman?"), Woods delivers a physical evocation of generations of black women working, rejoicing, and confronting the world. Her movement is wide and strong as her torso loops down to the ground and then arches up to the sky, catapulting her long legs out into the space around her. Her arms can be powerfully direct, as in the moment when she shoots her arm straight to the audience in a defiant gesture, or wonderfully generous, as when she reaches out to embrace the possibilities of the world around her. Suddenly, the slow, punctuated rhythm underlining Truth's speech switches gears and becomes upbeat and bouncy. Woods responds in kind until the final moment, which ends with a rolling strut offstage to Truth's declaration "And now I am here."

The next Eliza is a contemporary portrayal by Heidi Latsky, a short Jewish woman whose fierce dancing provides a tangible accompaniment to the story of abuse and betrayal she recites. In this section, we move from the archetypal figure of Eliza as an African-American woman struggling with crossing over from slavery to freedom to a contemporary portrait of Eliza as a survivor. Her text (which she speaks into a microphone held by the Stowe character as she moves across the stage) is potently embodied in Latsky's movement eruptions. "I believe . . . My father told me turn the other cheek . . . My mother told me not to expect much," contextualizes her dancing, which is marked by the contrast between clenching her body to herself and striking out at the forces around her. Pulling at her own body, Latsky seems, at times, to want to tear off her own skin. The lyrical movement of the historical Eliza changes here into the tight, explosive movement of a woman who desperately wants to resist society's admonishments to "be good." This Eliza is also caught between the shores of expectation and freedom, but the terms of her struggle have changed.

The next two Elizas similarly embody archetypal situations for women, but because their solos have no direct textual accompaniment, they are much less specific in narrative detail. The third Eliza is danced by Betsy McCracken, a tall, white dancer whose legs shoot out with military precision as she wields her staff around the stage. Her character is like a powerful Greek goddess, perhaps Athena, who directs the male corps de ballet into parade-like formations. Jones speaks of this Eliza as the one "who commands men—part Joan of Arc, part dominatrix, and part martial arts master."[23] This power is, of course, extremely tenuous, and it is exhausting to watch McCracken always on her guard, never able to release the tension in her body. Eventually she decides that this power isn't worth the stakes involved and, throwing her staff away, she runs offstage—free at last.

The fourth Eliza is Maya Saffrin, whom Jones describes in his autobiography as "exotically pretty," and whose dance is a metaphoric struggle between the various men who lift and pass her among themselves and the first Eliza, who tries to rescue her from their control. This Eliza is clearly the most disempowered. Almost zombi-like, her passive physical presence makes it seem as if she has no will of her own. Even when she dances a duet with the first Eliza, she is dancing her partner's movement, always looking at her friend for guidance. Although she is not floppy like a rag doll (which in some ways would be a sort of resistance, making it hard for anyone to lift or carry her), her energy is so contained that one wonders whether this Eliza would even have left the first shore, let alone have the strength of purpose actually to make it across to the promised land.

As this fourth Eliza exits, a fifth and final Eliza—one the audience has not previously seen—enters. This Eliza is danced by a very tall African-American man, Gregg Hubbard. He is wearing only a bright white miniskirt and white pumps. Perhaps the most contemporary of all, this Eliza is figured as a gay man in drag. Standing awkwardly on these heels, his almost naked body giving him a childlike innocence, he executes a series of gestural movements very much like Jones's signature gestures where the arms continually circle the upper body to form an elaborate frame. Tracing his hands over his head and down the front of his body, Hubbard stops to grab his crotch in a sudden gesture. Is he meant to surprise us or reassure himself? This brief moment of doubt changes into a "work it" attitude as he turns and walks off the stage with a body wave slyly snaking from his head down to his toes.

In the Alive From Off Center television special focusing on the making of *Last Supper* (aired in 1992), Jones details the process of creating these various Elizas. He speaks eloquently about the importance of the dancers involved in the making of these solos, especially with regard to the first two Elizas, whose own personas were so deeply embedded in their characters. Then Jones shifts to a discussion of the final Eliza and talks about this figure's own struggles between a different kind of slavery and freedom. Speaking as a gay man about this final Eliza, Jones declares: "Our sexuality exists on neither shore, that of femininity and that of masculinity. It is its own thing, but because of the strictures of our society, we are left suspended, doubtful, fearful even, of where we belong."

Jones clearly identifies the "Eliza on the Ice" section of his epic undertaking as a feminist statement of sorts. Certainly the progression from the historical Eliza to Hubbard's gay Eliza thoroughly deconstructs the static concept of woman so embedded in Western representation. *Woman* as a universal term actually meaning "white," "feminine," defined by her relationships to men, or even as suggesting a biological femaleness, is fractured by the different and contradictory embodiments of Eliza. Although Jones is playing here with the historical/fictionalized character of Eliza, he is also intent on underlining the universal dimensions of a liminal state, the way in which many people find themselves existentially "between two shores." The final Eliza could be problematic for feminists who are hesistant to fully deconstruct the category of woman altogether (for as Hubbard's crotch-grabbing gesture makes clear, a man in a skirt really hasn't given up his social power, it is merely hidden, available to be reerected, so to speak, at a moment's notice). Yet, for me, the crucial question is whether "her" appearance actually adds another dimension to this investigation of gender in our culture, or whether it serves to dismiss the earlier images of women's struggles. I believe that Jones consciously left Hubbard's Eliza out of the original lineup in order to give these female Elizas their own voices. Indeed, the autobiographical as well as historical character of their stories allows Jones to make the ideological connection—that gay men's sexualities are also suspended between two shores—without usurping the material and political realities of women's lives. Jones thus problematizes, even deconstructs, gender without rendering it a completely vacant category. This balance of realism and performative spectacle is absolutely critical to the genre of epic dance. The potency of the form lies precisely in its witnessing of people's stories as well as its reconstructing of their historical legacies. And too, there is the issue of merged identities here, for Jones has often declared the powerful influence that black women have had in his life, most notably his mother (who appears onstage in this piece) and his sisters. If we take the Hubbard character as Jones himself, one might argue that he is, in fact, trying to bring out the female embedded in the male persona.[24]

Nonetheless, Hubbard's appearance at the end of the Eliza section serves to return the focus of the narrative back to men. For, as with the majority of Jones's work, most of *Last Supper* concentrates on the telling of his/story. This story starts with that of Uncle Tom and is told and retold in various forms throughout the dance. This is the story of black men in a white man's world—the history of racism and tales of its (and their) survival. This authorial voice is evident from the beginning of the "Cabin" section, embodied in the onstage figure of the narrator by Justice Allen. Much like a master of ceremonies, Allen welcomes the audience to Uncle Tom's Cabin and introduces the figure of Harriet Beecher Stowe, played by Sage Cowles. Allen and Cowles take turns telling the story of *Uncle Tom's Cabin* until the figure of Uncle Tom is introduced into the scenerio. Uncle Tom is played by Andréa Smith, a strapping young man who infuses this character with a riveting stage presence. His powerful voice is first heard in sermon. The moment is striking because he is the first character within the staged drama to speak. Up to this point all the other characters' thoughts, feelings, and actions have been either mimed or narrated by someone else. The fact that Uncle Tom controls his own voice gives him an immediate dignity within this minstrel setting. In *Last Night on Earth*, Jones mentions the combination of optimism, gentleness, and sensuality that he thought Smith could embody in his portrayal of Uncle Tom. "Andréa was young in many senses of the word, and the openness and curiosity implied by his youth were necessary in recreating such a worn, misunderstood icon as Uncle Tom."[25]

Recreated by Jones's directorial vision, this Uncle Tom is vulnerable yet strong, young yet wise. Interestingly enough, Smith's presence onstage immediately stands out in contrast to the minstrel icons surrounding him. Whereas their movements are often puppet-like, repetitious, and spatially truncated, his physical presence is grounded but graceful, with his arms arching to the heavens. Working in union with his voice, his movement commands attention. While preaching, he stands above the others like a magnificent old tree whose branches dance in the wind, all the while being rooted deeply to the earth. Uncle Tom's spiritual and inspirational leadership is foregrounded by Jones's use of theatrical retrograde. After Uncle Tom is killed by Simon Legree and ascends to heaven, Stowe asks what is there for those who are left behind. The cast faces out and together shouts "Freedom!" Refusing closure in order to rewrite the possibilities of another kind of resistance back into the

story, Jones stops the play and all the characters backtrack through their movements until the scene where Legree tries to "break Tom's spirit." Here, Jones
reproduces, with a crucial difference, the stylized whipping of slaves by Legree. Instead of one or two characters, the whole cast comes back out without
masks and one by one lines up to confront Legree. Shaking their heads "NO!"
and circling their arms in front of their bodies in a defiantly martial gesture,
these people—black, white, young, old, male, female—refuse Legree's domination, even as he whips them. They line up again and again such that Legree
has a constant group of protesters in his face. Their perseverance and their refusal to become submissive (like Tom's refusal to be beaten down even as he
was beaten up) make Legree's relentless whipping gesture look increasingly
ridiculous.

In this section, Jones sets up a narrative logic that he will pursue throughout *Last Supper at Uncle Tom's Cabin/The Promised Land*. In scene after scene,
Jones highlights the importance of African-American men's experience and
then connects that experience to issues of power, exclusion, pain, and survival
that affect us all. Allen, Smith, Hubbard, and Arthur Aviles are spotlighted as
the central figures, as various embodiments of Christ in the Last Supper. In
the documentary on the making of this dance, Jones tells us that "this dance
is a dance about differences—race, sexual, class. About how we can work
through those differences and move to another place." The desire to balance a
sense of specific history with a sense of global harmony serves as the impetus
for the following sections of the dance ("The Supper" and "The Promised
Land") in which Uncle Tom becomes Bill T. Jones becomes Justice Allen becomes Christ becomes naked becomes us all.

After an interlude in which Bill T. Jones improvises to his mother's singing
and praying, "The Supper" begins with a live depiction of Leonardo da
Vinci's famous painting. Standing in front of the allegorical tableau is Justice
Allen, holding an imaginary basketball and dribbling in slow motion. He then
joins the tableau, which metamorphoses into a group dance, leaving Smith
and Allen standing facing one another on the table. Inching closer to one another, they seem to be arguing until it eventually becomes clear that their old-
fashioned-sounding language is not medieval English or even Shakespeare,
but rather Martin Luther King's famous "I Have a Dream" speech recited
backwards. All of a sudden, this long table is a meeting place where King's
speech becomes the connective tissue that draws Uncle Tom, an antebellum
fictional character as well as a layered iconic image that must be grappled
with, to Justice Allen, who provides an example of the conflicted life situations
in which many African-American men find themselves. As these two men

stand side by side, their attention (and the audience's) shifts to Arthur Aviles, who is dancing on the stage in front of them. The physical strength and fluidity of Aviles's dancing, the kinesthetic dynamism of his body offers a palatable release from the angst of their spoken words.

Eventually, Allen comes forward and sits down to tell us a rap version of his own life story. He begins the tale with "Young, gifted, and black was my identity." Caught up in a racist system, he goes to war and then to jail, describing himself as "just another nigger in a cracker box." At this point there is a chorus in which the company joins him, echoing the first words of each line.

SLAVE—three fifths of a man

BIAS—it's the law of the land

DEATH—better fight if you can, 'cause clubs is trumps in the corporal plan

TIME—the master of illusion

PAIN—the core of this confusion

LOVE—an emotional intrusion, survival tools were my only solution

The last two verses, which bring Allen's story up to the present performance, reveal a self-empowerment and a decision to take responsibility for his own future, ending with "now I'm rockin' 'round the world with Bill T. Jones."[26] A stunning tale of survival, Allen's autobiographical rap transforms Uncle Tom's faith in God and King's faith in humanity into a reconstructed faith in his own self. Allen's story is powerful not only because we believe its truthfulness and are activated by its rhythms, but also because it stands as part of the epic chain of black man's histories resurrected in Jones's work.

Resurrection in the sense of rebirth—even in the more literal sense of arising from the dead with a new knowledge—is one of the central themes in Urban Bush Women's *Bones and Ash: A Gilda Story*. In this epic her/story, choreographer Jawole Willa Jo Zollar and her company are joined by the writer Jewelle Gomez, the composer Toshi Reagon, and co-director Steven Kent in a dance/theater collaboration that recreates another nineteenth-century literary genre —that of the vampire story. Jewelle Gomez's lesbian vampire novel, *The Gilda Stories*, serves as the textual basis for *Bones and Ash*, although some features of the novel were dropped and others were added to make this story into a performance. In this retelling of a European genre, however, the self-indulgent, obsessive vampire figure is transformed into a caring, maternal angel cum lover, who is a spiritual guide for humanity. In the context of an African-American tradition, sharing blood is less an aspect of sadistic seduction than of a mutual exchange, marking a respect for balance based on African ideologies of ritual sacrifice. Gomez's work is much more surreal than Stowe's domestic novel, for it chronicles the evolution of the Girl character from her rescue as a runaway slave in 1850 and her conversion into a vampire called Gilda (what is called, somewhat euphemistically, the "long life") through the twentieth century right into the future in a chapter entitled "Land of Enchantment 2050." Although the need for theatrical coherence has limited the time frames of *Bones and Ash*, the performance still highlights a sense of history as a continuum of people—a literal bloodline that, interestingly enough, has little to do with biological family and more to do with emotional families. Epic in scale and mythic in genre, *Bones and Ash* traces historical change through the life of one body—one body, that is, that will live for hundreds of years.

Like Gomez's novel, *Bones and Ash* has two central vampire characters: Gilda (played by Deborah Thomas in the 1995 version I first saw, and now played by Pat Hall-Smith) and Bird (played by Emerald Trinket Monsod, a guest artist). These two women's historical knowledge gives them both the wisdom and the responsibility to guide their surrogate daughter, a runaway slave called Girl (played by company member Christine King). Gilda, who lived in Brazil several hundred years ago, runs a bordello with her lover, Bird, a Filipino woman who lived with the Lakota tribe before starting this life. It is the coming of yet another war, the Civil War, that compels Gilda to give up her eternal life. But before Gilda can cross over into the promised land, she and Bird must teach Girl how to understand her terrifying nightly dreams, which mix disturbing images of past fears and present realities. In effect, they must teach her how to understand her history fully so that she can begin to envision her future. These lessons take the form of a dancing apprenticeship in which Bird helps the Girl to literally re-member her own body by leading her through a series of martial dance forms that gives the Girl a renewed sense of agency and pride. It is only once she is physically present that the Girl can begin to remember and embrace her own history. "Of her home their mother spoke about, the Girl was less certain. It was always a dream place—distant, unreal. Except the talk of dancing. . . . Talking of it now, her body rocked slightly as if she had been rewoven into that old circle of dancers. She poured out the images and names, proud of her own ability to weave a story. Bird smiled at her pupil who claimed her past, reassuring her silently."[27]

Once the girl has reclaimed her past—found the voice with which she can tell her own history—Gilda can move on, bequeathing her spirit and her name to the Girl. Because Gilda is a vampire, her "gift of long life" takes place as an "exchange of blood," where the two individuals involved in the exchange suck blood (not from the neck, as one might expect, but from a space just below the breast). This motif of exchange—of blood, life, and body—reverberates throughout the individual biomythography of Jewelle Gomez. In her collection of writings, *43 Septembers*, Gomez has a piece entitled "Transubstantiation: This is my body, this is my blood." She begins this essay with a very simple summation of the contradictions that defined her childhood religious experience: "I was raised a Black Catholic in a white Catholic town."[28] Although Gomez has since revised her spirituality to accommodate more fully her life choices, the passion and the physical vitality of that early training have never really left her. Thus, the blood of communion becomes the blood of social action and a belief in the interconnectedness of people and their histories.

The key is in the sea change: the place where the small incident is transformed into the belief, the daily wine into the blood. In that change I am learning to treasure the things of my past without being limited by them. . . . To make the past a dimension of my life, but not the only perspective from which I view it. In that way my youth is not more important than my middle years; . . . my knowledge is not better or truer than anyone else's, its value comes when it is made useful to others."[29]

For Gomez, blood becomes the bond becomes the body that can change, through the redemptive power of love, the ordinary into the spiritual, life into history, and words into a dance.

In *Bones and Ash*, however, the exchange of blood is not the central event that it is in Gomez's novel. Rather it is the exchange of movement, of energy, of dancing among the company that signals the physical and spiritual interconnectedness of the women onstage. This is most striking in the dancing sections, which serve as metaphoric frames to the narrative action of the first act. The opening scene of *Bones and Ash* is a prologue spoken from the present about the past. The light comes up slowly to reveal a lone figure, moving through the shadows of the stage's dim lighting. An offstage voice is heard speaking memories about a life that has lasted many centuries. The woman onstage begins a solo that will parallel many of the emotional states called forth by the poetic prose. At times she lifts her arms slowly, fluidly, stretching her body luxuriously. Other times she skips lightheartedly, and yet other times she seems agitated. Although she is silent, it is clear that we are hearing her memories, her thoughts, her story. Images of cotton and blood are woven into a tapestry of reflection that speaks of slavery and a historical memory that is an ongoing puzzle. For the past, like the vampires at the center of this story, refuses to "lie down and die."

The shape of my life is motion through fields, through time, through blood. Each decade is woven into the nest, embroidered centuries draped across my shoulders, a rainbow of lives, every one my own. Behind me—one hundred and fifty years of those I've loved, those I've lost. All taking or giving blood. Dangerous, Reviving, Vital. The thin red line I follow down one row, up the next. A rhythmic dance draws the attention of the gods—Yemeya, Yellow Woman and many others. I am enamoured of motion.

Someone said to me once: It must be hard in this world being black, descended from slaves, 'buked and scorned, benign neglect. I said no . . . actually it's being two hundred years old that pulls my patience. To live forever is a puzzle. Each piece snapping into place beside the next, but the picture is never fully seen.[30]

This sense of life and history as movement is triply reflected in the figures of the Irissas who soon enter upstage. In the program for *Bones and Ash*, the characters of the Irissas are described as the oldest teachers, the wise elders who guide their vampire family through the ages.[31] Danced by Gacirah Diagne, Beverley Prentice, and Christine Wright, these dancing sages often appear behind the scrim or sheer curtains, as if they are protecting, by the mere fact of their presence and attention, those onstage. In the prologue, they haunt the upstage space, emerging from the shadows to follow the Girl's journey across the space. Quick and light-footed, breathy yet grounded and forceful, their dancing can shift unexpectedly from a slow, steady bowing and rising motion to a whirling dervish–like spinning that sweeps across the stage, sending energy out in every direction. Their breathing is often audible and sometimes they whisper or sing advice to the central characters. Half Greek chorus, half African shaman, the Irissas embody archetypal spirits whose presence underlines life's continuity.[32]

The Irissas' presence in *Bones and Ash* provides a historical metanarrative to the specific action going on downstage, for they embody the past as well as the future. In many ways, their otherworldly presence has an angel-like quality. The main characters may sense the Irissas as they move with or surround them, but they never seem to see these dancing spirits. Like the vampires in Gomez's novel, the Irissas can hear other people's thoughts and, entering their minds, change those thoughts into more positive ones. They remind me of the trenchcoated angel figures in Wim Wenders's film *Wings of Desire*, whose very presence next to someone on a subway can alter the most cynical and disheartened thoughts, bestowing the gift of hope. In the middle of the first act, the Irissas chant the mantra of life-enriching vampires: "We take blood not life. Leave something in exchange." Indeed the difference between good vampires, embodied by Gilda and Bird, and bad ones, embodied in the figure of Fox, is clearly demonstrated in the first act. When Gilda and Bird come upon a distressed figure who is flailing around the stage, obviously confused, they surround him with sympathy, embracing him more as sisters than vampires, even as they take the blood they need. When they leave him, his sense of purpose is restored. In contrast, Fox seduces a woman with a courtly dance, and then leaves her dead.

In her recent study of vampires in nineteenth- and twentieth-century literature, wittily entitled *Our Vampires, Ourselves*, Nina Auerbach expresses her frustration with what she calls the "anestheticizing virtue" of these good fairy vampires in Gomez's novel.

Instead of killing mortals, Gilda and her friends bestow on them edifying dreams after taking fortifying sips of blood. Vampirism is not bloodsucking or feeding or the dark gift; it becomes "the exchange," an act of empathy, not power, whose first principle is, "feel what they are needing, not what you are hungering for" (p. 50). Like the construction of lesbianism *The Gilda Stories* celebrates, vampirism is purged of aggression.[33]

Although they do not fit into Auerbach's own definition of power as domination, the vampires in both *The Gilda Stories* and *Bones and Ash* provide what I consider a radical new vision of humanity. It is certainly true that these vampires don't excite that frisson of dangerous seductivity that seems a mainstay of traditional vampire novels. Yet their commitment to a sense of common bond with others, even those very different from themselves (i.e., mortals), presents an intriguing reconfiguration of identity, desire, and love within this gothic genre. The vampire figure rewritten as storyteller, as griotte, as spiritual guide, is a compelling example of how *Bones and Ash* weaves an Afrocentric belief in the interconnectedness of the world into a Eurocentric literary genre. Drawing on performative traditions that include ritual possession as well as West African and diasporan dance cultures, Urban Bush Women's collaborative epic builds on these influences to create the climactic ending of act 1, where Gilda "crosses over" to her final death. Once Gilda has decided to leave this world, she first initiates the Girl into the vampire life. At this moment, the theatrical action or "plot" is temporarily suspended as Gilda and the Girl are joined by the Irissas in a ritual exchange of identity.

As Gilda's farewell letter is read by an offstage voice, Gilda begins her journey back to the earth. Alone onstage, Gilda emerges from the shadows with movements that suggest she is struggling to find the right pathway back. Her dancing becomes more convulsive as she continues, flinging her head first in one direction and then in another. Turning here and then there, bending down and arching up, twisting one way and then another, she seems to be fighting

Embodying History

Urban Bush Women in *Bones and Ash: A Gilda Story*. Photo by Tom Brazil.

with her own choice, dissatisfied with every available position. Slowly the background fills with the rest of the company, newly dressed in African robes. They line up at the back of the stage as if they are protecting her from what lies beyond. Drawn to their presence, Gilda moves back and forth across their space, trying to find the right fit—the right rhythm, the right pathway, the right expression for her death. A drummer enters the space, intermittently accompanying her movement with ambient sound. Soon, however, the company's breaths take on a rhythm of their own as they first speak and then sing to Gilda. The drummer joins their rhythm and then starts to intensify it as Gilda works herself into a state of divine possession. Suddenly, this energy quiets down as she opens her body to the voyage over. Two women help her to disrobe, and a priestess figure (played by Valerie Winborne) begins to sing "Coming Home Through the Morning Light," metaphorically washing Gilda down with her powerful voice. A slide of a river delta, then a closeup of the river are projected on the back scrim as Gilda opens the curtains and disappears into the water.

The exchange of energy between the company and Gilda in this last scene is paradigmatic of much of Urban Bush Women's work in which an individual transformation is assisted by the energy of the group. This sense of interconnectedness between self and community is reflective of both the present moment and a historical continuity—defining who your community is at present and who your community was several hundred years ago. As their name suggests, Urban Bush Women bring their ancestral roots into the twentieth century. In commenting on the diversity of African-American women within the company, Veta Goler describes what she calls the "stunning mosaic of black womanhood." Despite the clear celebration of individuality, Urban Bush Women's work usually focuses on the sense of community between women. Goler describes this legacy of collective experience:

Historically, black women have always established ways of coming together for mutual benefit. From the female networks in the family compounds of traditional African societies to the club movement and extended families of the New World, black women have supported and affirmed each other. Urban Bush Women's name evokes images of women assisting each other in maneuvering for their survival within challenging environments.[34]

Most of Zollar's choreography for Urban Bush Women centers on the cultural experiences of African-American women, creating what Goler calls a "cultural autobiography."

In many ways, the trope of the vampire allows Zollar literally to trace that cultural autobiography through different bodies. In this vein, vampires can help us to create a new sense of family, subverting the notion of bloodlines to fit different styles of familiar relationships. This is clearly a theme within Gomez's novel, which focuses on the vampire as lesbian more than *Bones and Ash* does. The lesbian perspective of Gomez's novel (which has several very steamy passages) is replaced by a less sexual and more womanist perspective in Zollar's choreography. What gets exchanged through the dancing in *Bones and Ash* is not so much desire, but memory and history. Urban Bush Women is the only professional African-American women's dance company, and Zollar and the company members are committed to making manifest that legacy of challenge, survival, and hope. In an essay entitled "The New Moderns: The Paradox of Eclecticism and Singularity," Halifu Osumare describes Zollar in terms that echo her sense of legacy: "In Jawole Willa Jo Zollar one sees Katherine Dunham's and Pearl Primus' fierce passion for roots, their bold adventurousness in walking the urban back alleys and the rural dirt villages to research their subject matter, and their ingenious artistic transformation of cultural information."[35]

Given her very conscious representations of African-American women's cultural experiences in her choreography, I was surprised to find out that Zollar doesn't see herself as directly addressing issues of race or gender in her work. This is not to say that Zollar is not acutely aware of racism or misogyny within representations of African-American women. Anyone who was present at her plenary talk at the 1990 Dance Critics Association conference in Los Angeles cannot doubt her commitment to these issues.[36] However, she doesn't foreground the categories of race and gender in quite the way that Jones does. Instead, she builds on a specific cultural experience right from the start, never framing race as a topic within the performance, but rather speaking right away in an Afrocentric idiom. This strategy allows Zollar to claim a black female voice while also refusing the problematic assumption that, by claiming that culturally rooted voice, you are speaking only to people with knowledge of that specific experience. Rather, Zollar believes, as does Jones, that ultimately, many experiences of exclusion and oppression, as well as inclusion and community, are shared across cultural differences.

Although Jones's epic originates in the historical perspective of an African-American gay man, his work continually interrogates these identities, even while claiming them. In "The Cabin" and "Eliza on the Ice" sections of his dance, which I discussed earlier in this chapter, Jones questions the constructions of race and gender. In almost every scene, the audience is confronted with the issues surrounding how we come to see "blackness," "maleness," and "femaleness." But what is also clear is that we are never allowed to see these performers, even when they are in blackface or drag, as statically defined objects of our gaze. In this work, performers claim and embody identities in ways that resist pat or simplistic constructions of race, gender, or sexuality. Thus, for example, when Justice Allen tells his life story, he fulfills a stereotype of the black criminal on drugs but at the same time refuses its deterministic rigor mortis by also claiming an identity as a writer and performer who is "rockin' 'round the world with Bill T. Jones."

Jones is a deconstructionist at heart and rarely gives his audience any answers to the questions he insistently asks. What he does give us is a through line of spectacular dancing. This is undeniably the role that Arthur Aviles (a self-described New York–rican, who is one of the company's most virtuosic dancers) takes on throughout *Last Supper*. Although Aviles doesn't have a speaking role and is never placed in a specific identity (such as Gregg Hubbard's drag scene at the end of "Eliza on the Ice"), his dancing serves as a sort of physical antidote to the existential quandaries implied by the text. This is true of the scene in which he is dancing downstage while "Uncle Tom" and Allen are speaking on the table. It is also Aviles's dancing that precipitates the final section of the dance, "The Promised Land," in which the stage is flooded with fifty-two naked people of all sizes and shapes who stand and face the audience.

I see Aviles's dancing as the physical metaphor for faith, the other focus of Jones's epic dance. Even as Jones doggedly deconstructs our assumptions about race, gender, life choices, family, and much more, he relies on a leap of faith to take his audience to the promised land. His improvisational questioning (maybe grilling is a more apt word) of a member of the clergy chosen from whichever community he is performing in is quite relentless. On the video of the premiere at the Brooklyn Academy of Music he is talking with Paul Abel, a gay minister. After asking him a series of questions including "What is faith? Is Christianity a slave religion? What is evil? Is AIDS punishment from God?" Jones probes Abel's feelings about serving a religion that doesn't recognize his own life choices. Yet this insistent line of questioning takes place after two scenes in which faith is reclaimed; Jones's improvising to his mother's praying, and his dancing to the story of Job as narrated by the clergy. In both instances, Jones's dancing, like Aviles's, fills an existential void with a very potent physical reality. Even though Jones questions faith in the midst of loss, he can still choreograph dances in which being present in the world with others takes on a healing spirituality. This is certainly the message of the final scene. In his autobiography, Jones sums it up this way:

The Promised Land, with its hordes of naked flesh coming wave after wave into the footlights, pubic patches, pert breasts, sagging breasts, wrinkled knees, blissful eyes, furtive expressions of shame, is a visual manifestation of my profound sense of belonging. This was my portrait of us. All of us. And this is who I am too. One of us. It was my battle to disavow any identity as a dying outcast and to affirm our commonality. In it, some one thousand people from thirty cities stood naked, took a bow, and said, "We are not afraid."[37]

This mass of naked humanity is meant to place the very real bodily differences of race, age, ability, and gender in the midst of a symbolic embodiment of vulnerability and sameness. One wonders, however, how different things really are once the euphoric final moments have subsided and everyone is clothed again. Although he began *Uncle Tom's Cabin/The Promised Land* with a searing critique of race, mimesis, and representation, Jones ends this epic dance rather blandly, bringing his audience through a potentially uncomfortable confrontation with histories of dominations and survival to a present-day *communitas*. Is community really that easy? Didn't the 1960s teach us that politics are harder to change than one's clothes?

Like Jones's piece, *Bones and Ash* draws on African-American memory and spirituality to stage the history of black women's bodies. Registering both the abuse and resistance of these women's lives, *Bones and Ash* celebrates a spirituality based on the interconnectedness of past, present, and future. In Gomez's and Urban Bush Women's vision, the exchange of self and other is considered an intersubjective act, not one of domination and subordination. This exchange of life force that does not destroy one partner (be it another person or the environment), but rather creates a mutual energy, is, of course, a wonderful model of performer/audience interaction—a model of responsiveness that is also grounded in African aesthetics and spirituality. Watching this piece, I came to appreciate the interconnectedness among the women onstage without feeling a need to identify their experience as my own. Unlike the final scenes in "The Promised Land" where difference is multiplied to the point of losing its meaning in a mass of humanity, *Bones and Ash* holds onto its own cultural moorings. I don't think that this differentiation is necessarily a problem. Indeed, it might be a very healthy distinction, one that recognizes the interconnectedness of our histories without erasing the importance of difference in choreographing the body's identity.

Appendix

Les Ballets C. de la B.

Ballets C. de la B. (Ballets Contemporains de la Belgique) was founded in 1984 by Alain Platel. Les Ballets C. de la B. employs dancers and actors, professionals and amateurs, adults and children, and its aesthetic is decidedly antiballet. Platel finds his inspiration for dances in everyday life, in minor flaws and insignificant gestures that he transforms into theatrical dance. Platel does not consider himself a choreographer, but rather refers to himself as a catalyst who helps to generate and organize those around him.

In the year of its creation, Les Ballets C. de la B. performed *Stabat Mater*, in which two men court the same woman who opts for an enormous cream cake. The company's current work, *La Tristeza Complice* (The Shared Sorrow), focuses on today's volatile youth culture facing a grim future of poverty and shattered dreams. A joint production with Het Muziek Lod, it is performed by ten dancers and two children to the music of Henry Purcell played on ten accordions and sung by a soprano. It has been performed throughout Europe, and in the United States and Canada.

Les Ballets C. de la B. is the third dance company to be recognized by the Ministère de la Communauté Flamande.

contact:
Les Ballets C. de la B.
Citadellaan 40, 9000 Ghent, Belgium
Phone: 32 09 221 75 01

Emery Blackwell

Emery Blackwell discovered dancing eight years ago in a DanceAbility workshop with Alito Alessi. Since then, he has created and performed in solo and group works, including *Hand Dance* and *Bumped*. With Alessi, Blackwell has choreographed several dances, including *There and Back Again*, and *Wheels of Fortune*. They have performed their work for the Governor's Arts Awards at the Hult Center in Eugene, Oregon, as well as for school children in Oregon and Austria. Blackwell has taught with DanceAbility throughout the United States and Europe. Blackwell views dance as a positive teaching tool and finds that, after seeing him—a man who gets around in a wheelchair—dance, audience members are more open to him.

Blackwell is past president of Oregonians for Independent Living (OIL), an advocacy group for people with disabilities, and owned and operated a bicycle taxi service for four years. He composes and performs music and has released an album entitled "Dreams and Nightmares."

contact:
Emery Blackwell
387 N. Polk
Eugene, OR 97402–4114
Phone/Fax: 541 484 7163

Candoco

Candoco is a British company of disabled and able-bodied dancers, founded and directed by Celeste Dandeker and Adam Benjamin. Dandeker was a dancer with the London Contemporary Dance Theatre when, during a performance, she suffered a fall that left her paralyzed. Benjamin, a dancer, was artist-in-residence at the Heaffey Centre in London, an integrated recreation center for disabled and able-bodied, when he saw *The Fall*, a film made about Dandeker in 1990. Together they developed an integrated dance workshop that led in 1991 to the formation of Candoco and new and inventive dancing.

Benjamin has since retired from dancing to become Candoco's resident choreographer. He also masterminds the company's workshops, which have been offered throughout Europe. Candoco's many performances at dance festivals have garnered critical acclaim.

Choreographer Victoria Marks, who was in the first class at the Heaffey Centre, created *The Edge of the Forest* for Candoco in 1991. Marks also choreographed *Outside In* for Candoco. This work was filmed by Margaret Williams for the BBC. Siobhan Davies, Darshan Singh Bhuller, Emilyn Claid, and Jodi Falk have also created works for Candoco.

contact:
Candoco
2L Leroy House

436 Essex Road
London N1 3Qp
Tel: 0171 704 6845
Fax: 0171 704 1645

Marie Chouinard

Marie Chouinard was born and resides in Quèbec and has earned an international reputation as a performance artist. Chouinard avoids the labels of dance or theater to describe her work, and instead prefers to call herself a "body artist." She has studied ballet, theater, modern dance, T'ai Chi, singing, Skinner releasing technique, and Body-Mind Centering.

After twelve years as a solo artist, Chouinard founded Compagnie Marie Chouinard in 1990, of which she is artistic director. Chouinard has more than thirty works to her credit, including *Cristallisation* (1979); *Marie Chien Noir* (1982); *Earthquake in the Heartchakra* (1985); *S.T.A.B. (Space, Time and Beyond)* (1986); *L'Après-midi d'un faune* (1987); *Les Trous du ciel* (Openings in the Sky) (1991); *The Rite of Spring* (1993); and *L'Amande et le Diamant* (The Almond and the Diamond) (1996).

Chouinard has taught in New York, Amsterdam, Vienna, and Montreal. She has performed at The Kitchen in New York City and the National Arts Center in Ottawa, as well as in Europe and Asia. Chouinard has been awarded the Jacqueline Lemieux Prize (1986); the Chalmers Award, Canada's most prestigious choreographic prize (1987); an Artist Lifetime Achievement Award (1993); and the Paper Boat Award (1994) (Glascow, U.K.), for *The Rite of Spring*.

contact:
Compagnie Marie Chouinard
Manon Forget, director
3981 Boul. St-Laurent #715
Montreal H2W 1Y5, Canada
Phone: 514 843 9036
Fax: 514 843 7616

Blondell Cummings

Choreographer and performer Blondell Cummings was an original member of Meredith Monk/The House. In 1978, she founded Cycle Arts Foundation, a multidisciplinary arts collaborative incorporating dance, theater, and visual, media, and literary arts. Cummings and Cycle Arts Foundation aim to use the collaborative artistic/creative processes to explore contemporary social, political, and personal issues that are cross-cultural in scope.

Cummings tours extensively throughout the United States, Europe, and Asia. She is the recipient of numerous fellowships from the National Endowment for the Arts, as well as fellowships from the New York Foundation for the Arts, the Jerome Foundation, and a land grant from the Harkness Center Foundation. Cummings has also led residencies in Japan with support from the U.S.-Japan Friendship Commission and the Asian Cultural Council. Cummings has taught at New York University, Cornell University, and Wesleyan, as well as in Japan and the Philippines.

Currently, Cummings is working on the ongoing collaborative project *Like Family*. Begun six years ago in conjunction with Duke University and with the support of a Lila Wallace grant, the work was conceived as a sprawling collaboration that changes and takes on the regional characteristics of the locales where Cummings holds "Like Family" workshops.

contact:
Blondell Cummings
Cycle Arts Foundation
1336 First Avenue
New York, NY 10021
Phone: 212 861 4305
Fax: 212 772 8713

Charlene Curtiss/Light Motion

Charlene Curtiss was a competitive gymnast and sports enthusiast when, at age seventeen, she permanently injured her spinal cord on a faulty set of uneven parallel bars. At first, she struggled with crutches and braces to avoid the stigma of "disabled." After experiencing the thrill of a National Wheelchair Competition, Curtiss purchased her first sports wheelchair. She went on to earn her law degree from Gonzaga University, and worked as an attorney in her own practice before retiring to dance. Her professional dance career began in 1989.

Curtiss utilizes Contact Improvisation in her work, and her original dance techniques in "front-end chair control" have redefined dance parameters and choreographic terminology of wheelchair movement work. She teaches regularly at the University of Washington Medical Center and is an artist-in-residence in the public schools of Washington State.

Curtiss's company, Light Motion, was established in 1988 to develop the artistic expressions of both disabled and nondisabled artists working together to enhance community awareness of disability issues through the arts. One of the company directives is to help disabled people discover the untapped, unexplored world of dance and artistic movement and to integrate the art of dance with mainstream professional productions. Light Motion has appeared in dance festivals in the United States and abroad.

contact:
Charlene A. Curtiss/Light Motion
1520 32nd Avenue South
Seattle, WA 98144
Phone: 206 328 0818

APPENDIX

Dancing Wheels/Mary Verdi-Fletcher

Mary Verdi-Fletcher, a native of Cleveland, Ohio, is principal dancer and director with Cleveland Ballet Dancing Wheels. Born with spina bifida, Verdi-Fletcher founded Dancing Wheels in 1980 to "Promote the collaboration and artistic talents of dancers with and without disabilities while demonstrating the diversity of dance and the abilities of artists with physical challenges." In 1990, Dancing Wheels was taken under the auspices of the Cleveland Ballet to form an educational outreach program. Cleveland Ballet Dancing Wheels gives lecture/demonstrations and performances throughout the United States, and is the first professional company of its kind in the United States. The company receives funding from Action Technology, the McGinty Foundation, and the Ohio Arts Council.

In addition to her work as an artist/administrator, and as a teacher of dance to others with disabilities, Verdi-Fletcher has worked in the field of independent living, rehabilitation, and disability rights. She presently serves as president of Professional Flair, Inc., a not-for-profit organization dedicated to providing career opportunities in the arts for people with disabilities.

Verdi-Fletcher is the 1990 winner of the "Outstanding Young Clevelanders Award," and the recipient of the 1992 ORACLE Award of Merit for Outstanding Outreach and Educational Programming in Ohio.

contact:
Cleveland Ballet Dancing Wheels
Mary Verdi-Fletcher
Professional Flair Inc.
1501 Euclid Ave., Suite 41
Cleveland, OH 44114
Phone: 216 621 2626

David Dorfman

David Dorfman, a native Chicagoan, toured internationally as a member of Susan Marshall & Co. before founding his own company, David Dorfman Dance, in 1985. Dorfman holds an MFA degree from Connecticut College. He has been guest artist at various institutions both across the United States and abroad.

In his choreography, Dorfman focuses on human situations and multicultural issues, as well as issues of love, loss, and survival. In two community-based projects, *Familiar Movements (The Family Project)* and *Out of Season (The Athletes Project)*, Dorfman engaged nondancers in residencies and performances. He won a 1996 New York Dance and Performance Award (Bessie) for outstanding choreographic achievement for *Familiar Movements*, which sought to "explore, examine, reverse or fabricate anew familial relationships." *The Athletes Project* has been produced throughout the United States and Europe, including the five boroughs of New York City.

Dorfman has been awarded four fellowships from the National Endowment for the Arts, including his 1997 award. He is the recipient of two New York Foundation for the Arts fellowships, an American Choreographer's Award, and the first Paul Taylor Fellowship from the Yard. David Dorfman Dance has toured widely in North and South America, Great Britain, and Europe.

contact:
David Dorfman Dance
Henry Liles, Manager
34 Morton St. #4C
New York, NY 10014
Phone: 212 255 2729
Fax: 212 243 3228

Joint Forces/Alito Alessi

Alito Alessi is the director of Joint Forces Dance Company, and has been involved with the evolution of Contact Improvisation for over twenty years. He is internationally known as a pioneering teacher and choreographer in the field of dance and disability.

Since 1982, Alessi has produced the Breitenbush Contact Improvisation Teachers and Performers Conference, which has become a major international networking event for those involved in the study, teaching, and performance of New Dance. Joint Forces also produces the annual New Dance Festival in Eugene, Oregon, a performance series featuring the work of internationally renowned dancers and performance artists.

Part of the New Dance Festival is the annual DANCEABILITY Project, a three- to five-day event where able-bodied, disabled, and hearing or visually impaired individuals come together to explore and create movement and dance. Alessi teaches and performs the DANCEABILITY work throughout the United States and Europe with Emery Blackwell, and has created finished and ongoing performing pieces for groups of able-bodied and disabled dancers. Residencies include the New Mexico School of the Deaf (Santa Fe) and the New Dance Lab of Minneapolis.

Alessi has received choreographer's fellowships from the National Endowment for the Arts in 1992, 1993, and 1995 and from the Oregon Arts Commission in 1992.

contact:
Joint Forces Dance
Alito Alessi
P.O. Box 3686
Eugene, OR 97403
Phone: 541 342 3273

Bill T. Jones/Arnie Zane Dance Company

Bill T. Jones began his dance training at the State University of New York at Binghamton, where he studied classical ballet and modern dance. Before forming Bill T. Jones/Arnie Zane Dance Company in 1982, Mr. Jones choreographed and performed internationally both as a soloist and as a duet company with his partner, Arnie Zane.

In addition to creating over forty works for his company, Jones has created dances for Alvin Ailey American Dance Theater, the Boston Ballet, and the Lyon Opera Ballet (where he was appointed resident choreographer in 1993), among others. His works for his company deal with love, loss, and current issues in Jones's life.

Jones has directed a number of operatic and theatrical works, among them works for the Guthrie Theater and the BBC. Notable dance works include *Still/Here* (1994); *Last Supper at Uncle Tom's Cabin/The Promised Land* (1990); and *D-Man in the Waters* (1989). Jones and media artist Gretchen Bender have directed a television version of *Still/Here*.

Jones has been the recipient of two New York Dance and Performance (Bessie) Awards, a Dorothy B. Chandler Performing Arts Award, the *Dance Magazine* Award, and, in 1994, a MacArthur Fellowship. Jones's autobiography, *Last Night on Earth*, was written with Peggy Gillespie and published in 1995 by Pantheon Books.

contact:
Bill T. Jones/Arnie Zane Dance Co.
Jodi Krizer, Manager
853 Broadway, Suite 1706
New York, NY 10003
Phone: 212 477 1850
Fax: 212 777 5263

Pooh Kaye/Eccentric Motions

Pooh Kaye is a filmmaker, a choreographer, and the director of the dance and film company Eccentric Motions. She holds a degree in Fine Arts from The Cooper Union in New York City. Pooh Kaye performed with Simone Forti from 1973 to 1979 as well as performing her own very physical brand of dance. In 1983, Kaye founded Eccentric Motions. The company has performed in the United States and abroad. Her interest in the representation of motion led Kaye to filmmaking. The combination of her experience as a choreographer and an interest in single-frame filmmaking eventually led Pooh Kaye to combine stop-action, two-dimensional animation and the human body in visually riotous dramas that could only exist on film.

Pooh Kaye has been awarded a Guggenheim Fellowship, as well as six NEA Fellowships, three state fellowships, eight NEA Dance Company grants, twelve NYSCA Dance Company Grants, in addition to numerous Special Project Grants for her work in choreography.

contact:
Pooh Kaye/Eccentric Motions
99 Vandam St.
New York, NY 10013

La La La Human Steps/Édouard Lock

Édouard Lock began working in dance at the age of nineteen. From 1975 to 1979, he worked with various Montreal dance companies, and in 1980, he formed his own company, Lock-Danseurs, which later became La La La Human Steps. His choreographies include *Oranges* (1981), for which he won the Jean A. Chalmers Award, Canada's highest choreographic honor; and *Businessman in the Process of Becoming an Angel* (1983), which earned the company's principal dancer, Louise Lecavalier, a New York Dance and Performance (Bessie) Award.

Lock won a Bessie Award in 1986 for the choreography of *Human Sex* (1985). *Infante, C'est Destroy* (1991) was a co-production of Theater Am Turm (Frankfurt), Theatre de la Ville (Paris), Centre National de Danse Contemporaine (Angers), the National Arts Centre (Ottawa), and the Festival International de Nouvelle Danse (Montreal). A one-hour version of the work was televised in the winter of 1996 on Radio-Canada's *Les Beaux Dimanches*, reaching an audience of nearly 360,000 viewers.

La La La Human Steps receives regular financial support from the Canada Council, the Department of Foreign Affairs and International Trade, the Conseil des Arts et des Lettres du Quebec, and the Conseil des Arts of the Montreal Urban Community.

contact:
La La La Human Steps
Anne Viau, Director of Communications
5655, Avenue du Park
Bureau 206
Montreal, Quebec H2V 4H2, Canada
Phone: 514 277 9090
Fax: 514 277 0862

Louise Lecavalier

Born in Montreal, Louise Lecavalier studied classical ballet and modern dance in Montreal and New York. A professional dancer since 1977, she has danced with companies in New York and Montreal, staging a solo performance entitled *No, No, No, I Am Not Mary Poppins*, in Montreal in 1982. Lecavalier joined La La La Human steps in 1981.

In 1985, Lecavalier became the first Canadian to merit New York's Bessie Award for her performance in Edouard Lock's *Businessman in the Process of Becoming an Angel*. She has twice received Canada Council grants and, in 1994, she received an advanced study grant from Quebec's Conseil des Arts et des Lettres.

contact: see La La La Human Steps

Zab Maboungou

Zab Maboungou was born in the Republic of the Congo and presently resides in Montreal. She has studied and worked in close collaboration with many masters of traditional African music and dance, among them Babatunda Olatunji from Nigeria and Lucky Zebila from the Congo, and has worked with various Congolese ballets in both Europe and America.

Maboungou is the artistic director of Compagnie Danse Nyata Nyata, which she founded in 1986. The company is dedicated to the promotion of contemporary African dance and is composed of dancers and percussionists of diverse ethnic origins. Compagnie Danse Nyata Nyata was the only dance company invited to perform in honor of Nelson Mandela's historic visit to Montreal in 1990, where Maboungou's trio, *Hommage*, was performed for an audience of ten thousand people.

In 1987, Maboungou opened Studio Danse Nyata Nyata, where African dance and art classes, as well as workshops, exhibitions, and video screenings, are available for adults and children. There Maboungou teaches courses that she calls "Rhythms and Movements from the Congo."

In May 1995, Maboungou appeared as a special guest speaker during the African Market for the Performing Arts (MASA) held in Abijan, Ivory Coast. Maboungou is the first professional African dancer to be awarded grants by the Canada Arts Council.

contact:
Zab Maboungou
Compagnie Danse Nyata Nyata
Paul Miller, General Manager
4374 Boul. St-Laurent, 3ieme étage
Montreal, Quebec, H2W 1Z5, Canada
Phone: 514 849 9781
Fax: 514 849 9781

Victoria Marks

Victoria Marks is currently a faculty member in the Department of World Arts and Cultures at UCLA. She has most recently returned to the United States from the United Kingdom, where for three and a half years she worked on a collection of choreographic projects and directed the choreography program at London Contemporary Dance School. Marks's choreography is created both for stage and film, and it reflects the distinctive community for whom it is made.

Marks recently choreographed *Outside In* for Candoco. It was filmed by Margaret Williams for BBC. For more than ten years, Marks has been involved creatively with an ongoing project with a group of high school girls in Eastchester, New York, in which dance and choreography provide a vehicle for an exploration of adolescence and identity. Her signature quartet, *Dancing to Music*, is a work for four women of four different generations.

Marks directed her own company from 1985 through 1993. She has been the recipient of grants from the National Endowment for the Arts, the New York State Council on the Arts, the New York Foundation for the Arts, and the London Arts Board, among others. She has received a Fulbright Fellowship in choreography, and numerous awards for her dance films.

contact:
Victoria Marks
578 Rialto Ave.
Venice, CA 90291
Phone: 310 452 5483

Jennifer Monson

In her evening-length works, improvisations, and antic line dances, Jennifer Monson explores extreme physical and emotional states, as well as issues of community. She teaches a wide range of workshops including "Falling (micro & macro)," releasing, improvisation, composition, and "instant line dances." She has taught at various colleges in the United States, as well as in Europe, Venezuela, Tanzania, and Cuba. In 1990, Monson was artist-in-residence at Movement Research, Inc.

Monson has an ongoing collaboration with composer Zeena Parkins in which they investigate the dynamic interplay of movement and music, and has also collaborated with Yvonne Meier. She has performed in works by DANCENOISE, Karen Finley, Eileen Myles & Ellen Fisher, Lisa Kraus, Fred Holland, John Zorn, Yoshiko Chuma, John Bernd, Pooh Kaye/Eccentric Motions, and Jennifer Miller's Circus AMOK, among others. Currently she is collaborating with John Jasperse and DD Dorvillier. In addition, Monson has curated several dance/music improvisation festivals and has a strong commitment to improvisation as a performance form.

Monson is the recipient of the NEA Choreographer's Fellowship for 1989, 1992, 1993–1994, and the NYFA Fellowship for 1989. Her work has been supported by NYSCA, the Jerome Foundation, the Mary Flagler Cary Charitable Trust, and the Martha Porter Fund.

contact:
Jennifer Monson
@The Matzoh Factory
319 Bedford Ave.
Brooklyn, NY 11211
Phone: 718 384 0568

Elizabeth Streb/Ringside

Elizabeth Streb presently resides in New York City. She began making dances in 1979, and formed Streb/Ringside in 1985. Streb has been awarded a three-year choreography fellowship from the National Endowment for the Arts, a Guggenheim, a 1988 New York Dance and Performance (Bessie) Award for her sustained investigation of movement, and a 1994–1995 National Dance Residency Program Award, sponsored by the Pew Charitable Trust.

For the past eight years, Streb has been on the faculty of the Harvard Summer Dance Center. She has taught lecture/demonstrations at several colleges and universities, including Rutgers, St. Lawrence, Princeton, Cornell, Sarah Lawrence, and Temple, and has hosted workshops in Europe and Israel. Streb has worked on several video projects with video artists Mary Lucier and Michael Schwartz, which have aired on the PBS series "Alive From OFF Center" and on "New Television."

Streb/Ringside has performed throughout the United States, Europe, and Canada, and has received funding from the National Endowment for the Arts, the New York

State Council on the Arts, and the New York City Department of Cultural Affairs, as well as numerous other sources.

contact:
Streb/Ringside
International Production Associates
584 Broadway, Suite 1008
New York, NY 10012–3253
Phone: 212 925 2100
Fax: 212 925 2426

Urban Bush Women/Jawole Willa Jo Zollar

Urban Bush Women was established in 1984 by Artistic Director Jawole Willa Jo Zollar. Using contemporary idioms and interdisciplinary forms, the company has created dance/theater works rooted in the folklore and spiritual traditions of African Americans. Through movement, live music, and *a cappella* vocalizations, Urban Bush Women explores the struggle, growth, transformation, and survival of the human spirit. The company seeks to foster cross-cultural exchange through educational seminars and workshops, as well as developmental residencies.

Urban Bush Women has presented major seasons in New York City and has toured extensively nationally and internationally. In 1992, Jawole Willa Jo Zollar and Urban Bush Women received a New York Dance and Performance (Bessie) Award for their collective work from *River Songs* (1984) through Praise House (1990), and in 1994 they received the Capezio Award.

Urban Bush Women designed, in collaboration with educator Lloyd Daniel, the Community Engagement Project to assist in the cultivation of a grassroots-led process through which a city's cultural traditions would be allowed to grow in greater harmony with already established plans for community-based neighborhood development and empowerment. The project was inaugurated in New Orleans in January and February 1992.

contact:
Urban Bush Women
Jawole Willa Jo Zollar, Artistic Director
Rhoda Cerritelli, Managing Director
225 Lafayette Street #201
New York, NY 10012
Phone: 212 343 0041
Fax: 212 343 2551

Notes

INTRODUCTION: WITNESSING DANCE (PP. xiii-xxvi)

1. I use the term *contemporary dance* here to delineate the experimental dance that has taken place over the past decade or so. Although it is rooted in Euro-American modern and postmodern dance, much of this work takes on the hybridity of contemporary culture, at once deconstructionist and visionary. Another reason that I chose the term *contemporary* was to avoid any historical confusion with the term *postmodern dance*. For an interesting debate over the currency of the term postmodern dance see Susan Manning's and Sally Banes's exchanges in *The Drama Review* 120 and 121 (Winter 1988 and Spring 1989).

2. I use the term *somatic* to suggest a bodily as well as a mental intelligence.

3. Don McDonagh's *The Rise and Fall and Rise of Modern Dance* (New York: New American Library, 1970); Marcia B. Siegel, *The Shapes of Change* (Boston: Houghton Mifflin, 1979; rprt. 1985, University of California Press); Suzanne Langer, *Feeling and Form: A Theory of Art* (New York: Scribner's, 1953); and Maxine Sheets-Johnson, *The Phenomenology of Dance* (Madison: University of Wisconsin Press, 1966).

4. Some examples of this new scholarly work are Barbara Browning's *Samba: Resistance in Motion* (Bloomington and Indianapolis: Indiana University Press, 1995); Ann Daly's *Done into Dance* (Bloomington and Indianapolis: Indiana University Press, 1995); Sally Banes's *Writing Dancing in the Age of Postmodernism* (Hanover, N.H., and London: Wesleyan University Press, 1994); Susan Manning's *Ecstasy and the Demon: Feminism and Nationalism in the Dances of Mary Wigman* (Berkeley and Los Angeles: University of California Press, 1993); Gay Morris, ed., *Moving Words* (London and New York, Routledge, 1996); Cynthia Novack's *Sharing the Dance* (Madison: University of Wisconsin Press, 1990); Maria Savigliano's *Tango and the Political Economy of Passion* (Boulder: Westview Press, 1995); and Susan Foster, ed., *Choreographing History* (Bloomington and Indianapolis: Indiana University Press, 1995), and *Corporealities* (London and New York, Routledge, 1996).

5. "Les Ballets C. de la B." is an abbreviated form of Les Ballets Contemporains de la Belgique. As the company's press materials attest: "The group adopted this name as a double-edged satiric twist on the typical generic name of state-sponsored dance companies common in Europe." That this company is not a ballet company will become clear in my description of their work.

6. "Mining the Dancefield: Spectacle, Moving Subjects and Feminist Theory," *Contact Quarterly* 12, no. 1 (Spring/Summer 1990).

7. John Martin, "Metakinesis," in *What Is Dance?* ed. Roger Copeland and Marshall Cohen (Oxford and New York: Oxford University Press, 1983), p. 23.

8. Jawole made this comment while she was a visiting artist-in-residence at Ohio State University. My class was fortunate enough to be graced with her presence one afternoon.

9. Although there may be some parallels between my notion of witnessing within a performance and the witnessing of trauma, I am not invoking notions of testimony and witnessing that are directly related to the Holocaust and the literature and oral history that document this event. For more references about witnessing and Holocaust testimonies see Shoshana Felman and Dori Laub, M.D., *Testimony: Crises of Witnessing in Literature, Psychoanalysis and History* (New York and London: Routledge, 1996). I am indebted to Wendy Hesford for conversations about witnessing.

10. In her introductory essay to the edited volume of *Choreographing History,* Susan Foster writes wittily and insightfully about the physical choreography of the historian's body and the reanimated bodies of history.

11. I would like to thank not only the dancers and choreographers whose work inspired me to write about contemporary dance, but also the company managers who worked so hard to get me the information and materials I needed when I needed them.

MINING THE DANCEFIELD (PP. 1–27)

1. Annette Kolodny, "Dancing Through the Minefield: Some Observations on the Theory, Practice, and Politics of a Feminist Literary Criticism," reprinted in *The New Feminist Criticism*, ed. Elaine Showalter (New York: Pantheon Books, 1985), pp. 151–57.

2. Ibid., p. 163.

3. Jane Desmond, "Embodying Difference: Issues in Dance and Cultural Studies," in *Cultural Critique* 26 (Winter 1993–1994), p. 34.

4. Ibid., p. 34.

5. Elizabeth Grosz, *Volatile Bodies* (Bloomington: Indiana University Press, 1994).

6. Sidonie Smith, *Subjectivity, Identity and the Body* (Bloomington: Indiana University Press, 1993).

7. Judith Butler, "Variations on Sex and Gender: Beauvoir, Wittig and Foucault," in *Feminism as Critique: On the Politics of Gender*, ed. Seyla Benhabib and Drucilla Cornell (Minneapolis: University of Minnesota Press, 1987), p. 133.

8. One of the most extreme examples of this marginalization that I know of was when the parents of a friend of mine refused to speak to her because she gave up her job as a secretary in order to pursue a graduate degree in dance.

9. Judith Butler, *Gender Trouble* (New York: Routledge, 1990), p. 33.

10. Ibid., p. 33.

11. Judith Butler, "Imitation and Gender Insubordination," in *Inside Out: Lesbian Theories, Gay Theories*, ed. Diana Fuss (New York and London: Routledge, 1991), p. 18.

12. Judith Butler, "Performative Acts and Gender Constitution: An Essay in Phenomenology and Feminist Theory," in *Theatre Journal* 40, no. 4 (December 1988), p. 519.

13. Teresa deLauretis, *Alice Doesn't: Feminism, Semiotics, Cinema* (Bloomington: Indiana University Press, 1984), p. 158.

14. Ibid., p. 159.

15. Ibid.

16. Virginia Woolf, *A Room of One's Own* (London: Hogarth Press, 1931), p. 7.

17. Théophile Gautier. Review originally published in *La Presse*, July 30, 1846, and reprinted in *Gautier on Dance*, ed. Ivor Guest (London: Dance Books, 1986), pp. 173–74.

18. Laura Mulvey, "Visual Pleasure and Narrative Cinema," *Screen* 16, no. 3 (Autumn 1975), p. 17.

19. For an insightful analysis of the gendered apparatus of representation in Balanchine's ballets see Ann Daly's article "The Balanchine Woman: Of Hummingbirds and Channel Swimmers," in *The Drama Review* 31, no. 1 (Spring 1987).

20. I am indebted to Wendy Kozol for pointing out this work to me. For examples of work that addresses oppositional gazes see Jane Gaines, "White Privilege and Looking Relations: Race and Gender in Feminist Film Theory," *Screen* 29, no. 4 (1988); bell hooks, "The Oppositional Gaze: Black Female Spectators," in *Black Looks: Race and Representation* (Boston: South End Press, 1992); and E. Deidre Pribram, ed., *Female Spectators: Looking at Film and Television* (London: Verso Press, 1988).

21. Elizabeth Hollander, "On the Pedestal: Notes on Being an Artist's Model," *Raritan* 6 (Summer 1986), pp. 26–37.

22. Ibid., pp. 32–33.

23. Ibid., p. 30.

24. Gordon Craig, quoted in *Your Isadora*, ed. Francis Steegmuller (New York: Random House and the New York Public Library, 1974), p. 23.

25. Ann Daly, "Dance History and Feminist Theory: Reconsidering Isadora Duncan and the Male Gaze," in *Gender in Performance*, ed. Lawrence Senelick (Hanover: University Press of New England, 1992), p. 243.

26. One of the problems that I have with Kristeva's notion of the "chora" is that she too easily accepts the traditional body/mind dichotomy by assuming that this realm of bodily experience is "non-symbolic" and therefore distinguishable from linguistic discourse. Her writing also suggests that the "chora" is precultural. While I do not think that Western culture as a whole has been particularly successful at articulating bodily knowledge, I do not believe that it is necessarily nondiscursive. Obviously one of my goals in writing this book is to try to articulate more fully those very interconnections of bodily and linguistic (both of which are cultural) knowledges.

27. Daly, "Dance History and Feminist Theory," p. 252.

28. Ibid., p. 253.

29. Yvonne Rainer, *Work 1961–1973* (Halifax and New York: The Press of the Nova Scotia College of Art and Design and New York University Press, 1974), p. 51.

30. Ibid., p. 46.

31. Sally Banes, *Terpsichore in Sneakers: Post-Modern Dance* (Middletown: Wesleyan University Press, 1977), p. 44.

32. Ibid., p. 46.

33. Conversation with the artist, Montreal, October 1995.

34. For some recent examples, see *African Culture: The Rhythms of Unity*, ed. Molefi Kete Asante and Kariamu Welsh Asante (Westport, Conn.: Greenwood Press, 1985); *African Dance: An Artistic, Historical, and Philosophical Inquiry*, ed. Kariamu Welsh Asante (Trenton: Africa World Press, Inc., 1996); Jacqui Malone, *Steppin' on the Blues: The Visible Rhythms of African American Dance* (Urbana and Chicago: University of Illinois Press, 1996); and Brenda Dixon Gottschild, *Digging the Africanist Presence in American Performance: Dance and Other Contexts* (Westport, Conn.: Greenwood Press, 1996).

TECHNO BODIES (PP. 28–55)

1. La La La Human Steps Press Packet, 1993.

2. Judith Butler, *Gender Trouble: Feminism and the Subversion of Identity* (New York: Routledge, 1990), p. 93.

3. Diana Fuss, *Essentially Speaking: Feminism, Nature and Difference* (New York: Routledge, 1989) pp. 5–6.

4. Ibid., p. 6.

5. Robert Walser, *Running with the Devil: Power, Gender and Madness in Heavy Metal Music* (Hanover: Wesleyan University Press/University Press of New England, 1993), p. 108.

6. At the fall 1994 CORD conference, an argument broke out about whether Lecavalier could build up to this heightened muscularity without the use of steriods. What interests me here is not whether she uses steriods or not, but the fact that her body so profoundly disturbs our notions of the "natural" female body that even progressive feminists found themselves arguing that Lecavalier needed drugs to alter her "natural" body so fundamentally.

7. Program notes from January 20, 1996, performance at the Ohio Theater, Cleveland.

8. Judy Burns, "Wild Bodies/Wilder Minds: Streb/Ringside and Spectacle," *Women and Performance* 7, no. 1 (issue 13), (1994), p. 101.

9. Streb/Ringside Press Packet, 1996.

10. Besides herself, Streb's women dancers for her 1995–1996 tour were: Hope Clark, who joined the company in 1991; Alma Largey, who joined the company in 1995; and Christine Knight, who joined in 1994.

11. Elizabeth Dempster, "Women Writing the Body: Let's Watch a Little How She Dances," in *Grafts*, ed. Susan Sheridan (London: Verso Press, 1988), pp. 37–38.

12. Gloria Steinem, *Moving Beyond Words* (New York: Simon and Schuster, 1994).

13. Ibid., p. 93.

14. Ibid., pp. 97–98.

15. Ibid., p. 102.

16. Although I find it a highly intriguing topic, it is not within the scope of this study to examine the interconnections between the emergence of identity politics in the last decade and the parallel commercialization and packaging of identity "looks."

17. Susan Bordo, "Reading the Slender Body," in *Body/Politics*, ed. Mary Jacobus, Evelyn Fox Keller, and Sally Shuttleworth (New York: Routledge, 1990), pp. 94–95.

18. For a cogent analysis of the discourse of femininity within this film, see Anne Marie

Balsmo, *Reading the Gendered Body in Contemporary Culture: 1980–1990* (Ph.D. dissertation, University of Illinois at Urbana-Champaign, 1991); and Annette Kuhn, "The Body and Cinema: Some Problems for Feminism," in Sheridan, *Grafts*.

19. Susan Bordo, *Unbearable Weight: Feminism, Western Culture, and the Body* (Berkeley: University of California Press, 1993), p. 27.

20. Alan M. Klein, *Little Big Men: Bodybuilding Subculture and Gender Construction* (Albany: State University of New York Press, 1993), p. 189.

21. Elizabeth Grosz, *Volatile Bodies: Towards a Corporeal Feminism* (Bloomington: University of Indiana Press, 1994), p. 224, n.7.

22. Diane Griffin Crowder, "Lesbians and the (Re/De)Construction of the Female Body," in *Reading the Social Body*, ed. Catherine Burroughs and Jeffery Ehrenreich (Iowa City: University of Iowa Press, 1993), p. 71.

23. Ibid., p. 73.

24. See M. Merleau-Ponty, *Phenomenology of Perception* (London: Routledge and Kegan Paul, 1962).

25. Iris Young, *Throwing Like a Girl and Other Essays in Feminist Philosophy and Social Theory* (Bloomington: Indiana University Press, 1990), p. 150

26. The following detailed analysis of Lecavalier's movement style would have been impossible without the generosity of the company in lending me a video tape of several sections of the spectacle. I am deeply grateful to Anne Viau for accommodating my request.

27. Quote from *The Gazette*, January 15, 1992, contained in La La La Human Steps Press Packet.

MOVING ACROSS DIFFERENCE (PP. 56–92)

1. Théophile Gautier, review originally published in *La Presse*, July 30, 1846; reprinted in *Gautier on Dance*, ed. Ivor Guest (London: Dance Books, 1986) pp. 173–74.

2. Ynestra King, "The Other Body: Reflections on Difference, Disability, and Identity Politics," *Ms.* 3, no. 5 (March/April 1993) p. 73.

3. Nancy Mairs, "On Being a Cripple," in *Plaintext* (Tucson: University of Arizona Press, 1986) pp. 9–10.

4. Ibid., p. 10.

5. Barbara Hillyer, *Feminism and Disability* (Norman: University of Oklahoma Press, 1993), p. 28.

6. Mairs, *Plaintext*, p. 9

7. King, "The Other Body," p. 72

8. Michelle Fine and Adrienne Asch, eds., *Women with Disabilities: Essays in Psychology, Culture and Politics* (Philadelphia: Temple University Press, 1988), p. 4.

9. Ibid., p. 15.

10. King, "The Other Body," p. 75.

11. "Thisability, an Interdisciplinary Conference on Disability and the Arts," University of Michigan, Ann Arbor, May 1995.

12. Mary Russo, "Female Grotesques: Carnival and Theory," in *Feminist Studies/Critical Studies*, ed. Teresa de Lauretis (Bloomington: Indiana University Press, 1986), p. 219.

13. Gus Solomons, Jr., "Seven Men," *Village Voice*, March 17, 1992.

14. Melinda Ule-Grohol, *Dance Movements in Time* (Cleveland: Professional Flair, 1995), p. 1.

15. Cleveland Ballet Dancing Wheels press packet, 1993.

16. Steve Wright, "Disabled Girl, 6, Beams as Dancers Wheel through Ballet," included in Cleveland Ballet Dancing Wheels press packet, 1993.

17. In a recent phone conversation (January 1997), Mary Verdi-Fletcher expressed concern that my analysis of Cleveland Ballet Dancing Wheels was based on earlier work that was very different from the current repertory of the company. I have tried to keep up with the company's changes and in the following discussion I compare dances from 1992 to 1995. My goal here is not to categorize all of the company's productions, but rather to use performances of specific work in order to articulate the issues at stake in the representations of dis/ability.

18. Ule-Grohol, *Dance Movements in Time*, p. 61.

19. Ibid., p. 74.

20. King, "The Other Body," p. 74.

21. L. M. Vincent, *Competing with the Sylph: Dancers and the Pursuit of the Ideal Body Form* (Kansas City, Mo.: Andrews and McMeel, 1979).

22. Suzanne Gordon, *Off Balance: The Real World of Ballet* (New York: Pantheon, 1983); Christy Adair, *Women and Dance: Sylphs and Sirens* (New York: New York University Press, 1992); Gelsey Kirkland with Greg Lawrence, *Dancing on my Grave: An Autobiography* (New York: Doubleday, 1986).

23. Roberta Galler, "The Myth of the Perfect Body," in *Pleasure and Danger: Exploring Female Sexuality*, ed. Carol Vance (Boston: Routledge and Kegan Paul, 1984), p. 166.

24. Ibid., p. 167.

25. Nancy Mairs's most recent collection of essays focuses on dis/ability. See *Waist-High in the World: A Life among the Nondisabled* (Boston: Beacon Press, 1996).

26. Nancy Mairs, *Carnal Acts* (Boston: Beacon Press, 1996), p. 33.

27. Just as I was finishing this manuscript, Rosemarie Garland Thomson's book on images of disability, *Extraordinary Bodies* (New York: Columbia University Press, 1997), came out. In an introductory section entitled "Politicizing Bodily Difference" she provides important background information on the ADA.

28. One might argue that this is no mere historical coincidence, but rather a very specific social backlash against proactive groups working on disability issues. For further discussions of how society molds bodies into its own ideal images, see Susan Bordo, *Unbearable Weight: Feminism, Western Culture, and the Body* (Berkeley: University of California Press, 1993), and Emily Martin, *Flexible Bodies: The Role of Immunity in American Culture from the Days of Polio to the Age of AIDS* (Boston: Beacon Press, 1994).

29. King, "The Other Body," p. 74.

30. Arlene Croce, "Discussing the Undiscussable," *The New Yorker*, December 26, 1994/January 22, 1995, p. 55.

31. Ibid., p. 54.

32. Marcia Siegel, "Survival by Drowning," *New York Press*, April 17, 1989.

33. Certainly the extraordinary influence of Japanese Butoh on contemporary American dance lies in Butoh's brilliant synthesis of the grotesque and classical bodies. Through the use of repetition, dramatic changes in speed and level, and vocal sounds, Butoh reveals

the grotesque within the classical and vice versa. As my description of their latest work in the introduction attests, another company that works back and forth across this continuum is Les Ballets C. de la B.

34. Adam Benjamin, "In Search of Integrity," *Dance Theatre Journal* 10, no. 4 (Autumn 1993), p. 45.

35. Ibid., p. 44.

36. Chris de Marigny, "A Little World of Its Own," *Ballet International* 16, no. 3 (June 1993), p. 30.

37. Ibid., p. 29.

38. I am indebted to Jodi Falk for lending me a copy of the British TV program "Here and Now" that contained a spot on Toole's retirement. In her presentation at the 1996 CORD conference, Falk quoted a June 1996 review of Can*doco* that lamented his departure, calling the rest of the company a "competent but unremarkable bunch of dancers." See "Questioning the Dancing Body" by Jodi Falk in the 1996 CORD conference proceedings.

39. Delphine Goater, "Et Pourtant Ils Dansent," *Les Saisons de la Danse* no. 256 (May 1994), p. 23.

40. Charlene Curtiss, quoted in "Wheelchair Dancer Teaches Moves to Disabled Performers," *Tri-City Herald* (Seattle), June 1, 1993 (article contained in artist's press packet).

41. Cynthia Novack, *Sharing the Dance: Contact Improvisation and American Culture* (Madison: University of Wisconsin Press, 1990), p. 186. For references to Judson Dance Theater see Sally Banes's work on the era, especially *Terpsichore in Sneakers* and *Democracy's Body: Judson Dance Theater 1962–1964*.

42. Curt Siddall, "Contact Improvisation," *East Bay Review* (September 1976), cited in John Gamble, "On Contact Improvisation," *The Painted Bride Quarterly* 4, no. 1 (Spring 1977), p. 36.

43. Steve Paxton, "3 Days," *Contact Quarterly* 17, no. 1 (Winter 1992), p. 13.

44. Ibid., p. 16.

45. Ibid., p. 14.

46. This is one reason why Contact rarely works on a proscenium stage. Most often Contact concerts are presented in alternative spaces, sometimes in the round.

47. Russo, "Female Grotesques," p. 213.

INCALCULABLE CHOREOGRAPHIES (PP. 93–118)

1. After studying a multitude of diverse movement techniques, including ballet, T'ai Chi, modern dance, and Contact Improvisation, Chouinard began to shape her own style of performance in 1978. For a long time her publicity information insistently underscored her solo status ("Marie Chouinard's work is resolutely personal. . . . An independent choreographer, she dances solo and interprets only her own pieces."). But recently, she has begun to work with her own dance company. During the eighties, Chouinard's work coincided with an explosion of experimental dance in Québec, and she is well known as part of the dance renaissance in Montreal.

2. Jacques Derrida and Christie McDonald, "Choreographies," *Diacritics* 12, no. 2 (Summer 1982), pp. 66–76.

3. Ibid., p. 69.

4. For a more in-depth discussion of this problematic move in Derrida see Jane Flax, *Thinking Fragments* (Berkeley: University of California Press, 1990), pp. 213ff; and Diana Fuss, *Essentially Speaking: Feminism, Nature, and Difference* (New York: Routledge, 1989), pp. 12ff.

5. Derrida and McDonald, "Choreographies," p. 69.

6. Ibid., p. 76.

7. *Marie Chien Noir* was originally premiered in 1982. I saw the first section, "Mimas, Lune de Saturne," at Dance Theater Workshop in New York City in October 1985.

8. "Panel: Canadian Choreography, The Development and Practise of the Craft," transcript published in *The Dance Connection* 6, no. 1 (March/April 1988), pp. 19–29.

9. In an interview with the author (Montreal, October 15, 1988) Chouinard registered her exasperation with the critical reception of her work, which focuses only on the afterimage of her body, not the actual presence of its performance: "It's incredible! . . . they [the critics] never speak of my dance, how I move, only the impression I made upon them."

10. "She is part woman, part animal, switching back and forth until one loses any sense of her as human. She becomes a mythic vision from another world, a creature who moves and screeches, warbles and screams with unparalleled intensity" (Linda Howe-Beck, *Montreal Gazette*, April 1986). "Chouinard dances like an extraterrestrial creature" (Ine Rietsap, *N.R.C.* Amsterdam 1986). Out of ten reviews of Chouinard's work (describing three different dances), eight described her persona as either a "creature," "sorceress," or "witch."

11. Hélène Cixous and Catherine Clément, *The Newly Born Woman* (Minneapolis: University of Minnesota Press, 1986); Hélène Cixous, *"Coming to Writing" and Other Essays*, ed. Deborah Jenson (Cambridge: Harvard University Press, 1991).

12. Cixous, "Coming to Writing," p. 9.

13. The relationship of the body to writing has been extremely problematic in feminist theory. During the 1980s, this discussion often ended up being staged as a debate between Anglo-American and French feminist theorists. The scope of my study does not allow me to take up the terms of this debate, but many anthologies and essays have focused on this issue. For general discussions of French feminist thought see: *New French Feminisms*, ed. Elaine Marks and Isabelle de Courtivron (New York: Schocken Books, 1981); Toril Moi, *Sexual/Textual Politics* (New York: Methuen, 1985); and *Revaluing French Feminism*, ed. Nancy Fraser and Sandra Lee Bartky (Bloomington: Indiana University Press, 1992). For discussions of the role of "feminine writing" in Cixous's work specifically, see *The Body and the Text: Hélène Cixous, Reading and Teaching*, ed. Helen Wilcox, Keith McWatters, Ann Thompson, and Linda Williams (New York: St. Martin's Press, 1990); and Verena Conley, *Hélène Cixous: Writing the Feminine* (Lincoln: University of Nebraska Press, 1984).

14. See Diana Fuss, *Essentially Speaking*, especially ch. 1.

15. Cixous and Clément, *The Newly Born Woman*, p. 95.

16. Ibid., p. 83.

17. Ibid., p. 90.

18. Ibid., p. 91.

19. Cixous, "Coming to Writing," p. 24.

20. Ibid., p. 52.

21. Cixous, "Sorties," from *The Newly Born Woman*, p. 92.

22. Marie Chouinard, publicity materials from press packet, 1985.

23. Cixous and Clément, *The Newly Born Woman*, pp. 94–95.

24. Jane Flax, *Thinking Fragments*, p. 215.

25. Mary Ann Doane, "The Voice in the Cinema: The Articulation of Body and Space," *Yale French Studies*, no. 60 (1980), p. 50.

26. Ibid., p. 35.

27. Ibid., p. 41.

28. Ibid., p. 42.

29. Kaja Silverman, *The Acoustic Mirror: The Female Voice in Psychoanalysis and Cinema*. Bloomington: Indiana University Press, 1988), p. 141.

30. Jacques Derrida, "Pas," in *Parages* (Paris: Éditions Galilée, 1986), p. 54.

31. Cixous, "Coming to Writing," p. 23.

32. "This Strange Institution Called Literature," an interview with Jacques Derrida by Derek Attridge in Jacques Derrida, *Acts of Literature*, ed. Derek Attridge (New York: Routledge, 1992), p. 41.

33. Ibid., p. 62.

34. Cixous, "Difficult Joys," in Wilcox et al., eds., *The Body and the Text*, p. 14.

35. Ibid.

36. This work premiered on July 9, 1987, at the Ottawa National Arts Center. I saw it two days later at the U.S. premiere on July 11, 1987, at the Pepsico Summerfare Festival in New York. Chouinard's dance is based on photographs of Nijinski in *L'Après-midi d'un faune* by Adolphe de Meyer. These photographs were published in 1983 in a book of the same name by Dance Horizons Press, New York. Although the 1987 programs give the title as *La Faune*, later publicity packets—in an interesting slippage of the original and the copy—refer to the dance as either *Le Faune*, or *L'Après-midi d'un faune*.

37. Lynn Garafola, *Diaghilev's Ballets Russes* (New York: Oxford University Press, 1989), p. 56.

38. Chouinard, publicity materials, 1987.

39. Interview with the author, Montreal, October 15, 1988.

40. Cixous, "Difficult Joys," p. 27.

DANCING BODIES AND THE STORIES THEY TELL (PP. 119–149)

1. Certain sections of this chapter are published in "Auto-Body Stories," in *Meaning in Motion*, ed. Jane Desmond (Durham: Duke University Press, 1997).

2. In Paul Eakins, *Fictions in Autobiography: Studies in the Art of Self-Invention* (Princeton: Princeton University Press, 1985).

3. This same pattern can be seen in Jones's recently published autobiography, *Last Night on Earth* (New York: Pantheon Books, 1995).

4. Amanda Smith, "Autobiography and the Avant-Garde," *Dance Magazine* (January 1985), p. 50.

5. Johanna Boyce, quoted in Amanda Smith, "Making the Personal Political," *Village Voice*, April 24, 1984.

6. Julinda Lewis, *Other Stages*, February 19, 1983.

7. I am thinking of groups such as Liz Lerman/Dance Exchange and Dancers of the

Third Age, as well as companies that do specific community projects such as David Dorf-man Dance Company's "The Athletes Project" and "The Family Project," and Blondell Cummings' work with intergenerational women.

8. Sidonie Smith, *Subjectivity, Identity and the Body: Women's Autobiographical Practices in the Twentieth Century* (Bloomington: Indiana University Press, 1993), p. 5.

9. bell hooks, *Talking Back: thinking feminist, thinking black* (Boston: South End Press, 1989), p. 9.

10. Sidonie Smith, *A Poetics of Women's Autobiography* (Bloomington: Indiana University Press, 1987), p. 175.

11. In the last chapter, I discussed the importance of voice within the theatrical perfor-mances of Marie Chouinard. In that context, I thought of voice quite literally, as a calling out across space, arguing that Chouinard's amplified voice was at once an extension of her corporeality and a way of denaturalizing her body. Oftentimes, however, feminist scholar-ship metaphorizes voice as a kind of immediate calling forth of women's subjectivity. While I applaud these very performative literary works (such as Cixous's *The Newly Born Woman*) I want to make it clear that I am thinking of voice as a mode of representation and not as a pure expression.

12. Nancy Miller, "Writing Fictions: Women's Autobiography in France," in *Subject to Change: Reading Feminist Writing* (New York: Columbia University Press, 1988), p. 60.

13. Ibid., p. 61.

14. Anna Kisselgoff, "Music's Absence Marks Five Dances," *New York Times*, March 14, 1971.

15. Veta Goler, "Dancing Herself: Choreography, Autobiography, and the Expression of the Black Woman Self in the Work of Dianne McIntyre, Blondell Cummings and Ja-wole Willa Jo Zolar," Ph.D dissertation, Emory University, 1994, pp. 237–39. Goler's disser-tation provides a wonderful overview of Cummings's artistic development and choreo-graphic work.

16. For instance, one of Cummings's latest projects came out of an artistic residency in Japan. The residency culminated in a performance with Junko Kikuchi entitled *Women in the Dunes*, which premiered at Japan Society December 14 and 15, 1995.

17. Marianne Goldberg, "Transformative Aspects of Meredith Monk's 'Education of the Girlchild.'" *Women and Performance* 1, no. 1, (Spring/Summer 1983), pp. 19–28.

18. Linda Small, "Best Feet Forward," *Village Voice*, March 10, 1980.

19. Paula Sommers, "Blondell Cummings: Life Dances," *Washington Post*, November 30, 1984.

20. Quoted in ibid.

21. Goler, *Dancing Herself*, p. 261.

22. Ibid., pp. 248–49.

23. Burt Supree "Worlds Apart," *Village Voice*, December 17–23, 1980.

24. Goler, *Dancing Herself*, p. 256.

25. Quoted in Debra Cash, "Blondell Cummings Melds Two Worlds of Dance." *Boston Globe*, January 1985 (courtesy of artist's press packet).

26. Nancy Goldner, "Electric Cooking," *Saturday Review* (May/June 1983).

27. Toni Morrison, "The Site of Memory," in *Inventing the Truth*, ed. William Zinsser (Boston: Houghton Mifflin Co., 1987), p. 115.

28. *New York Times*, August 7, 1988.

29. Interview with the author in New York City, 7 February 1989.

30. Interview in Michael Blackwood's film *Retracing Steps*, 1988.

31. Susan Friedman, "Women's Autobiographical Selves: Theory and Practice," in *The Private Self*, ed. Shari Benstock (Chapel Hill: University of North Carolina Press, 1988), p. 34.

32. Ibid., p. 40.

33. Quoted in Regina Blackburn, "In Search of the Black Female Self: Afro-American Women's Autobiographies and Ethnicity," in *Women's Autobiography: Essays in Criticism*, ed. Estelle Jelinek (Bloomington: Indiana University Press, 1980), p. 139.

34. Trinh T. Minh-ha, *When the Moon Waxes Red* (New York: Routledge, 1991), p. 157.

35. Sidonie Smith, *Subjectivity, Identity and the Body*, p. 23.

36. Jamaica Kincaid, 1987. This text was commissioned for *Basic Strategies V*.

37. Elizabeth Grosz, *Volatile Bodies: Towards a Corporeal Feminism* (Bloomington: Indiana University Press, 1994), p. 209.

38. For an insightful analysis of how the body has been constructed as a fortress against disease, etc., see Emily Martin's recent book *Flexible Bodies: Tracking Immunity in American Culture—From the Days of Polio to the age of AIDS* (Boston: Beacon Press, 1994).

39. David Dorfman quoted in Iris Fanger, "Looking Up: David Dorfman's Ascending Boundaries," *Dance Magazine* (April 1992), pp. 59–61.

40. Veta Goler, "Living with the Doors Open: An Interview with Blondell Cummings," in *High Performance* (Spring/Summer 1995), p. 21.

EMBODYING HISTORY (PP. 150–177)

1. Although these days it is customary to hyphenate African-American only when it is used as an adjective (African-American performance) and not when it is used to describe a people (African Americans), I still think it is valuable to recall Trinh T. Minh-Ha's concept of the hyphenated realities of underrepresented peoples. Indeed, I rather like the inseparability of African-American, suggesting that this is an identity that, while contradictory, is a whole, not the sum of two parts.

2. Toni Morrison, "The Site of Memory," in *Out There: Marginalization and Contemporary Cultures*, ed. Russell Ferguson, Martha Gever, Trinh T. Minh-ha, Cornel West (New York: New Museum of Contemporary Art; and Cambridge, Mass.: MIT Press, 1990), p. 303.

3. Trinh T. Minh-ha, *Woman, Native, Other: Writing Postcoloniality and Feminism* (Bloomington: Indiana University Press, 1989), p. 119.

4. Ibid., p. 121.

5. Ibid., p. 122.

6. This is the excuse that Sue-Ellen Case uses in her simultaneous recognition and dismissal of theater by women of color at the end of her book *Feminism and Theater* (New York: Methuen, 1988). For an interesting analysis of her critical position see Michael Awkward's book *Negotiating Difference: Race, Gender, and the Politics of Positionality* (Chicago: University of Chicago Press, 1995), pp. 87–90.

7. Awkward, *Negotiating Difference*, p. 60.

8. Ibid., p. 60.

9. Ibid., p. 61.

10. Rich, quoted in Awkward, *Negotiating Difference*, p. 41.

11. Richard Yarborough, "Strategies of Black Characterization in *Uncle Tom's Cabin* and the Early Afro-American Novel," in *New Essays on Uncle Tom's Cabin*, ed. Eric J. Sundquist (Cambridge and New York, Cambridge University Press, 1986), p. 63.

12. Jane Tompkins, *Sensational Designs: The Cultural Work of American Fiction 1790–1860* (Oxford and New York: Oxford University Press, 1985), p. 124.

13. Eric Lott, *Love and Theft: Blackface Minstrelsy and the American Working Class* (Oxford and New York: Oxford University Press, 1993), p. 214.

14. Ibid., p. 221.

15. *New York Daily Times*, July 27, 1853, quoted in Lott, *Love and Theft*, p. 217. For more on Germon's acting see Thomas Gossett, *Uncle Tom's Cabin and American Culture* (Dallas: Southern Methodist University Press, 1985), pp. 278–79.

16. Lott, *Love and Theft*, p. 228.

17. Bill T. Jones, *Last Night on Earth* (New York: Pantheon Books, 1995), p. 205.

18. Ibid., p. 206.

19. Lott, *Love and Theft*, p. 236.

20. In *Love and Theft*, Lott elaborates the multiple and complex layers of meaning and subversion in the American minstrel tradition, complicating the analysis of blackface that serves only to reveal its racist stereotypes by asking what kinds of unconscious desires and conscious class connections are also negotiated in blacking up.

21. Harriet Beecher Stowe, *Uncle Tom's Cabin or, Life Among the Lowly* (New York: Penguin, 1987), p. 44.

22. Jacqueline Shea Murphy, "Unrest and Uncle Tom: Bill T. Jones/Arnie Zane Dance Company's *Last Supper at Uncle Tom's Cabin/The Promised Land*, in *Bodies of the Text: Dance as Theory, Literature as Dance*, ed. Ellen W. Goellner and Jacqueline Shea Murphy (New Brunswick: Rutgers University Press, 1995), p. 82.

23. Jones, *Last Night on Earth*, p. 207.

24. I thank Caroline Jackson-Smith for pointing out this reading to me.

25. Ibid., p. 207.

26. Allen's text is printed in the program for the world premiere of *Last Supper at Uncle Tom's Cabin/The Promised Land*.

27. Jewelle Gomez, *The Gilda Stories* (Ithaca, NY: Firebrand Books, 1991), p. 39.

28. Jewelle Gomez, *43 Septembers* (Ithaca, NY: Firebrand Books, 1993), p. 69.

29. Ibid., pp. 78–79.

30. This quotation is a transcription of the narrator's voice-over during this section of the piece.

31. I saw a performance of *Bones and Ash* in Columbus, Ohio, on September 23, 1995, and another one in New York City in November 1996. I am grateful to the company for providing me with an early video of their performance in Iowa City (September 15, 1995). These are the sources for my movement descriptions in the piece. As with any performance work, the dancing and even the text can go through various and multiple revisions. Recently, Pat Hall-Smith has replaced Deborah Thomas as Gilda in the first act.

32. Although the Irissas are not featured in Gomez's *The Gilda Stories* per se, there are teacher characters like them in the novel, particularly Sorel and Anthony.

33. Nina Auerbach, *Our Vampires, Ourselves* (Chicago: University of Chicago Press, 1995), p. 185.

34. Veta Goler, "Dancing Herself: Choreography, Autobiography, and the Expression of the Black Woman Self in the Work of Dianne McIntyre, Blondell Cummings and Jawole Willa Jo Zollar," Ph.D. dissertation, Emory University, 1994, p. 167.

35. Halifu Osumare, "The New Moderns: The Paradox of Eclecticism and Singularity," in *African American Genius in Modern Dance*, ed. Gerald E. Myers (Durham, N.C.: American Dance Festival, 1993).

36. See the printed version of Zollar's talk in *Looking Out: Perspectives on Dance and Criticism in a Multicultural World*, ed. David Gere (New York: Schirmer Books, 1995).

37. Jones, *Last Night on Earth*, p. 223.

Selected Bibliography

Adair, Christy. *Women and Dance: Sylphs and Sirens*. New York: New York University Press, 1992.

Albright, Ann Cooper. "Mining the Dancefield: Spectacle, Moving Subjects, and Feminist Theory," *Contact Quarterly* 12, no. 1 (Spring/Summer 1990).

Asante, Molefi Kete, and Kariamu Welsh Asante. *African Culture: The Rhythms of Unity*. Westport, Conn.: Greenwood Press, 1985.

Asante, Kariamu Welsh, ed. *African Dance: An Artistic, Historical, and Philosophical Inquiry*. Trenton: Africa World Press, Inc., 1996.

Attridge, Derek. "This Strange Institution Called Literature," an interview with Jacques Derrida. In *Acts of Literature*, ed. Derek Attridge. New York: Routledge, 1992.

Auerbach, Nina. *Our Vampires, Ourselves*. Chicago: University of Chicago Press, 1995.

Awkward, Michael. *Negotiating Difference: Race, Gender, and the Politics of Positionality*. Chicago: University of Chicago Press, 1995.

Balsmo, Anne Marie. "Reading the Gendered Body in Contemporary Culture: 1980–1990." Unpublished Ph.D. dissertation, University of Illinois at Urbana-Champaign, 1991.

Banes, Sally. *Terpsichore in Sneakers: Post-Modern Dance*. Middletown: Wesleyan University Press, 1977.

———. *Democracy's Body: Judson Dance Theater 1962–1964*. Ann Arbor: UMI Research Press, 1983.

———. *Writing Dancing in the Age of Postmodernism*. Hanover and London: Wesleyan University Press, 1994.

Benhabib, Seyla, and Drucilla Cornell. *Feminism as Critique: On the Politics of Gender*. Minneapolis: University of Minnesota Press, 1987.

Benjamin, Adam. "In Search of Integrity," *Dance Theatre Journal* 10, no. 4 (Autumn 1993).

Benstock, Shari, ed. *The Private Self: Theory and Practice of Women's Autobiographical Writings*. Chapel Hill: University of North Carolina Press, 1988.

Bordo, Susan. "Reading the Slender Body." *Body/Politics*. New York: Routledge, 1990.

———. *Unbearable Weight: Feminism, Western Culture, and the Body*. Berkeley: University of California Press, 1993.

Brodzki, Beth, and Celeste Schenck, eds. *Life/Lines: Theorizing Women's Autobiography*. Ithaca: Cornell University Press, 1988.

Browning, Barbara. *Samba: Resistance in Motion*. Bloomington: Indiana University Press, 1995.

Burns, Judy. "Wild Bodies/Wilder Minds: Streb/Ringside and Spectacle," *Women and Performance* 7, no. 1 (issue 13) (1994).

Butler, Judith. "Performative Acts and Gender Constitution: An Essay in Phenomenology and Feminist Theory," *Theatre Journal* 40, no. 4 (December 1988).

———. *Gender Trouble: Feminism and the Subversion of Identity*. New York: Routledge, 1990.

Cixous, Hélène. "Difficult Joys." *The Body and the Text*. New York: St. Martin's Press, 1990.

———. *"Coming to Writing" and Other Essays*, ed. Deborah Jensen. Cambridge and London: Harvard University Press, 1991.

Cixous, Hélène, and Catherine Clément. *The Newly Born Woman*. Minneapolis: University of Minnesota Press, 1986.

Conley, Verena. *Hélène Cixous: Writing the Feminine*. Lincoln: University of Nebraska Press, 1984.

Contact Quarterly. "Dancing with Different Populations," vol. 17, no. 1 (Winter 1992).

Copeland, Roger, and Marshall Cohen, eds. *What is Dance?* New York: Oxford University Press, 1983.

Croce, Arlene. "Discussing the Undiscussable," *New Yorker*, April 17, 1989.

Crowder, Diane Griffin. "Lesbians and the (Re/De)Construction of the Female Body." *Reading the Social Body*. Iowa City: University of Iowa Press, 1993.

Daly, Ann. "The Balanchine Woman: Of Hummingbirds and Channel Swimmers," *The Drama Review* 31, no. 1 (Spring 1987).

———. "Dance History and Feminist Theory: Reconsidering Isadora Duncan and the Male Gaze." *Gender and Performance*. Hanover: University Press of New England, 1992.

———. *Done into Dance: Isadora Duncan in America*. Bloomington: Indiana University Press, 1995.

DeLauretis, Teresa. *Alice Doesn't: Feminism, Semiotics, Cinema*. Bloomington: Indiana University Press, 1984.

————, ed. *Feminist Studies/Critical Studies*. Bloomington: University of Indiana Press, 1986.

deMarigny, Chris. "A Little World of Its Own," *Ballet International* 16, no. 3 (June 1993).

Dempster, Elizabeth. "Women Writing the Body: Let's Watch a Little How She Dances." In *Grafts*, ed. Susan Sheridan. London: Verso, 1988.

Derrida, Jacques. "Pas," *Parages*. Paris: Éditions Galilée, 1986.

Derrida, Jacques, and Christie McDonald. "Choreographies," *Diacritics* 12, no. 2 (Summer 1982).

Doane, Mary Ann. "The Voice in the Cinema: The Articulation of Body and Space," *Yale French Studies* 60 (1980), pp. 33–50.

Eakins, Paul. *Fictions in Autobiography: Studies in the Art of Self-Invention*. Princeton: Princeton University Press, 1985.

Fanger, Iris. "Looking Up: David Dorfman's Ascending Boundaries," *Dance Magazine* (April 1992).

Fine, Michelle, and Adrienne Asch, eds. *Women with Disabilities: Essays in Psychology, Culture and Politics*. Philadelphia: Temple University Press, 1988.

Flax, Jane. *Thinking Fragments*. Berkeley: University of California Press, 1990.

Foster, Susan Leigh, ed. *Choreographing History*. Bloomington: Indiana University Press, 1995.

————. *Corporealities: Dancing Knowledge, Culture and Power*. New York and London: Routledge, 1996.

Fraser, Nancy, and Sandra Lee Bartky, eds. *Revaluing French Feminism*. Bloomington: Indiana University Press, 1992.

Fuss, Diana. *Essentially Speaking: Feminism, Nature and Difference*. New York: Routledge, 1989.

————, ed. *Inside Out: Lesbian Theories, Gay Theories*. New York and London: Routledge, 1991.

Gaines, Jane. "White Privilege and Looking Relations: Race and Gender in Feminist Film Theory," *Screen* 29, no. 4 (Winter 1988).

Gamble, John. "On Contact Improvisation," *The Painted Bride Quarterly* 4, no. 1 (Spring 1977).

Garafola, Lynn. *Diaghilev's Ballets Russes*. New York: Oxford University Press, 1989.

Gates, Henry Louis, Jr., ed. *Bearing Witness: Selections from African-American Autobiographies in the Twentieth Century*. New York: Pantheon Books, 1991.

Goater, Delphine. "Et Portant Ils Dansent," *Les Saisons de la Danse* 256 (May 1994).

Goellner, Ellen W., and Jaqueline Shea Murphy, eds. *Bodies of the Text: Dance as Theory, Literature as Dance*. New Brunswick: Rutgers University Press, 1995.

Goldner, Nancy. "Electric Cooking," *Saturday Review* (May/June 1983).

Goler, Veta. "Dancing Herself: Choreography, Autobiography, and the Expression of the Black Woman Self in the Work of Dianne McIntyre, Blondell Cummings and Jawole Willa Jo Zolar." Unpublished Ph.D. dissertation, Emory University, 1994.

SELECTED BIBLIOGRAPHY

Gomez, Jewelle. *The Gilda Stories*. Ithaca: Firebrand Books, 1991.

Gordon, Suzanne. *Off Balance: The Real World of Ballet*. New York: Pantheon, 1983.

Gossett, Thomas. *Uncle Tom's Cabin and American Culture*. Dallas: Southern Methodist University Press, 1985.

Gottschild, Brenda Dixon. *Digging the Africanist Presence in American Performance: Dance and Other Contexts*. Westport, Conn.: Greenwood Press, 1996.

Grosz, Elizabeth. *Volatile Bodies: Towards a Corporeal Feminism*. Bloomington: Indiana University Press, 1994.

Guest, Ivor, ed. *Gautier on Dance*. London: Dance Books, 1986.

Hillyer, Barbara. *Feminism and Disability*. Norman: University of Oklahoma Press, 1993.

Hollander, Elizabeth. "On the Pedestal: Notes on Being an Artist's Model," *Raritan* 6, no. 1 (Summer 1986).

hooks, bell. *Talking Back: thinking feminist, thinking black*. Boston: South End Press, 1989.

————. *Black Looks: Race and Representation*. Boston: South End Press, 1992.

Jelinek, Estelle, ed. *Women's Autobiography: Essays in Criticism*. Bloomington: Indiana University Press, 1980.

Jones, Bill T. *Last Night on Earth*. New York: Pantheon Books, 1995.

King, Ynestra. "The Other Body: Reflections on Difference, Disability, and Identity Politics." *Ms.* 3, no. 5 (March/April 1993).

Kirkland, Gelsey, with Greg Lawrence. *Dancing on My Grave: An Autobiography*. New York: Doubleday, 1986.

Kisselgoff, Anna. "Music's Absence Marks Five Dances," *New York Times*, March 14, 1971.

Klein, Alan M. *Little Big Men: Bodybuilding Subculture and Gender Construction*. Albany: State University of New York Press, 1993.

Kolodny, Annette. "Dancing Through the Minefield: Some Observations on the Theory, Practice, and Politics of a Feminist Literary Criticism." In *The New Feminist Criticism*, ed. Elaine Showalter. New York: Pantheon Books, 1985.

Kuhn, Annette. "The Body and Cinema: Some Problems for Feminism." In *Grafts*, ed. Susan Sheridan. London: Verso, 1988.

Langer, Suzanne. *Feeling and Form: A Theory of Art*. New York: Scribner's, 1953.

Lott, Eric. *Love and Theft: Blackface Minstrelsy and the American Working Class*. Oxford: Oxford University Press, 1993.

McDonagh, Don. *The Rise and Fall and Rise of Modern Dance*. New York: New American Library, 1970.

Mairs, Nancy. *Plaintext*. Tucson: The University of Arizona Press, 1986.

————. *Carnal Acts*. Boston: Beacon Press, 1996.

————. *Waist-High in the World: A Life Among the Nondisabled*. Boston: Beacon Press, 1996.

SELECTED BIBLIOGRAPHY

Malone, Jaqui. *Steppin' on the Blues: The Visible Rhythms of African Dance*. Urbana and Chicago: University of Illinois Press, 1996.

Manning, Susan. *Ecstasy and the Demon: Feminism and Nationalism in the Dances of Mary Wigman*. Berkeley and Los Angeles: University of California Press, 1993.

Marks, Elaine, and Isabelle de Courtivron, eds. *New French Feminisms*. New York: Schocken Books, 1981.

Martin, Emily. *Flexible Bodies: The Role of Immunity in American Culture from the Days of Polio to the Age of AIDS*. Boston: Beacon Press, 1994.

Merleau-Ponty, M. *Phenomenology of Perception*. London: Routledge and Kegan Paul, 1962.

Miller, Nancy. *Subject to Change: Reading Feminist Writing*. New York: Columbia University Press, 1988.

Minh-ha, Trinh T. *Woman, Native, Other: Writing Postcoloniality and Feminism*. Bloomington: Indiana University Press, 1989.

Moi, Toril. *Sexual/Textual Politics*. New York: Methuen, 1985.

Morris, Gay, ed. *Moving Words: Rewriting Dance*. New York and London: Routledge, 1996.

Morrison, Toni. "The Site of Memory." *Out There: Marginalization and Contemporary Cultures*. New York: Museum of Contemporary Art; and Cambridge, Mass.: MIT Press, 1990.

Mulvey, Laura. "Visual Pleasures and Narrative Cinema." *Screen* 16, no. 3 (Autumn 1975).

Murphy, Jacqueline Shea. "Unrest and Uncle Tom: Bill T. Jones/Arnie Zane Dance Company's *Last Supper at Uncle Tom's Cabin/The Promised Land*." *Bodies of the Text: Dance as Theory, Literature as Dance*. New Brunswick: Rutgers University Press, 1995.

Myers, Gerald E., ed. *African American Genius in American Dance*. Durham, N.C.: American Dance Festival, 1993.

Novack, Cynthia. *Sharing the Dance*. Madison: University of Wisconsin Press, 1990.

Paxton, Steve. "Three Days," *Contact Quarterly* 17, no. 1 (Winter 1992).

Pribram, E. Deidre, ed. *Female Spectators: Looking at Film and Television*. London: Verso, 1988.

Rainer, Yvonne. *Work 1961–1973*. Halifax and New York: The Press of the Nova Scotia College of Art and Design and New York University Press, 1974.

Savigliano, Marta. *Tango and the Political Economy of Passion*. Boulder: Westview Press, 1995.

Sheets-Johnson, Maxine. *The Phenomenology of Dance*. Madison: University of Wisconsin Press, 1966.

Showalter, Elaine, ed. *The New Feminist Criticism*. New York: Pantheon Books, 1985.

Siegal, Marcia B. *The Shapes of Change*. Boston: Houghton Mifflin, 1979.

———. "Survival by Drowning," *New York Press*, April 17, 1989.

Silverman, Kaja. *The Acoustic Mirror: The Female Voice in Psychoanalysis and Cinema*. Bloomington: University of Indiana Press, 1988.

Small, Linda. "Best Feet Forward," *Village Voice*, March 10, 1980.

Smith, Amanda. "Making the Personal Political," *Village Voice*, April 24, 1984.

———. "Autobiography and the Avant-Garde," *Dance Magazine* (January 1985).

Smith, Sidonie. *A Poetics of Women's Autobiography*. Bloomington: Indiana University Press, 1987.

———. *Subjectivity, Identity, and the Body*. Bloomington: Indiana University Press, 1993.

Solomons, Gus, Jr. "Seven Men," *Village Voice*, March 17, 1992.

Sommers, Paula. "Blondell Cummings: Life Dances," *Washington Post*, November 30, 1984.

Stanton, Domna C., ed., *The Female Autograph*. Chicago and London: University of Chicago Press, 1984.

Steegmuller, Francis, ed. *Your Isadora*. New York: Random House and the New York Public Library, 1974.

Steinem, Gloria. *Moving Beyond Words*. New York: Simon and Schuster, 1994.

Supree, Burt. "Worlds Apart," *Village Voice*, December 17–23, 1980.

Thomson, Rosemarie Garland. *Extraordinary Bodies*. New York: Columbia University Press, 1997.

Tompkins, Jane. *Sensational Designs: The Cultural Work of American Fiction 1790–1860*. Oxford and New York: Oxford University Press, 1985.

Ule-Grohol, Melinda. *Dance Movements in Time*. Cleveland: Professional Flair, 1995.

Vance, Carol, ed. *Pleasure and Danger: Exploring Female Sexuality*. Boston: Routledge and Kegan Paul, 1984.

Vincent, L. M. *Competing with the Sylph: Dancers and the Pursuit of the Ideal Body Form*. Kansas City: Andrews and McMeel, 1979.

Walser, Robert. *Running with the Devil: Power, Gender and Madness in Heavy Metal Music*. Hanover: Wesleyan University Press/University Press of New England, 1993.

Wilcox, Helen, Keith McWatters, Ann Thompson, and Linda Williams, eds. *The Body and the Text: Helen Cixous, Reading and Teaching*. New York: St. Martin's Press, 1990.

Woolf, Virginia. *A Room of One's Own*. London: Hogarth Press, 1931.

Yarborough, Richard. "Strategies of Black Characterization in *Uncle Tom's Cabin* and the Early Afro-American Novel." In *New Essays on Uncle Tom's Cabin*, ed. Eric J. Sundquist. Cambridge and New York: Cambridge University Press, 1986.

Young, Iris. *Throwing Like a Girl and Other Essays in Feminist Philosophy and Social Theory*. Bloomington: Indiana University Press, 1990.

Index

Note: Page numbers for illustrations are in *italics*.

UNIVERSITY PRESS OF NEW ENGLAND

publishes books under its own imprint and is the publisher for Brandeis University Press, Dartmouth College, Middlebury College Press, University of New Hampshire, Tufts University, and Wesleyan University Press.

ABOUT THE AUTHOR

A performer and feminist scholar, Ann Cooper Albright is an associate professor in the dance and theater program at Oberlin College, Ohio. Combining her interests in dancing and cultural theory, she is currently involved in teaching a variety of dance, performance studies, and women's studies courses that seek to engage students in both the practice and the theory of the body. She enjoys making academics dance and dancers write, and is a founding member of the Flaming Bitches, an interdisciplinary feminist study group that helps to keep life interesting in Oberlin, Ohio.

LIBRARY OF CONGRESS CATALOGING-IN-PUBLICATION DATA

Albright, Ann Cooper.
        Choreographing difference : the body and identity in contemporary dance / Ann
    Cooper Albright.
            p.   cm.
        Includes bibliographical references and index.
        ISBN 0–8195–6315–3 (alk. paper). — ISBN 0–8195–6321–8 (pbk. : alk. paper)
        1. Modern dance—Social aspects. 2. Modern dance—Psychological aspects.
    3. Body image. 4. Identity (Psychology) 5. Sexuality in dance. I. Title.
    GV1588.6.A43 1997
    792.8—dc21   97–17034